The eighteenth century poet, W
is now recognized as one of the most important
fore-runners of the Romantic Movement, and
there is intense interest in his life and writings.
Attempts to write his biography have been made
at various times, but as Collins lived a mysterious
and secluded life and was uncommunicative
about his private affairs even to his intimate
friends, it has until now been impossible to trace
his career except in the vaguest outline.

P. L. Carver's new biography, however, has
gleaned new information from a number of
sources likely and unlikely, including wills,
poems attributed to a Scottish minister, and a
collection of letters in a ducal library. When
Collins died in 1759, he was virtually unknown
to the reading public. The only contemporary
who has left on record a critical appreciation of
his now famous "Odes" was Gray, the author of
the "Elegy". Gradually, towards the end of the
century, interest in Collins increased, with
Wordsworth, Coleridge, and Hazlitt among his
ardent admirers. Today, P. L. Carver's new
discoveries not only contribute to our knowledge
of Collins' life, but to the better understanding of
his poems, among them the great "Ode to
Evening" and "How sleep the Brave".

EDMUND BLUNDEN says in his Foreword
to this book: ". . . a complete biography. And
happily here it is. The power of looking
steadily and critically at memoranda is one of the
advantages which Mr. Carver has in composing
his book . . . Collins' life was largely in his poetry
and his art of writing, and there also the vigilance

PATRICK LANGWORTHY CARVER,
Ph.D., graduated in English Language and
Literature from the University of Leeds. He has
subsequently taught at various times at Ample-
forth College, the University of Manitoba, and
Queen's University. He has contributed
numerous articles and reviews to the *Review of
English Studies*, the *Modern Language Review*, the
Journal of English Notes and Queries, among other
periodicals.

THE LIFE OF A POET

a biography of

WILLIAM COLLINS

THE LIFE OF A POET

a biography of

WILLIAM COLLINS

by

P. L. CARVER

With a Foreword by
Edmund Blunden

HORIZON PRESS
NEW YORK

Printed in Great Britain

To

B.E.C. and F.M.D.

Contents

Acknowledgments

I think it right to place first the name of the late Professor A. S. P. Woodhouse, to whom, as explained elsewhere, this book owes the beginning of its existence. Mr. Edmund Blunden, whose election to the Chair of Poetry at Oxford made the only cheerful news in the papers of the year 1966, took a helpful interest in the project as soon as he knew of it, and I have a treasured collection of his letters which date back to the time when the articles on Collins were appearing in *Notes and Queries*. I am very grateful to several correspondents who have taken far more trouble to answer enquiries than can be adequately acknowledged by a mention in the Notes, particularly Mr. J. M. G. Blakiston and Mr. John Harvey, both of Winchester College; Mrs. Heseltine and Miss Audrey Jennings, of Chichester; and to Mr. Noel Blakiston.

Also to the late Lord Sempill; the late Sir Sidney Burrard; the Rev. C. W. F. Bennett, of Chichester; the Rev. David Scriven, of Inveresk; and Mrs. Carlyle-Bell. Also for several valuable suggestions, to Professor A. D. McKillop, of Houston, Texas. To these names I should like to add that of my cousin, the late Miss A. B. Staniforth, who spent much time in verifying references at the British Museum when I was far away from London, and who tragically lost her life in a road accident in 1962. My thanks are due also to the publishers, Messrs. Sidgwick and Jackson, for taking the book under their wing, and to the printers and proof-readers.

Foreword by Edmund Blunden

SOME years have passed since readers of *Notes and Queries*
found in that valuable periodical a series of papers by Mr. P. L.
Carver, in which much accurate information was given concerning the life of the poet William Collins. I was one of those readers
and a reader of the works of Collins, and moreover I had myself
attempted a biographical sketch of that favourite poet; the difficulties were well known to me; accordingly it seemed to me
devoutly to be wished that Mr. Carver would one day extend his
studies into a complete biography. And happily here it is.

Nobody will ever supersede the beautiful and touching memoir
of Collins which his friend Dr. Johnson left us, but the *Lives of
the Poets* are perhaps character-studies and portraits in prose
rather than fully detailed records of the subjects; and so, many
hands have tried to put together a copious Life of Collins, notwithstanding Dr. Johnson – who incidentally, as is well known,
assigned Collins's death to the year 1756, three years too
early. Other statements made by Johnson are occasionally inexact,
and probably everyone who has hitherto published a Life of
Collins has relied on early 'evidences' which indeed demanded a
much more severe scrutiny. The power of looking steadily and
critically at memoranda, however long and generally they may
have enjoyed a reputation for veracity, is one of the advantages
which Mr. Carver has in composing his book. For example, he is
not bewitched by the agreeable personal note of the recollections
of Collins by John Ragsdale, but treats them with caution so far

as likelihood and logic require. Or again, about the old tale of Collins burning the unsold copies of his 'Odes', and there must have been a great many, Mr. Carver is sceptical as Sherlock Holmes might be.

Besides, the new biography affords glimpses of the living Collins which, theoretical as they are, arise from well-considered facts; and one of these persuasive speculations connects what we know of Collins's religious conversion with his closing years of mental disorder, and the not infrequent occurrence of such troubles among highly sensitive and imaginative people of that age.

The startling discovery of new poems or poetical fragments by Mr. J. S. Cunningham, given to the public in 1956, has duly been taken into consideration by Mr. Carver in his critical pages: Collins's life was largely in his poetry and his art of writing, and there also the vigilance and reflection of his new biographer yield all his admirers new light and new pleasure. The book is directed skilfully throughout in the search for the real Collins and what his poetry was and was intended to be; yet it has variety and picturesque relief. There is much in it for the reader who enjoys his eighteenth-century England, and at last the brilliant and hapless William Collins is seen much less as a solitary figure in old Chichester than in many of the descriptions : Mr. Carver, with the documents that he has unearthed and his great interest in the theme, gives quite a company of personalities around his poet, and revives the music and paintings and country places and properties which were part of that poet's world as he grew up. Old wills, as in this instance, can become eloquent.

Preface

THIS little book traces its origin to a time nearly thirty years ago, though it has not evolved during the interval by a continuous process. In 1938 it was suggested by the late Professor Woodhouse, of Toronto, who knew that I was interested in Collins, that we should collaborate in an edition which it was hoped might prove to be definitive: a hope which, as I now know, would have been frustrated by later discoveries. Woodhouse was to write the General Introduction on lines to be extended from those laid down in his *Collins and the Creative Imagination,* published a few years earlier. The Biographical Introduction was to be left to me, and the Notes were to be divided between us.

Accordingly I set to work to make what discoveries I could about Collins's life; but the war was already casting its shadow before, and I thought it best to publish what I had collected immediately, so as to make it available to some future gleaner in case conditions favourable to the exploration should ever return, which at that time seemed unlikely. Woodhouse, who had now returned to Canada, willingly agreed, and I then, very hurriedly, threw together a series of short articles which appeared in *Notes and Queries* at weekly intervals during the autumn of 1939. That series, of course, includes some facts which, as facts are unalterable, have had to be repeated, but I do not think it can be considered as anticipating the present volume.

It was not until about 1958, when I found myself free of other work, that I thought of Collins again. The Collins Exhibition held at Winchester in 1959 brought a further reminder. The project of a new edition of the poems had long been abandoned, but the possibility occurred to me of writing a biography in book form if enough material could be collected. This I managed to do in the course of the next two years, and the manuscript was sent to Woodhouse and benefited by his criticism. When I last saw him, in the summer of 1964, he had recently retired, and was looking forward to spending long years of leisure in an immense undertaking of which his *Puritanism and Liberty*, now accepted as a standard work, had marked the first stage. His sudden death at the end of that year, when he was apparently in robust health and certainly at the height of his power, was a blow to English scholarship which is still felt far beyond the bounds of his native Canada.

Bexhill-on-Sea, Sussex
December 1966

I

The Collins Family

ANYONE who has explored the mountain of manuscript described in the British Museum Catalogue as 'Materials for a History of the County of Sussex', and more generally known as the 'Dunkin Collection', will have found himself becoming familiar with the name of Roger Collins. To the county historian it is not a name of greater importance than those of many other obscure clergymen who flourished in the later seventeenth century, and made, or neglected to make, the necessary entries of births, marriages, and deaths in their registers. In the matter of keeping his Parish records Roger Collins was careful and conscientious; but the fact which invests him with a special interest as we think of him today is that he turns out to be the grandfather of the author of the ode *To Evening*. That is apparent from his will, which Dunkin has summarized, and from that of his son Charles, as will be shown later.

If, having made that discovery, we decide on a journey to Chichester in the hope of tracing the career of Roger Collins – and most people would welcome an excuse to re-visit that city of mellow memories – the probability is that we shall find ourselves beginning our enquiries at the wrong end; for the only information which we are likely to discover, without an extensive search of the surrounding parishes, is furnished by the inscription on a memorial tablet in the ancient church of St. Olave. From that we learn that Roger Collins died on 21st November, 1707, at the age of eighty-three; that his wife, who had died fifteen years earlier, was

1

buried with him, as also were two sons (probably infants) whose names are not recorded; and that he claimed a coat of arms, described in heraldic terms thus: 'Vert, a griffin segreant or, with a mullet for difference. Impaling: Argent, a chevron sable between three Cornish choughs.'(1) We may be reminded at this point that the arms *Vert, a griffin segreant or* were displayed on the memorial to several members of the Collins family erected in the church of St. Andrew by Anne, the poet's sister.(2)

After copying the inscription, and making some further enquiries in the neighbourhood, we shall probably decide to return to London, for any information to be gleaned from parish records has been brought together in a much more accessible form by Dunkin. We have found reason already to doubt the traditional belief that the forebears of Collins had been established in Chichester since the sixteenth century as 'tradesmen of the higher order': a phrase repeated from one memoir to another on the ultimate authority of Dallaway, the Sussex historian. Roger Collins, as we have seen, came of an armorial family, and there is no trace of that family in Sussex, though the surname is not uncommon, earlier than the Restoration.

A little further research will lead to the discovery that a griffin segreant or, on a field vert, is distinctive of the family of Collins or Collin (subject to much variation of spelling) of Kent and Essex.(3) The pedigree of that family is available in the Manuscript Room of the British Museum, and from it we learn that Edward Collin or Collen, second son of William of that name, of Beauchamp Roding, in Essex, had a son Roger.(4) This Roger appears, so far as we can tell in the absence of exact dates, to have been contemporary with the Roger Collins who afterwards appeared in Chichester, and it is probable that the two were identical. The 'mullet for difference' included by Roger Collins of Chichester is the sign of a third or fourth son, and would not be transmitted to descendants. The impaled arms are those of the Duffields of Buckinghamshire,(5) a family undistinguished but of long descent.

From the Dunkin Collection, to which we now return, we can compile an impressive list of Roger Collins's clerical appointments. He was ordained Deacon by the Bishop of Chichester on 28th November, 1662.(6) A month later he was ordained Priest,

2

and was appointed immediately to be Rector of St. Olave's. If this seems incredibly rapid advancement, we must remember two things. In the first place, it was in 1662 that some two thousand clergymen seceded from the Church of England rather than subscribe to the Act of Uniformity, and the consequent shortage of clergy must have created difficult problems throughout the country. Secondly, Roger Collins was a man of nearly forty when he was ordained, and his age, and perhaps his personal qualities, would weigh in the balance against his lack of clerical experience. It is very regrettable that we have no knowledge whatever of his earlier career. He would have been just old enough for military service at the outbreak of the Civil War, and if he fought at all we may feel assured that it was not on the side of Cromwell. We may even amuse ourselves with the fancy that he had carried on some kind of passive resistance to the Puritan régime, and been concerned in plots and conspiracies and narrow escapes. Though he has earned the gratitude of local historians by the fullness and accuracy of his Parish Registers, in which he has recorded trades as well as names, his handwriting is said to have been strangely clumsy for a person of his profession.(7) That, perhaps, is a sign that he had not led a sheltered life before his ordination.

In January, 1663, almost immediately after his appointment to St. Olave's, he was admitted Vicar Choral of the Cathedral of Chichester. If he had any real qualifications in music that would make him a particularly valuable recruit to the Church after the Puritan régime. He retained this office, as well as the Rectorship of St. Olave's, for the rest of his life, but his responsibilities did not end there. He was Rector of Rumboldswyke from 1670 to 1693; Rector of East Wittering from 1688 to 1707, resigning a few months before his death; Vicar of Hunston, united, then as now, with North Mundham, for the last year of his life; and Sequestrator of St. Andrew's, Chichester, for the last eight years.(8) Apparently he lived at Hunston during his short period of office as Vicar, as he describes himself as 'of Hunston' in his will.

On 26th February, 1664, at the village of Tangmere, Roger Collins married Wilmot Duffield,(9) then a resident of Tangmere but probably, in view of the arms of her family already noticed, a native of Buckinghamshire. Mr. Edmund Blunden has observed

3

that the city of Chichester 'remains to this day a resting-place for antiquity and tradition, and may be said to be the most intimate relic of the life of William Collins that now exists'.(10) For that reason we cannot without a certain reluctance arrive at the conclusion that neither of the poet's grandparents, on his father's side, had any original connexion with the city, or even with the county of Sussex, and must console ourselves with the thought that Roger Collins was by this time a Cicestrian by adoption. In the Register he is described as 'of the Close of the Cathedral Church of Chichester, Clerk', and we know on other authority that he still occupied a house in the Cathedral Close in 1670, and was liable for hearth tax.(11)

Charles, the elder son, was baptized in the Cathedral on 8th February, 1666.(12) His name may be taken as a sign of the father's loyalty to the Stuarts, for it was then very uncommon. We shall hear of him again in his later life; he was to have some discernible influence upon the career of his nephew William, for whom he had an evident affection.

The elder daughter, Judith, was baptized in the Cathedral on 17th April, 1667.(13) She is a shadowy figure among Collins's older relatives, and the little that we know of her does not indicate that she had a happy life. On 21st January, 1707, she was married to John Scott, of Eltham, in Kent.(14) The marriage is recorded in the Register of Hunston, and in the margin beside the entry, in a contemporary hand, are the frightening words, 'Woeful Day'. She is named as the executrix of her father's will, drawn up on 1st May, 1707, and his principal heir, and it is worth remarking that one of the witnesses to this document is Thomas Scott, presumably a relative of John, who signs by mark as an illiterate.

It appears that John Scott, soon after his marriage, migrated to Chichester. On 3rd February, 1709, he was bound in the sum of £100 for the due performance by his wife of the terms of Roger Collins's will, and in the record of the proceedings he is described as 'of the city of Chichester, gentleman'.(15) We know from a recent discovery that in 1720 a man named John Scott was living as tenant in a house in Chichester which some twenty-five years later was inherited by Collins, under the will of his uncle Charles. Of that we shall have occasion to say more.

4

The two other children of Roger Collins who survived were Anne and William. We do not know when either was born, and must suppose that both were baptized at St. Olave's, the registers of which, for long periods, are missing. It is probably for the same reason that we have no record of the date of Anne's marriage. At some time about the turn of the century she became the wife of William Payne, of Midhurst, and her name is revealed by the will of her husband. William Payne died in 1723, leaving bequests to his wife Anne Payne, his children, George, William and Anne, and his brother-in-law, 'William Collins of the City of Chichester in the said County of Sussex Haberdasher', the latter being appointed executor. The elder son, George Payne, whose name is familiar in memoirs of Collins, was born not later than 1703. In 1737 he gave evidence before the Barons of the Exchequer in the action *Collins* v. *Diggens,* in which the Plaintiff was his aunt by marriage, Mrs. Elizabeth Collins, the mother of the poet. He stated that his age at that time was thirty-four.(*16*)

William Collins, whom we remember today as the father of the poet, was probably the youngest of the family, and certainly the younger son. It is unfortunate that the exact date of his birth is unknown. According to the memorial tablet in St. Andrew's he died in 1734 aged sixty; but in her evidence in the action *Collins* v. *Diggens* his widow stated that he died on 30th September, 1733, and that accords with the fact that his will was proved on 5th November of that year. If his daughter, who erected the memorial, could be mistaken about the year of his death, she is far more likely to have been mistaken about his age, or, from lack of exact knowledge, to have arrived at 'sixty' in round figures as a rough estimate. In that case we must admit the possibility that William Collins's true age at his death was no more than fifty-six, so that the choice of his name may have been suggested by the marriage in 1677 of William, Prince of Orange, to Princess Mary, elder daughter of James, Duke of York. It was at that time a name no less agreeable to a Royalist than the names given by Roger Collins to two of his other children, Charles and Anne. The year 1688 was then very far distant, and no one could have imagined Prince William as King William the Third of England or his bride as Queen Mary the Second.

5

It was not unusual for the son of a country clergyman to go into trade. According to tradition the elder William Collins was a hatter – 'a hatter of good reputation', as Dr. Johnson says – and that is confirmed by the record of his marriage and also by the records of two other marriages for which he stood as sponsor;(17) though he seems to have grown into a haberdasher by 1720, as he is so described in the will of his brother-in-law, William Payne. Moy Thomas, in the memoir of the poet prefixed to his edition of 1858, observes that in the accounts of John Caryll, the Sussex magnate and friend of Pope, there are 'numerous entries' reading 'To Collins of Chichester for a hat'. A recent search among the household accounts of the Caryll family preserved in the British Museum did not reveal any such entry, but if Moy Thomas is right perhaps we should conclude that Collins's hats did not wear well. The site of his shop, now occupied by a bank, is very close to St. Andrew's Church, and it is probable that his choice of premises was in some way connected with his father's tenure of the living of St. Andrew's. In that case he must have opened his business at some time later than 20th December, 1699.

In the Parish Register of the village of Ernley, near Chichester, is recorded the marriage on 13th February, 1703, of 'Mr. Wm. Collins of Chich[este]r Hatter and Eliz[abeth] Martin of West Wittering'.(18) The bride was the daughter of Edmund and Magdalen Martin of Southcott Farm, in the neighbourhood of Cackham Tower, between East and West Wittering. A daughter, Elizabeth, was born in 1704.(19) She is mentioned in the will of her grandfather, Roger Collins, who leaves her five pounds on her attaining the age of twenty-one. A second daughter, Anne, was born about a year later.(20) For many years these were the only children.

Throughout his active life William Collins the elder served his native city conscientiously and with some distinction, though not in such a way as to achieve even a local immortality in his own right. There is no sign that he inherited his father's devotion to the cause of the Stuarts, or made any difficulty about accepting the principles of the Revolution and the Hanoverian succession. He was Mayor of Chichester in 1714,(21) and had, presumably, been elected an Alderman at some earlier date. He was one

6

of the City Fathers who in 1716 provided a banquet to celebrate the expected visit of the Prince of Wales; when the Prince, having heard of the banquet or being informed of the menu, changed his route so as to avoid Chichester, and the Aldermen consumed the feast themselves.(22) In this and the following year, and probably earlier and later, he was one of the Churchwardens of St. Peter the Great.(23) In 1721 he was Mayor of Chichester for the second time,(24) and on 1st January of that year his only son, William, was baptized.(25)

A search in the Public Record Office has revealed that in 1727 Alderman Collins entered into a commercial transaction which was to lead to litigation with some of his neighbours, extending to the end of his life and beyond it. The Church of St. Bartholomew had been destroyed by artillery fire in the siege of Chichester during the Civil War, and the ground belonging to the Rectory, about two acres, had been cultivated ever since as farm land. About 1682 the Dean and Chapter granted a lease of the land to Paul Burrard, of Lymington. Burrard thereupon claimed that he was entitled to tithes at the rate of 4s. 4d. a year from each of the parishioners, being the occupant, by a legal fiction, of the non-existent Rectory. The parishioners, or some of them, resisted the claim, but Burrard succeeded in enforcing it by an action at law in 1690, and all went well for a number of years.(26)

Paul Burrard died in 1706,(27) and at some uncertain date about twenty years later(28) his son and successor granted a sublease of the land to Alderman Collins. The Alderman in his turn claimed the right to tithes, and brought actions at law against several defaulters, first in 1727 and again in 1730.(29) In 1735, two years after the Alderman's death, Paul Burrard the second died, and a new lease was granted by Dean Hayley to Mrs. Elizabeth Collins, the Alderman's widow. Again there was trouble about the payment of tithes, and in 1737 Mrs. Collins brought the action *Collins* v. *Diggens,* already mentioned as the one in which George Payne was called as a witness.(30) That action has a recognized place in legal history, and is summarized in Hutton Wood's *Tithe Cases.*

The value of the tithes has been estimated at £15 a year,(31) by no means a negligible revenue in the eighteenth century. In

1747, after Mrs. Collins's death, the rights under the lease were sold for £260 to John Backshell and Thomas Ball, 'during the lives of Lucy Burrard, widow of Paul Burrard, Esq. [the second] deceased, Harry Burrard,(32) son of the said Paul and Lucy, and William Collins, son of Elizabeth Collins, widow, deceased, and the life of the longest liver of them.'(33)

It is very regrettable that the Burrard family papers have not survived, for we might have expected to find documents among them bearing Collins's signature, or even personal letters. The collection was dispersed, and possibly destroyed, in 1885, when the Burrard of that day, the sixth baronet, met with financial disaster, and, to the bitter regret of his cousin, who succeeded to the title as Sir Sidney Burrard, his estate and possessions were sold.

That is all that can be said of the affairs of Alderman Collins, except that he left the whole of his property to his wife with directions to sell as much as might be necessary to pay his debts. It is certain that the debts did not amount to much, for if we compare his will with that of his widow we shall find that Mrs. Collins, when her time came, was able to dispose of the whole estate left by her husband. That seems a sufficient answer to the story, of uncertain origin, that the Alderman borrowed money on a large scale from his brother-in-law, Colonel Martin, and died hopelessly in debt.

No contemporary has left any impression of the character of William Collins the elder. From the facts recorded we should suppose that he was first and last a man of business, competent, industrious, and successful. It may be conjectured that it was from him that the second daughter, Anne, derived a certain mercenary strain, while her brother's feeling for music and poetry and haziness about the laws of economics – qualities which may also be discerned in his uncle Charles – were inherited from his grandfather, the Rector and Vicar Choral. Of Mrs. Collins we know little, but that little indicates that she was a good manager and had nothing to learn about the value of money. We know even less of the elder daughter, Elizabeth, but her will reveals a methodical mind and a desire to act fairly in arranging her affairs.

NOTES TO CHAPTER I

1. For an account of St. Olave's and its monuments, with full notes on the memorial to Roger Collins, see Lindsay Fleming, *The Little Churches of Chichester*, pp. 7-16.

2. The Collins arms have somehow disappeared, and that, perhaps, accounts for the failure of modern writers to trace the poet's descent from Roger Collins. They are described by Burrell as having been there in his time, inscribed on a lozenge at the top of the monument. (B.M. Add. MS. 5699, f. 171r; see also Lindsay Fleming, *The Little Churches of Chichester*, p. 19.)

3. Harl. MS. 5181, f. 6. Illustrated in Add. MS. 14307, f. 10v.

4. Harl. MS. 1398, f. 5. See also Harl. MS. 1541, f. 224v.

5. Harl. MS. 1533, f. 49.

6. For this and his subsequent appointments see B.M. Add. MS. 39326 (22), ff. 1878-85.

7. See Mr. W. D. Peckham's Introductions to his transcripts of the Parish Registers of St. Olave's, Chichester, and Rumboldswyke in the Library of the Society of Genealogists.

8. See note 6. The appointment of a Sequestrator indicates that there was some doubt whether the living was technically vacant, as the person last appointed had not resigned and could not be proved to have died; but for practical purposes the Sequestrator was Vicar of the parish.

9. B.M. Add. MS. 39326 (22), ff. 1879, 1882.

10. *Poems of William Collins*, p. 3.

11. William Durrant Cooper in *Sussex Archaeological Collections*, Vol. xxiv, p. 84.

12. B.M. Add. MS. 39326 (22), f. 1879; 5699, f. 180v.

13. Ibid. 5699, f. 183.

14. Ibid. See also *Sussex Marriage Licenses* (Sussex Record Society), p. 131.

15. B.M. Addit. MS. 39326 (22), f. 1892.

16. P.R.O. E.133/37/76

17. Those of John Groome of West Grinstead, on 27th April, 1711, and Randall Stanton, of Havant, on 10th January, 1711/12. See *Sussex Marriage Licenses* (Sussex Record Society), pp. 188, 192.

18. B.M. Add. MSS. 5699, f. 221; 29456, f. 59.

19. Baptized at St. Peter the Great on 6th March. B.M. Add. MS. 5699. f. 184.

20. No record has been found. Anne was certainly the younger daughter, and is said to have been eighty-five at the time of her death in 1789 (see p. 180 below); but it is not likely that her age would be known with perfect accuracy.

21. Hay, *History of Chichester*, p. 572.

22. *Sussex Archaeological Collections*, Vol. xix, p. 147.

23. B.M. Add. MS. 39461, f. 105.
24. See note 21.
25. Register of St. Peter the Great, Chichester.
26. Dallaway, *A History of the Western Division of the County of Sussex,* Vol. I, p. 171; Burrell's notes in B.M. Add. MS. 5689, f. 21. See also P.R.O. E.112/1301/43.
27. Sir Sidney Burrard, *The Families of Borard and Burrard,* p. x.
28. Mrs. Collins told the Court of Exchequer in her action against Diggens and others that her husband took over the lease from Burrard on 10th March, 1727; but her husband had told the same Court in 1730 that he had then held the lease for seven years or thereabouts.
29. P.R.O. E.112/1301/7, 43.
30. P.R.O. E.112/1302/54. For the Depositions see E.134/11, George II, Mich. 8.
31. B.M. Add. MS. 5689, f. 21.
32. Afterwards General Sir Harry Burrard, a distinguished soldier. He lived till 1791.
33. P.R.O. C.P. 25 (2) 1224, George II, Hil. 21.

II

Winchester

HOW and where the infant Collins learnt his letters is a question which need not detain us long, though it has given rise to some speculation. It has been sometimes assumed, and sometimes stated as if it were an ascertained fact, that he attended for a time the Prebendal School, Chichester. There is no evidence that he did so, and it is, in fact, unlikely. The Prebendal School was a charity school for a limited number of sons of the poor, and Alderman Collins could never have counted himself as belonging to that order of society even if he did, at times – and of that there is no proof – experience some financial stress. The function of a preparatory school was usually performed in the eighteenth century by the poorer clergy, and the safest assumption is that Collins received his earliest instruction from some curate in the neighbourhood.

With the real beginning of his education we are on firmer ground. In 1733, the year in which his father died, he was admitted to Winchester College as a Scholar.(1) Probably his grandfather's position in the Church helped toward his election. Mr. Garrod under-rates the family's social pretensions when he says of Collins later in his career: 'His father, the "hatter of good reputation", had wished to make a gentleman of him, or at least a clergyman.'(2) Of his contemporaries at the school, the one best remembered is Joseph Warton, who has a place of his own in literary history, and was to be his friend for life; among the others

11

were William Whitehead, a future Poet Laureate, James Hampton, the future translator of Polybius, and John Mulso, the friend of Gilbert White and the brother of Mrs. Chapone. The memory of Mrs. Chapone has faded with the reputation of her book, *Letters on the Improvement of the Mind*, but her name was once a household word.

Mr. J. M. G. Blakiston, the present Librarian of the College, and Mr. John Harvey, the Archivist, responded generously to a request for information about Collins's career at Winchester by making an exhaustive search, and what they have discovered may be safely assumed to be all that is discoverable. There is an Election Indenture 'Ad Winton' of 1733, which reads: 'Guliel: Collins de Chichester Com. Sussex. Bapt. 1 Jan: 1722.' The Register contains a record of his admission as Scholar on 23rd February, 1733/4. In the Register of Oaths of Scholars (aged fifteen and over) for 1728 to 1783 there is an entry under 3rd September, 1737: 'Guliel: Collins de Chichester Comit. Sussex.'

From the Long Rolls, or School Lists, made up about October each year, we may learn something of Collins's progress during seven years. The following extracts are given in the exact form in which they have been supplied by Mr. Blakiston:

    1733 Collins 'ad Winton' (11th on roll).
    1734 5th Book Jun. (15th), 7th Chamber.
    1735 5th Book Mid. (15th), 7th Chamber.
    1736 5th Book Sen. (16th), 4th Chamber.
    1737 5th Book Sen. (4th), 4th Chamber.
    1738 6th Book   (13th), 4th Chamber, and 'ad Oxon'
                               (14th on roll).
    1739 6th Book   (7th), 5th Chamber, and 'ad Oxon'
                               (9th on roll).
    1740 (not in text of roll of school). 'Ad Oxon'
                               (3rd on roll).

Mr. Blakiston explains that ' "Book" is the local term for "form" or "class". The "Chamber" is the Scholars' living-room in one of which is the marble to Otway. The "ad Oxon" list appears at the foot of the roll.'

The mention of the 'marble to Otway' refers to No. 82 in the

Collins Exhibition, held at the College in 1959, the two hundredth anniversary of the poet's death, and organized by Mr. Blakiston. The description is: ' "Marble" to the memory of Thomas Otway in Sixth Chamber, Winchester College, erected by W. C. and J. W., generally thought to be William Collins and Joseph Warton. n.d.' There can be no serious doubt that the initials are those of Collins and Warton,(3) and it is interesting to find Collins while still at school displaying that devotion to Otway which he professed more than once in his later career.

In *William Collins: Drafts and Fragments,* a collection of poems which Mr. J. S. Cunningham rescued from oblivion in 1956, and of which more will be said later, there is printed as an Appendix a Latin oration signed by Collins and inscribed, in another hand, 'Declamatio ad portas by Collins.' Mr. Cunningham says of it:

> The custom still survives at Winchester College of welcoming distinguished guests in a Latin oration delivered by the senior scholar. During his schooldays, Collins must have heard several such orations on the occasion of the visit of the New College electors. The speeches are traditionally the work of the Headmaster or some other adult classical scholar, not of the boys. The present example was probably written by Collins as a school exercise. Similar exercises by other Winchester boys are to be found among the Trinity College Warton papers.

The Latin is by no means impeccable, even when allowance is made for some obvious printer's or copyist's errors, but the sense is sufficiently clear. Collins begins by speaking of a lamentable event which has plunged the College into grief, making it difficult to display the happiness appropriate to the present occasion and sanctioned by custom; but as there would be something ungracious in tearful silence, which might show them deficient in the noble fortitude so finely exemplified by their late Warden, now summoned to Heaven, it was fitting that they should receive the visitors with some measure of restrained joy. And while they remembered with what bountiful erudition and kindliness the deceased Warden had instructed their youthful minds and guided

13

their studies they were assured that his successor was likewise of shining merit, and that Wykehamist scholarship still blossomed with its pristine splendour.

It may be helpful at this point to insert a few words of explanation for which thanks are due, again, to Mr. Blakiston and Mr. Harvey, and which enable us to date this composition within very narrow limits. The deceased Warden was Henry Bigg, whose death must have occurred between 28th June, 1740, when he is known to have been still active, and the following 11th August, when his will was proved. His successor, Warden Coxed, elected on the 18th August, had been Warden of New College, where a vacancy was now created. 'Consequently,' says Mr. Blakiston, 'the New College electors who came down to Winchester in 1740 were headed by the Sub-Warden of New College, Thomas Coker, not apparently mentioned in this speech.' The two Electors who accompanied him were Richard Eyre, Scholar 1719, Fellow of New College 1722-44, and Lancelot Mitchell, Scholar 1714, Fellow of New College 1723-56. The former is described by Kirby in *Winchester Scholars* (1880) as 'The Traveller', that, adds Mr. Blakiston, being 'Clearly a translation of "Peregrinator eximius" in the MS. Register of the Fellows of New College, which Kirby consulted.'

In the continuation Collins first addresses himself to Eyre, beginning with some pseudo-Ciceronian compliments which would be applicable to almost any visitor of academic distinction; he then proceeds to tell him how happy they are to see him back in his own country and among them again after his long absence. During his sojourn in his beloved Italy he had been constantly in their thoughts, and whatever Latin author they studied had brought his image vividly before their eyes. A work of Virgil, a kindred spirit, would suggest the fancy that perhaps at that moment he was prostrate before his tomb, and drawing inspiration from his shade; and if they turned to Cicero they found the same patriotic zeal and the same eloquence contending, with the same power though with greater success, for the institutions and threatened religion of his country.

Of the other visitor it is said that, without having been abroad, he has devoted himself with no less assiduity to humane studies;

14

from his rural retreat, as from another Tusculum, he had explored the fountains of wisdom and formed his life and character on the ancient models. The youth of Winchester had had experience of his noble qualities not long ago, and they wished that they themselves might enjoy the same privilege. Both visitors were welcome as they returned with loyal affection to the home of which they had deserved so well, from which they had gone forth with such high distinction, and from which, in the course of time, so many and so great men, as nearly as possible like themselves, might be expected to emerge.

At the time of this composition Collins had already made some experiments in the field of English poetry. At the age of twelve, according to tradition, he composed a satire entitled 'The Battle of the Schoolbooks', a title which presumably owed something to Swift. The one line which has come down to us, 'And ev'ry Gradus flapp'd his leathern wing,' is its own guarantee of authenticity. Mr. Garrod has remarked that the phrase *leathern wing* 'Collins thought sufficiently well of to embody it later in his *Ode to Evening.*'(4)

'The Battle of the Schoolbooks', we should suppose, was written merely for private amusement, but later in their school career both Collins and Warton achieved the distinction of having some of their verses printed. Collins's earliest publication appears to have been an ingenious trifle in rhymed couplets entitled 'Hercules', not included in any edition of his poems.

A claim on behalf of 'Hercules' to be the work of Collins was made tentatively in 1828, when *The Crypt,* a Winchester periodical, printed it with an introductory note. The Editor explains that the manuscript 'was formerly in the possession of the great Thomas Warton, to whom it probably passed from his brother, the school-fellow and friend of Collins', and that in the Warton family it has always passed, he understands, 'as a youthful production of the "Cicestrian bard".' That is strong evidence, and the fact that the poem is signed 'Collins' would seem to settle the question; but there is a date as well as a signature, and the date is 'Jun. 1747'. Remembering that Collins left Winchester for Oxford in 1740, the Editor made searching enquiries into the possible claims of other boys of the same name, and finally satis-

15

fied himself that 'to none of them is there any reasonable probability for attributing the verses in question.'

The Editor adds the suggestion that the date on the manuscript
may be that of the transcription, and concludes that the tradition
in favour of William Collins must 'be permitted, in lack of more
substantial authority, to predominate'. It is unfortunate that no
notice has been taken of his discovery. A little rummaging among
the likely volumes of the *Gentleman's Magazine* will reveal that
'Hercules' appeared anonymously in that journal in January,
1738. The manuscript dated 1747 must, therefore, be a copy, and
the date of composition belongs to the time when Collins was still
at Winchester and is known to have been a contributor to the
Gentleman's Magazine.

'Hercules', we need not hesitate to say, is worthy of the place
claimed for it in the Collins canon. It is a fanciful satire on Walpole, then at the height of his power, and the horde of lordly time-
servers who supported his Administration in return for honours
and sinecures. The argument is that, just as in the earliest ages
the earth was infested by 'strange Hydras, and Dragons, and
things without name', until Hercules was raised up by Jupiter
to destroy them, so now the political world is threatened by a new
kind of monster.

> But Hercules dy'd, – and alas! we behold
> How Monsters are made not by nature but gold;
> And wear such disguises, I'm told without joke,
> That some have a Garter and Star for a cloke;
> And some, yet more sly, are disfigur'd with lawn,
> And look on all monsters less cunning with scorn.

So we should implore Jupiter to send a second Hercules to complete the work of the first. It then occurs to the poet that the new
Hercules may do his work too thoroughly, and that he himself
may be mistaken for a monster; so he ends with the prayer:

> Then, lest I should share in the general drub,
> Transform me, O Jupiter, into – his club.

It seems unlikely, if we may judge by his associations a few years

16

later, that Collins was ever a Tory, but he was certainly hostile to Walpole. Apparently he sympathized with the group of dissident Whigs who were then beginning to organize themselves into a regular Opposition with Pitt as their leader, and who ultimately, in 1742, brought down the Walpole Government.

Three years earlier than the first appearance of 'Hercules' Thomson had published the first Book of his poem *Liberty*, with a fulsome dedication to Frederick, Prince of Wales. 'The Prince,' writes Thomson's latest biographer, 'must have handsomely rewarded the poet for a work which is not only a history of liberty, but an attack upon Walpole and his administration. Thomson lost no opportunity which his subject offered to arraign those ministers who corrupt a people by bribery and prevent their greatness by pacific policies, and his gibes at Walpole could not have been mistaken by even the most stupid reader. The opposition must have been delighted by such lines as these,

> *Corruption's Toils,*
> Foul Ministers, dark-working by the Force
> Of secret-sapping Gold.(5)

It is very likely that Collins read Thomson's poem at Winchester, and found in it the inspiration for his juvenile satire. Thus, when he met Thomson at Richmond some years later, and became one of his circle of friends, the elder and the younger poet would find that they had more than one interest in common.

Collins's only other direct contribution to the *Gentleman's Magazine*, so far as we can say with any approach to certainty, appeared in October, 1739. Wooll, the biographer of Joseph Warton, tells us that he found this note, in Warton's handwriting, on page 545 of Volume IX: '*Sappho's Advice* was written by me, then at Winchester School; the next, *Beauty and Innocence*, by Tomkyns; and the sonnet by Collins.' In speaking of the poem last mentioned as a 'sonnet' Warton refers to the fact that it was printed with that single word as the title; actually its formal structure has no resemblance to that of a sonnet, consisting of two stanzas of four lines each, of four and three feet alternately. For a schoolboy, even a senior schoolboy, it shows extraordinary precosity, not so much in intellectual development as in acquaintance with the mind and literary pursuits of the great world. It is very likely that Lord Chesterfield read it, and if he did we may be sure that he was green with envy. But if we recognize the 'Sonnet' as a typical product of the age in which it was written, we feel at the same time that only Collins could have written it. He adapted himself to the prevailing taste, but he did so as an artist adapts himself to his environment without ceasing to be himself.

We might have guessed that, after contributing to the *Gentleman's Magazine*, Collins would think of a more ambitious project. The evidence that he did so is furnished by a unique copy of his *Persian Eclogues*, in the Dyce Collection at South Kensington. In this copy the modest Ciceronian motto on the title-page has been struck out, and a line adapted from the *Aeneid* has been substituted in Collins's handwriting: 'Quos primus equis Oriens afflavit anhelis.'(6) Below, also in Collins's handwriting, are the words, 'Written at Winchester School', and on the reverse of the title-page Joseph Warton has written: 'Mr. Collins gave me this Copy with his own Hands when I & my Brother visited Him for the Last time at Chichester.'

From this it seems probable that Warton had a high opinion of the Eclogues, or at least a certain affection for them. If that is so he differed from the author, for Collins himself lived to despise this youthful production, and to speak disparagingly, according to Dr. Johnson, of his 'Irish Eclogues'. The possibility suggests itself that it was Warton who proposed the subject to Collins during their last two years at Winchester, and that that was the reason for his special interest in the volume.

We do not know when Warton began the translation of the Eclogues of Virgil which he completed in or before 1752, but we cannot believe that his pen was altogether idle when Collins was engaged with his shepherds and camel-drivers. If the two friends were both writing pastoral verse at the same time it would be natural that they should read one another's work, exchange opinions, and even, to some extent, collaborate. The internal evidence clearly suggests that something like this happened.

Besides a general similarity of style and diction, there are lines and couplets which would harmonize equally well with either poem, and some which could even be said to be interchangeable. One example may be given from Warton's version of the First Eclogue:

> We leave our country's bounds, our much-loved plains.
> We from our country fly, unhappy swains!

That will pass as a more than usually accurate rendering of the original (*Nos patriae fines, et dulcia linquimus arva; Nos patriam fugimus*), but Warton could have given a very fair reproduction of the sense by borrowing two lines from the Fourth Eclogue of Collins:

> Far fly the Swains, like us, in deep Despair,
> And leave to ruffian Bands their fleecy Care.

Collins, in his turn, could have fitted some of Warton's couplets into his poem without making any noticeable change in the structure. In the continuation of his Fourth Eclogue he has written:

> Fair scenes! but, ah! no more with Peace possest,
> With Ease alluring, and with Plenty blest.
> No more the Shepherds' whit'ning Seats appear,
> Nor the kind Products of a bounteous Year;
> No more the Date with snowy Blossoms crown'd,
> But Ruin spreads her baleful Fires around.

The effect would be much the same if for Collins's couplets we substituted three of Warton's:

> Ah! shall I never once again behold,
> When many a year in tedious round has roll'd,
> My native seats? – Ah! ne'er with ravisht thought
> Gaze on my little realm, and turf-built cot?
> What! must these rising crops barbarians share?
> These well till'd fields become the spoils of war?

If we agree that Collins's verse, whether directly influenced by

19

c

Warton or not, has its leading qualities in common with that of Warton, it is easy to understand why his Eclogues proved to be acceptable to the contemporary public and why they are not characteristic of Collins at his best. The art of Warton – an art carried to its final perfection by Gray in the 'Elegy' – is the art of expressing familiar truths in exquisite language. He himself, we may suppose, would have been the first to acknowledge this, for he observes in his Preface that the excellence of the Latin poets, including Virgil in his Eclogues as the supreme example, 'was owing to their exerting all their powers, in dressing up those thoughts and ideas that were ready found to their hands'.

Whether that is true of Virgil is disputable, even if we restrict our view to the Eclogues. It would certainly be true if applied to Warton himself. It is clearly not true of Collins, judged by the poems by which he is remembered; but in *Persian Eclogues* he was striving after a style not genuinely his own, and the result is a poem suited to the taste of the time because it could have been mistaken for the work of Warton. Such popularity as it attained, in contrast with the failure of the Odes, can be explained by a remark which Warton in his Preface quotes with approval from Boileau: that 'the number is greater of those whom custom has enabled to judge of words, than whom study has qualified to examine things'.

In speaking of *Persian Eclogues* we are not obliged to make any considerable allowance for the poet's youth. We expect a poet to display his powers early, and Collins, as we have seen, was nineteen when he left Winchester. But even so we shall agree that his literary production so far – *Hercules*, the *Sonnet* and *Persian Eclogues* – amounts to a creditable achievement, even if we assume that the Eclogues underwent some revision at Oxford before their publication. It may be thought a promising beginning.

20

NOTES TO CHAPTER II

1. T. F. Kirby, *Winchester Scholars*, p. 238.
2. *Collins*, p. 55.
3. Mr. Blakiston replied to a request for further information by quoting from an article by 'our most distinguished antiquarian, the late Herbert Chitty', who wrote in *The Wykehamist* in 1928:

   Another well known fact is that there is a marble on the south wall of the VIth Chamber, which is inscribed in three lines, 'Thomas Otway

   $$\left.\frac{\text{W.C.}}{\text{J.W.}}\right\} \text{Pos.} - 1670.\text{'}$$

   The initials stand for William Collins and Joseph Warton, who had the marble erected, probably in the year 1739-40, while they were College Prefects. I believe that Otway is the only Commoner who has ever been honoured by a commemorative marble set up in a College Chamber. Unfortunately the date which Collins and Warton assigned to Otway's residence in College, though not far wrong, is not quite accurate, for it is now known that Otway matriculated at Oxford, as a member of Christ Church, on 27 May, 1669. See Foster's *Alumni Oxonienses*.
4. *Collins*, p. 14.
5. Douglas Grant, James *Thomson*, pp. 146-7. See also Mr. Grant's remarks on the Walpole Government (p. 135), and compare Macaulay's very different account in his essay on Horace Walpole.
6. Cf. *Aeneid*, V, 239: 'Et me saevus equis Oriens afflavit anhelis.'

III

Oxford

THE visit of the Electors in 1740, when Collins composed his 'Oratio ad Portas', was in accordance with the intention of William of Wykeham, the common founder, that the best scholars of Winchester should proceed to New College, Oxford. Collins was placed first on the list, with Warton second and Mulso third, but his success was unrewarded. He had proved his claim to any vacancy there might be, but actually there was no vacancy at New College that year. Dr. Johnson says that 'this was the original misfortune of his life',(1) and as he knew Collins intimately for a short time the statement must be accepted, but it does not appear from his actions that Collins took his disappointment as a disaster of the first magnitude. The dates here are a little confusing, but according to the Register of Magdalen College, as edited by Bloxam,(2) he had already, on 22nd March, 1739-40, matriculated at Queen's, and it was after having thus made himself secure of a refuge in case of need that, 'remaining still at Winchester', he made his attempt to enter New College. At Queen's he spent, so far as we know, an uneventful year. On 29th July, 1741, he was elected a Demy of Magdalen, of which college his cousin, William Payne, the younger brother of George, was a Fellow.(3).

One anecdote of his life at Magdalen is recalled by Gilbert White, who, by rescuing it from oblivion, may be said to have made amends for the unfriendly and somewhat spiteful tone of some of his other references to Collins:

22

It happened one afternoon at a tea-visit, that several intelligent
friends were assembled at his rooms to enjoy each other's conversation, when in comes a member of a certain college, as remarkable at that time for his brutal disposition as for his good
scholarship;(4) who, though he met with a circle of the most
peaceable people in the world, was determined to quarrel; and,
though no man said a word, lifted up his foot and kicked the
tea-table, and all its contents, to the other side of the room.
Our poet, tho' of a warm temper, was so confounded at the
unexpected downfall, and so astonished at the unmerited insult,
that he took no notice of the aggressor, but getting up from
his chair calmly, he began picking up the slices of bread and
butter, and the fragments of his china, repeating very slowly,
'Invenias etiam disiecti membra poetae'.(5)

This story, besides being interesting in itself, may be found helpful in the interpretation of the ode *On the Poetical Character*.

It is certain that Collins the undergraduate did not fulfil the
promise of Collins the schoolboy. Gilbert White, who knew him
well, says that 'he brought with him . . . too high an opinion of his
school acquisitions, and a sovereign contempt for all academic
studies and discipline'. We know enough of the state of Oxford
in the middle eighteenth century to suspect that Collins's superior
airs may have been in some measure justified, and that it was not
without reason that he was 'always complaining of the dullness
of a college life'. Perhaps he felt that anything that Oxford could
teach him he could learn better in his own way. However that may
be, he took his Bachelor's degree in 1743,(6) 'and then', in the
words of Dr. Johnson, 'suddenly left the University; for what
reason I know not'.

At this point, and later, we must take account of the well-known
narrative of John Ragsdale, who came to know Collins after he
had settled at Richmond, and entertained him at his house. In
1783, when he must have been an old man, and when Collins's
position in literature was beginning to be established, Ragsdale
wrote his recollections of the poet, besides a good deal that he
could not have recollected, in the form of a long letter to William
Hymers, of Queen's College, Oxford, who was collecting materials

23

LIFE OF A POET: WILLIAM COLLINS

for a biography. His veracity is not in doubt, but he had never learnt to distinguish between what he knew to be true and what he thought a probable conjecture. He tells Hymers of his belief that he is the only one of Collins's intimates who has lived to be able to 'give a true account of his family and connexions', and that belief, in a man unaccustomed to being consulted as an authority, and conscious of his importance, is not conductive to scrupulous accuracy.

According to Ragsdale Alderman Collins at his death had left his affairs 'rather embarrassed'. He continues:

> Colonel Martin, his wife's brother, greatly assisted his family, and supported Mr. William Collins at the University, where he stood for a fellowship, which, to his great mortification, he lost, and which was his reason for quitting that place – at least, that was his pretext. But he had other reasons: he was in arrears to his bookseller, his tailor, and other tradesmen. But, I believe a desire to partake of the dissipation and gaiety of London was his principal motive.

We shall find reason later to doubt the allegation that Collins or his family was in any degree dependent on Colonel Martin for financial assistance. It is possible that he was in debt to his bookseller and his tailor – such cases have been known – but, of the two other reasons suggested by Ragsdale for his departure from Oxford, the first and the third are hardly compatible. Readers of Gibbon will not be easily convinced that a young man who in 1743 hankered after the dissipation and gaiety of London could at the same time have been ambitious to take his place among the Fellows of Magdalen.

A more probable account is given in passing by an anonymous contributor to the *Gentleman's Magazine* for October, 1823, who claims to have received it by direct tradition. Writing of Magdalen College, he says:

> We speak from impression; for many a morning between chapel and breakfast have we lounged in its *cloisterd* walk, and turned back when we came to the naked trees; ... we have admired

24

the spur royals from the secret treasures of *Domus*; eaten veni-
son with contemporaries of Collins the poet; and learned from
them that he was a pock-fretted man, with small black eyes;
associated very little; and was introduced into Magdalen by
Dr. Payne, an uncle, whom he offended by refusing to pay
attention to him, and therefore left the University.

Actually, as we know, Dr. Payne was Collins's cousin, not his
uncle, but that would be a natural error if the information had
come down in a direct line from people who had seen them together. William Payne was sixty-one at the time of his death in
1772, and must, therefore, have been some ten years older than
Collins. If he conformed to the pattern of a Fellow of Magdalen
according to Gibbon's description, the relationship between them
would easily be misunderstood.

Oxford was to Collins a stage on the journey from Winchester
to London. It was as a Demy of Magdalen that in 1742 he published *Persian Eclogues* with the firm of Roberts. Of that work
enough, and perhaps too much, has been said already. In December, 1743, he published with the firm of Cooper, under the pseudonym 'A Gentleman of Oxford', his *Verses Humbly Address'd to
Sir Thomas Hanmer, on his Edition of Shakespear's Works,* more
conveniently known as the 'Epistle to Hanmer'. If *Persian Eclogues*
looks back to Winchester, the 'Epistle to Hanmer' looks forward
to London. The title suggests that it is designed as an appeal for
the opulent Baronet's patronage, but, except for a fantastic com-
pliment in the closing lines, obviously not intended to be taken
seriously, there is a remarkable absence of the kind of servile adulation to which the public was accustomed in such addresses.
Though there is a good deal about the Romans, Sir Thomas is not
hailed as the Maecenas of the age; nor is it even hinted that he is
the reincarnation of Caesar, Cicero and Virgil rolled into one.

Mr. Garrod, in his Warton Lectures of 1928, has brought down
to earth any of the poet's admirers whose judgment had been
clouded by enthusiasm.(7) Here we have all Collins's faults observed, set in a note-book, learned, and conned by rote, and it
is, perhaps, the final proof of his genius that he still has some
merit left when Mr. Garrod has done with him. The 'Epistle to

Hanmer' is passed over lightly, but one couplet is quoted with qualified approbation and another with unqualified disfavour. 'Lines,' we are told, 'like

> Too nicely *Johnson* knew the Critic's Part;
> Nature in him was almost lost in Art

may perhaps be called both good criticism and competent verse. On the other hand, when, addressing Shakespeare, Collins writes

> O blest in all that Genius gives to charm,
> Whose morals mend us, and whose Passions warm,

I should call the criticism bad and the verse both incompetent and without spirit.'(8)

Now it must be said, with all respect to Mr. Garrod's authority, that this is not the way to criticize the 'Epistle to Hanmer', or any of Collins's poems with the possible exception of *Persian Eclogues*. It could be applied with more fairness to Pope, for Pope's verses stand or fall by the excellence of the component parts rather than by the architectural design. If we compare the *Essay on Criticism* with the 'Epistle to Hanmer' we shall agree that Pope's couplets in general are more skilfully fashioned, or polished, or chiselled, or whatever the correct term of appreciation may be, though it would not be very difficult to find some to which Mr. Garrod's words would apply: the criticism is bad and the verse both incompetent and without spirit. The *Essay on Criticism* lends itself to this kind of minute analysis because whatever life it has is cellular life, contained within the couplet. The 'Epistle to Hanmer' has some pretension, at least, to organic unity, and, for that reason, must be judged as a whole.

The lines which Mr. Garrod has selected for condemnation occur at a point where we recognize an unavoidable pause before a change of direction, an example of what Quiller-Couch has called the 'flat interval', which even Milton sometimes managed awkwardly. Collins has traced the history of the drama from Greece, the home of its origin, to Rome, where comedy flourished but tragedy declined; from Rome to Italy and Provence, and so to Elizabethan England. After Shakespeare,

> No second growth the Western Isle could bear,
> At once exhausted with too rich a Year.

Then follows some mild disparagement of Ben Jonson in the lines which Mr. Garrod has quoted, and then some faint praise of Fletcher. After a glance at the French drama, with perfunctory compliments to Corneille and Racine, the poet returns to England and to Shakespeare, who

> alone to ev'ry Scene could give
> Th' Historian's Truth, and bid the Manners live.

He describes how he responds to Shakespeare's admiration for Henry the Fifth, his pity for the murdered Princes and his horror at the villainy of Richard,(9) and how he delights in the pastoral scenes of *As You Like It,* in the magic of the *Midsummer Night's Dream,* and in the supernatural strangeness of *The Tempest.* We should expect him to continue in this strain towards the natural conclusion; instead, after the 'flat interval' already noticed, he turns aside to lament that pictorial art has not kept pace with the drama or with music. He longs for the time when a new Raphael shall depict Antony pleading with the mob over the body of Caesar, and Coriolanus yielding to his mother's tears. Finally, as if by an afterthought, Sir Thomas Hanmer is compared to the 'former Hanmer' who first collected the Homeric fragments and shaped them into a harmonious whole.

It is an interesting possibility that the lines from the 'flat interval' to the end have been substituted for others in consequence of a change of plan. There are signs that Collins's first intention was to survey the progress of the drama, without reference to Hanmer or his edition of Shakespeare, from the earliest times to his own day. As his main concern would be with the English drama Shakespeare was certain to be the dominant figure, but when the praise of Shakespeare was exhausted the poem would continue in the natural way with Ben Jonson, Fletcher and the lesser Elizabethans; then Davenant, Otway, Wycherley, Congreve and Addison would follow, and so to Colley Cibber and the contemporary favourites. Before he was in sight of the end it may have occurred to him that the appearance of Sir Thomas Hanmer's edition of Shakespeare provided a suitable occasion for a complimentary poem; the verses already written, up to line 112 of the poem as we have it ('And Spring diffusive decks th' enchanted Isle') could easily be adapted, but the continuation would have to be altered so as to be brought within the chronological limits of the new scheme. The lines following line 112 were therefore struck out, and there was substituted for them a further tribute to Shakespeare under the guise of a prayer for a second Raphael, worthy to illustrate his scenes.

On the understanding that this is merely conjecture, I will add the further suggestion that the lines deleted from the 'Epistle to Hanmer' may be those numbered Eight in Mr. Cunningham's *Drafts and Fragments*. They begin:

> Yet this wild pomp so much in vain pursued,
> The Courtly Davenant in our Thames renew'd.
> For who can trace thro' Time's oer-clouded maze
> The dawning stage of old Eliza's days?
> What Critic search its rise, or Changes know,
> With all the Force of Hollingshead or Stow?
> Yet all may gain, from any a worthless page,
> Some lights of Charles and his Luxurious age.

Collins proceeds, in terms which would certainly have scandalized his Royalist grandfather, to denounce the Restoration and all its works, political, social and literary:

> Vain all the Truth of just Dramatic Tales!
> Nought pleas'd Augustus, but what pleased Versailles!

He pours contempt upon 'the Froth, and Foppery of Wit', the 'Mob of Coxcombs' who 'swelld their loud applause' at 'that Pride of Pantomime, the rich Machine', the 'Witlings' all of whom

> could talk how *Betterton* was drest
> And gave that Queen their Praise, who curtsied Best.

28

At the point where the fragment ends he seems just about to arrive at the reign of Queen Anne.

That these lines have some relation to the 'Epistle to Hanmer' has been noticed by Mr. Cunningham, who says: 'In the *Verses Address'd to Sir Thomas Hanmer* (1743), Collins reviewed the progress of drama up to the time of Jonson and Fletcher. The present lines consider Davenant and Otway, and the excesses of the Restoration stage.' It is also true, as Mr. Cunningham observes, that 'they resemble in some points what Johnson said of the decay of the theatre in his Drury Lane Prologue, 1747', but that resemblance we must take to be accidental. The point of immediate interest is that they could belong to an earlier version of the 'Epistle to Hanmer'.

There is another poem in Mr. Cunningham's collection which invites comparison with the 'Epistle to Hanmer', though for a different reason. It is entitled 'Lines Addressed to James Harris', and Mr. Cunningham's note reminds us that Harris published his *Three Treatises* in 1744. 'The second treatise in particular. "A Discourse on Music, Painting, and Poetry", prompted Collins to address him in these lines.' Harris, afterwards Under-Secretary of State, was the nephew of the third Earl of Shaftesbury, the author of *Characteristicks*, and was himself a man of some considerable social importance as well as a minor politician. We should suppose, therefore, that Collins thought of turning to this

> Gentlest Patron born to grace
> And add new Brightness ev'n to Ashley's race

when his 'Epistle to Hanmer' failed to evoke a response. Whether Harris ever saw the lines we do not know. Possibly it was soon after writing them that Collins changed his plans and thought of entering the Church, as he did at some time during the summer of 1744.

A line in the 'Epistle to Hanmer' in its final form, 'The Sister Arts shall nurse their drooping Fires', has supplied Mr. J. H. Hagstrum with the main title of his interesting study, *The Sister Arts: The Tradition of Literary Pictorialism and English Poetry from Dryden to Gray*. In his chapter on Collins Mr. Hagstrum

29

observes that in the 'Epistle to Hanmer' we find expressed the notion that 'all the arts are sisters, notably painting and poetry'. Poetry is viewed 'as in a special way the inspirer of painting', and this is illustrated by the lines:

> O might the Muse with equal Ease persuade
> Expressive Picture to adopt thine Aid!
> Some pow'rful *Raphael* shou'd again appear,
> And Arts consenting fix their Empire here.

To that it may be added that in the lines to James Harris there is the same desire to unite the powers of painting and poetry, but with the important difference that these two arts are to co-operate in the service of music, which is supreme over both.

> These would I sing – O Art for ever dear
> Whose Charms so oft have caught my raptur'd Ear
> O teach me Thou, if my unpolish'd lays
> Are all too rude to speak thy gentle praise
> Oh teach me softer sounds of sweeter kind
>
> .   .   .   .
>
> Then let the Muse and Picture Each contend
> This plan her Tale, and that her Colours blend
> With me tho' both their kindred charms combine
> No Pow'r shall emulate or equal thine!

In both poems the sister arts are three: poetry, painting and music. In the 'Epistle to Hanmer' comparatively little is said about music because Collins's main concern is to assert the claims of pictorial art, but it is implied that music is present with poetry already –

> There ev'ry Scene the Poet's Warmth may raise,
> And melting Music find the softest Lays –

and it is desired that 'some pow'rful *Raphael* shou'd again appear' so that his art might complete the trio:

Thus, gen'rous Critic, as thy Bard inspires,
The Sister Arts shall nurse their drooping Fires;
Each from his Scenes her Stores alternate bring,
Spread the fair Tints, or wake the vocal String.

If, in the 'Epistle to Hanmer', music is accorded somewhat less than its due prominence, the lines to James Harris might have been designed to redress the balance. In the concluding lines of the fragment as we have it the poet hopes to learn from Philosophy, by Harris's guidance,

Why all my soul obeys her pow'rfull Art
Why at her bidding or by strange surprise
Or wak'd by fond degrees my Passions rise
How well-form'd Reeds my sure attention gain
And what the Lyre's well-measur'd strings contain
The Mighty Masters too unprais'd so long
Shall not be lost, if Thou assist my Song,
They who with Pindars in one Age bestowd
Cloath'd the sweet words which in their numbers flowd
And Rome's and Adria's Sons – if Thou but strive
To guard their Names, shall in my Verse survive.

The poets who have been equally devoted to music and to painting must be very few, and Collins must be counted as one of that small number.

NOTES TO CHAPTER III

1. Where no other reference is given, all quotations from Johnson are from his 'Life' of Collins in the *Lives of the English Poets*.
2. And also according to Foster's *Alumni Oxonienses*, as Mr. John Harvey has pointed out.
3. Bloxham, *Register of St. Mary Magdalen College, Oxford,* Vol. VI, pp. 254-5.
4. A footnote adds, 'The translator of Polybius'. He is identified as James Hampton, who had been at Winchester with Collins.
5. *Gentleman's Magazine,* Vol. LI, p. 11.
6. Bloxam, op. cit. VI, 255.

7. This was written, and, in fact, the whole book was complete in manuscript, before I read the announcement of Mr. Garrod's death. After some consideration I have thought it best not to revise any of those passages in which I have referred to his study of Collins, because I do not feel that he would have resented anything that I have said if it had appeared in his lifetime and had come his way. His book is an important contribution to the subject, and cannot be ignored; but it is, and was intended to be, a provocative book, and it would be a poor tribute to its excellence to receive every one of its challenging statements with passive acquiescence.

No one will take literally Mr. Garrod's assertion in his Preface that some of his commentary will seem 'ungracious and fault-finding'. He was incapable of writing in any way to which those terms could fairly be applied; but perhaps he was partly right when he admitted the possibility that 'I have not kept a just control of my emphasis'. The reason for that, so far as it is true, is that he was impatient of the exaggerated praise lavished upon Collins by certain earlier critics, particularly Swinburne, which 'makes him less interesting than he is'. He attempted to redress the balance, and in doing so he has, I think, somewhat overweighted the scale on the other side; but the attempt was in the interest of truth, and has been of better service to truth than the blind adulation which he condemned.

8. *Collins*, pp. 16-17.
9. I mean, of course, Richard as Collins portrays him, following Shakespeare. It would not be relevant to discuss the evidence here, but my own feeling is that a strong case has been made out by those who contend that Richard was innocent of the murder and that the real villain was his successor on the Throne, the first Tudor.

IV

'A Literary Adventurer'

DR. JOHNSON tells us that Collins 'came to London a literary adventurer, with many projects in his head, and very little money in his pocket'. The words must have dropped easily from Johnson's pen, for he must have realized that they would have been equally true of himself, and of several others of his friends besides Collins. After speaking of Collins's 'irresolution', and of 'the frequent calls of immediate necessity' which 'broke his schemes, and suffered him to pursue no settled purpose', he continues: 'A man, doubtful of his dinner, or trembling at a creditor, is not much disposed to abstracted meditation or remote enquiries.'

The first of the literary projects, we may say with certainty, was what Johnson calls a 'History of the Revival of Learning'. We are told that he published proposals for such a work, but 'probably not a page of the *History* was ever written'. That assumption we now know to be incorrect. In the *Review of English Studies* for January, 1927, Mr. H. O. White drew attention to an announcement of forthcoming publications in *A Literary Journal* for December, 1744. At the head of the list is 'A Review of the Advancement of Learning from 1300 to 1521, by Wm. Collins, 4to'. We still cannot believe that the book was ever published, as no trace of it has ever come to light, but it must have had, in some form, a recognizable existence. Ragsdale mentions that he had a copy of the printed proposals in his possession at the time of writing.

It is well known that John Mulso, who had been Collins's contemporary at Winchester, refers to him more than once in his letters to Gilbert White. On 18th July, 1744, he writes:

I saw Collins in Town, he is entirely an Author, & hardly speaks out of Rule: I hope his subscriptions go on well in Oxford: he told me that poor Hargrave was quite abandon'd, that He frequented night Cellars; I am sure you will be sorry for it, it really concerns me when I think of it, that so sprightly a Genius & so much good-nature should be thrown away.(*I*)

This was rather more than six months after Collins's arrival in London. The literary work in which he was absorbed, as Mulso implies by the expression 'entirely an Author', was presumably his 'Review of the Advancement of Learning'. Of 'poor Hargrave' we are to hear again very soon. Both Collins and Mulso seem to have been concerned at the dissipated habits of the young man, while acknowledging his natural charm.

It has always been believed, on the ultimate authority of Hay, the historian of Chichester, that Collins when he left Oxford thought of applying for a Commission in the Army, that with this intention he went to Flanders to ask for the help of Colonel Martin, his uncle, and that Colonel Martin advised him to enter the Church instead. There is some substance of truth in the story, but we shall find reason to believe that it was not until some time after July, 1745, more than eighteen months after his leaving Oxford, that he went to Flanders to interview Colonel Martin. What has not been understood is that in the late summer of 1744 Collins wrote to the Duke of Richmond to ask a favour of some kind without consulting Colonel Martin, and it is probable that the two applications have been confused.

'In 1733 or 1744,' according to Hay,

he quitted the College [Magdalen]; and at the desire of his mother's brother, Lieutenant-Colonel Martin, of Guy's Regiment of Foot, went to Flanders, where the Colonel then was; who would have provided for him in the Army, but found him too indolent, even for the Army; and besides, his mind was fixed on letters, and the improvement of his intellect.

It can be said at once that Hay is mistaken in speaking of Colonel Martin as 'of Guy's Regiment of Foot'. The Colonel belonged to the Fifty-Seventh Foot, known as 'Price's Regiment' until 23rd June, 1743, when Colonel Price was transferred to the Fourteenth Foot, and succeeded by Colonel Murray. The Fifty-Seventh Foot, known from this time as 'Murray's Regiment', had 'received orders to proceed to North Britain' in October, 1743,(2) and in North Britain it remained until some time later than 1st May, 1745, on which date Colonel Martin was transferred to the King's Regiment.(3) If, therefore, at any time within eighteen months of his leaving Oxford, Collins had responded to an invitation from his uncle to talk over his affairs, he must have travelled not to Flanders but to Scotland.

What he actually did is revealed by a collection of letters addressed to the second Duke of Richmond, edited and published in 1910 by the Earl of March of that day, afterwards Duke of Richmond and Gordon, in a volume entitled 'A Duke and his Friends'. As the second Duke was an active and prominent politician his correspondence is important mainly to the historian of the age of Pitt, but one of the letters affords welcome and unexpected help to the biographer of Collins. It appears that one of the Duke's occasional correspondents was Colonel Edmund Martin, of the Fifty-Seventh Foot, whose privilege it often was, says Lord March, 'to enjoy the Duke's hospitality at Goodwood as well as to join the merry throng that assembled at Charlton during the hunting season'. On 17th September, 1744, Colonel Martin writes from Fort William, Scotland:

Nothing could give me greater pleasure than ye rec[ei]pt of Your most kind and most obliging Letter. I was afraid I had the misfortune of Displeasing You, and had not ye Courage to write, tho' I attempted it two or three times and as often burnt it. I am extremely sorry my Nephew had ye Impudence to apply to You; I knew nothing of it, if I had he should not have done it; I never thought an Oxford Education was fit for any-

D

one but a Parson, and they a Nuisance to ye Comonwealth.(4)

What, then, was the nature of Collins's request to the Duke of Richmond? For the answer we must turn back to Hay's narrative, which we take to be true in substance though erroneous in the matters of place and time and in some points of detail. Hay continues, after the passage already quoted:

> Returning, therefore, to England, he applied, by the Colonel's desire, to Mr. Green, who gave him a title to the curacy of Birdham, of which Mr. Green was Rector, and letters of recommendation to the Bishop (Doctor Mawson) then in London. With these, and the necessary credentials, he went to London; but did not go to the Bishop's, being dissuaded from the clerical office by Mr. Hardham the tobacconist.

We remember that on 18th July Collins had been described by Mulso as 'entirely an Author', being absorbed, as we suppose, in his 'Review of the Advancement of Learning'. But the mere title of that work is enough to indicate that it would be a very considerable undertaking, and, if he did not abandon it entirely, Collins may well have decided to go about it in a more leisurely way, perhaps spreading it over several years instead of attempting to finish it in haste. The death of his mother in July, presumably obliging him to return to Chichester for a time, may have been the occasion of his revising his plans. However that may be, it is apparent that soon after his talk with Mulso he decided to enter the Church, and wrote to the Duke of Richmond asking for a recommendation to the Bishop as a candidate for Holy Orders. The Duke at this time had as his domestic Chaplain Richard Green, a typical hunting parson of the period, who was also Rector of Birdham.(5) It is evident, then, from Hay's account, that the Duke referred Collins's application to his Chaplain, that the Chaplain replied that he could make use of the services of a Curate at Birdham, and that Collins then arranged to present himself to the Bishop of Chichester for ordination. Then – to imitate the dramatic swiftness of the turn of events as Hay relates it – 'Enter John Hardham'.

36

Mr. Garrod says that he 'would give much to know a little more of this wealthy and, we must suppose, worldly tobacconist'.(6) We are not obliged to make the latter supposition, for John Hardham was, in fact, a philanthropist. He was a native of Chichester, and remained all his life, in spite of his migration to London, intensely loyal to his native city. He was also an ardent lover of the theatre, and on friendly terms with the leading actors and dramatists, and he is probably the only tobacconist who has been distinguished by a place in the *Dictionary of National Biography*. Garrick, to whom he had rendered some small services, had recommended a certain brand of snuff which Hardham prepared from a secret formula, and which came to be known as 'No. 37' from the number of the jar in which it was stored. The business is still carried on in premises in the Strand close to those of the original Hardham, and still has possession of the secret formula, so that people who care to sample the aroma of the eighteenth century may see in operation the identical Jar 37 which has supplied Garrick, Johnson, Sir Joshua Reynolds and a host of other people remembered and unremembered, probably including Collins.

> A name is all – from Garrick's breath a puff
> Of praise gave immortality to snuff;
> Since when each connoisseur a transient heaven
> Finds in each pinch of Hardham's Thirty-seven.(7)

By the time of his death in 1772 Hardham had amassed a considerable fortune, which he left for the benefit of the aged poor of Chichester, and many lives have been brightened in their closing years by the Hardham Trust. It is evident from the facts of his career that this prince of tobacconists owed his prosperity to other causes besides the smile of Garrick. He must have been one of those people of forceful personality who possess unconsciously the gift of radiating influence.

It would not take Hardham long to discover that Collins came from Chichester; that fact alone would excite his interest, especially, if, as is very likely, he remembered Alderman Collins and his family. In the course of conversation he would easily ascertain the state of affairs: that the young man had come up to London in the hope of making literature his profession, having already published some verses; that so far, though he had worked hard, he had reaped very little material reward; and that he had now decided, reluctantly, to renounce the vocation of a man of letters and to enter the Church.

Hay's story ends with the statement that Collins was 'dissuaded from the clerical office' by Hardham, but it is natural to suppose that his new friend and counsellor suggested an alternative. Remembering that Hardham's interest in the drama amounted to a passion, we may be reasonably sure that it was under his influence that Collins attempted to write a tragedy, as, according to Dr. Johnson, he did. We can almost hear the eloquent tobacconist arguing, with much force and many examples, that no man could live by poetry alone, however it might have been in the past; that the future was with the drama, and that his young friend, having learned at Oxford how a tragedy ought to be constructed, as well as having a natural gift, was just the man to conquer this limitless field.

Dr. Johnson remembered that 'he planned several tragedies, but he only planned them'. It is unlikely that any of them progressed within sight of the Fifth Act, as even the titles have eluded contemporary gossip. Langhorne, who was the first to attempt a complete edition of Collins's poems, and had the advantage of writing within six years of his death, says with laborious irony that he 'proceeded so far towards a tragedy – as to become acquainted with the Manager'. The statement accords with Ragsdale's recollection, from which we gather that Collins was for a time on familiar terms with dramatists, and, even though not a dramatist himself, was recognized by the profession as having equivalent status:

> He was an acceptable companion everywhere; and among the gentlemen who loved him for a genius, I may reckon the Doctors Armstrong, Barrowby, and Hill, Messrs. Quin, Garrick, and Foote, who frequently took his opinion on their pieces before they were seen by the public. He was particularly noticed by the geniuses who frequented the Bedford and

Slaughter's Coffee Houses. From his knowledge of Garrick, he had the liberty of the scenes and green-room, where he made diverting observations on the vanity and false consequence of that class of people; and his manner of relating them to his particular friends was extremely entertaining.

Judging by the date of Colonel Martin's letter, 17th September, 1744, we should suppose that it was some time in August, perhaps a month after his conversation with Mulso, that Collins made his decision to enter the Church; for we must allow time for correspondence between London and Goodwood and again between Goodwood and Scotland, and must remember also that the Duke of Richmond did not write to Colonel Martin immediately after hearing from Collins. It is very likely that by the middle of September, when Colonel Martin replied to the Duke, Collins had already met Hardham and been dissuaded from his plan. We can be sure that from this time he looked in frequently at Hardham's establishment, which is within an easy walk of Drury Lane, and it was most probably by Hardham's introduction that he met Garrick and began to move freely in theatrical circles.

About the beginning of October Collins changed his place of residence. Where he had been living up to this time is not known, but after his talk with Hardham and his decision to remain in London he may have felt justified by his prospects in looking for greater domestic comfort.

'In London I met him often,' says Gilbert White, 'and remember that he lodged in a little house with a Miss Bundy, at the corner of King's Square Court, Soho, now a warehouse, for a long time together.' Another resident of King's Square Court at this time was Mulso, and we have it on his authority that Collins was living there on 8th October, 1744, and was still there, as we shall see later, on 28th May, 1746, which explains Gilbert White's phrase, 'for a long time together'. On the first of these dates Mulso writes to Gilbert White:

Collins is now my next neighbour. I breakfasted with him this morning, & Cap[tai]n Hargrave play'd on ye Harpsichord, which he has not forgott quite so much as He has Himself.(8)

We remember that Captain Hargrave has been mentioned before by Mulso, and as he was on visiting terms with Collins, in spite of his unconventional behaviour, we should like if possible to find out more about him. There can be little doubt that he is identical with the writer of a number of letters preserved in the Manuscript Room of the British Museum: a certain Thomas Hargrave whose father, Dr. James Hargrave, had been Dean of Chichester until his death in 1741.(9) In 1742, at the age of sixteen, Thomas Hargrave had matriculated at Christ Church, Oxford.(10) Collins, Mulso and Gilbert White were all at Oxford at this time, and the son of Alderman Collins might well have taken a friendly interest in the son of Dean Hargrave, in spite of the difference of seniority. Early in 1744, as we gather from his own statements, Hargrave had obtained a commission in the Army,(11) and, as Collins left Oxford about the same time, it is possible that they went up to London together. Dean Hargrave had been in high favour with the magnificent Duke of Newcastle since the days when they were together at Cambridge.(12) The son entertained great expectations from the Duke's patronage, and he did not hope in vain; for it was the Duke, as is apparent from the correspondence, who sent him to Oxford and established him in the Army, even providing his uniform and personal necessaries. Then, or soon afterwards, began a series of errors or indiscretions. The opening paragraph of a letter dated 28th July, 1745, is typical of the numerous appeals that are to follow:

After the many hardships and inconvenience which through your Grace's displeasure I have justly suffered, I hope my sincere repentence and change of Behaviour will so far intercede for me as to give me leave to lay before you, how willing I am to undergo whatever your Grace shall please to lay upon me, and how entirely I am incapable of making Provision for my Voyage to Minorca.(13)

In the continuation he says that he has 'been upon duty with the imprest men at the Tower ever since I was in the Regiment'. That grain of information is useful in helping us to identify him with Collins's guest, as it reveals that he must have been in London at the time when Mulso was writing to Gilbert White. So far as we can judge by his letters, all of which are pitiable appeals for help in extricating himself from troubles and difficulties obviously of his own making, he was weak, unstable and shamelessly parasitic, though we may suspect that these defects were accompanied, as they often are, by more attractive qualities. His handwriting is beautifully neat and clear, with signs of artistic taste. If it was the author of this fine penmanship who played on the harpsichord in Collins's rooms we may be sure that he touched the instrument with a certain natural grace, and can understand Mulso's grudging admiration of his skill.

We have arrived at the autumn of 1744, and must suppose that until the end of the year, and beyond it, Collins continued to plan tragedies, to share in the gossip of Drury Lane, to chat with Hardham and occasionally to entertain Mulso and other friends in King's Square Court. It is very likely that about the end of the year he was called back to Chichester to attend to business arising out of the death of his uncle Charles, which would distract his mind from literary work. Of that more shall be said in the next chapter.

At some time before the end of the year Collins received one of the few signs ever vouchsafed to him that the reading public had some appreciation of his verses, or at least was aware of their existence. His 'Epistle to Hanmer', though it had not elicited any response from Sir Thomas, had proved to be a saleable product, and a second edition was required. The publisher, Thomas Cooper, had died about the beginning of the year, but his widow, Mrs. Mary Cooper, was carrying on the business with the experienced assistance of Dodsley,(14) and it was probably on Dodsley's initiative that the second edition, extensively revised, was undertaken.

With the second edition there appeared for the first time 'A Song from Shakespeare's *Cymbelyne*'. The contemporary public received it with indifference, and Collins's editors, so far, have hardly attempted to make amends. It is regrettable that Hazlitt, who includes it in a short list of poems which he considers 'the proofs of his capacity', has not given a reason for the faith that was in him. It is the first of Collins's poems which gives promise of the powers afterwards to be revealed in the ode *To Evening*. Collins, like Browning, has been criticized for the double fault of obscurity and harshness. In the 'Song from *Cymbelyne*' there is neither, but there is something of the art of Browning practised with a lighter touch. As when we approach the Dark Tower, or as when we heard Andrea del Sarto comparing Raphael's picture with his own, we do not consciously use our imagination in response to that of the poet; it is more as if the poet had possessed himself of our imagination and were using it in his own way. 'The sounds,' says Hazlitt, speaking of the ode *To Evening*, 'steal over the ear, like the gradual coming on of evening itself.' The critic who could say that could have spoken the last word in appreciation of the 'Song from *Cymbelyne*', and it could be wished that he had done so.

NOTES TO CHAPTER IV

1. *Letters to Gilbert White of Selbourne from ... the Rev. John Mulso* (ed. Holt-White), p. 3.
2. R. Cannon, *Historical Record of the Forty-Sixth, or the South Devonshire Regiment of Foot; originally numbered the Fifty-seventh Regiment*, p. 3. See also the manuscript Marching Orders in the Public Record Office (W.O. 536, passim).
3. For particulars of Colonel Martin's career see Dalton, *George the First's Army*, Vol. II, p. 165; *Historical Record of the King's Liverpool Regiment of Foot* (1905), p. 42; *Notes and Queries*, 12th Series, I, 245; State Papers 44 in the Public Record Office.
4. *A Duke and His Friends*, p. 460.
5. There are frequent references to him in the Duke of Richmond's correspondence. See *A Duke and His Friends*.
6. *Collins*, p. 55.
7. Colton, *Hypocrisy*, quoted by the *D.N.B.* under 'Hardham'.
8. *Letters to Gilbert White*, p. 7.
9. He had formerly, according to Nichols, been Rector of East Hoadley, Sussex, Rector of St. Margaret's, Westminster, and Chaplain-in-Ordinary to the King. (*Literary Anecdotes*, Vol. 1, p. 416.)
10. Foster, *Alumni Oxonienses*, p. 607.
11. On 2nd March, 1750, he tells Mrs. Spence that he had held a Commission 'now about six years, three and a half of which I have been a Lieutenant'. On 23rd October, 1755, he reminds the Duke of New-

castle that he has been 'eleven Years an Officer'. (B.M. Add. MSS. 32724, f. 159, and 32860, f. 146.)

12. Nichols, *Literary Anecdotes,* Vol. I, p. 416. See also the Dean's numerous letters in the Newcastle Correspondence (B.M. Add. MSS. 32698-33087).
13. B.M. Add. MS. 32704, f. 535.
14. See Plomer. *Dictionary of Booksellers and Printers, 1726-1775,* p. 60.

V

Financial Problems

IT has already been mentioned that Collins's mother died in July, 1744, about seven months after he had settled in London. That he rejoined his family in Chichester at this time cannot be stated with certainty, but it is natural to suppose that he did so. In that case the progress of his 'Review of the Advancement of Learning' would be interrupted, and it may have been immediately or soon after his return to London that he decided to postpone it and to enter the Church. His presence in Chichester would not be required by the lawyers, as his two sisters, Elizabeth and Anne, were the joint executrices of his mother's will.

In her will Mrs. Collins directed that her property, consisting mainly of copyhold land within the manor of Cackham, should be sold, and the proceeds divided equally, after payment of her debts, between her three children. It has always been assumed that the property in question was Southcott Farm, the original home of the Martin family, and Moy Thomas, drawing on his imagination, adds that it was 'secured by his mother's marriage settlement to her children'. He then, taking Hay as his principal authority, tells the story of Collins's supposed visit to Colonel Martin in Flanders, the offer of the Curacy of Birdham and the meeting with Hardham, and continues:

From that time Collins appears to have adopted the precarious profession of a man of letters. He disposed of the property in-

44

herited from his mother to his relative Mr. George Payne, and probably subsisted on the proceeds. He became a frequenter of the leading coffee-houses, and contracted an acquaintance with actors and the theatre. He soon dissipated his small fortune, and fell into pecuniary embarrassments. About this time he made the acquaintance of Johnson.(*1*)

In what follows there is no wish to refute Moy Thomas for the pleasure of doing so, but we have to recognize that for a hundred years his account has been taken as authoritative, and is followed by such cautious writers at Birkbeck Hill, the editor of Johnson's 'Lives of the Poets', Bronson and Mr. E. G. Ainsworth. His own principal authorities, besides Hay, are Johnson, Ragsdale and Warton, and as all three knew Collins more or less intimately we may hesitate to challenge his statements on points of fact. On the other hand, we have to remember that Collins himself seems to have been uncommunicative. Of those writers, contemporary and later, who have spoken of his poverty and his dependence on his relatives, not one professes to have derived his information from the person principally concerned. All seem to have exaggerated the wealth which he inherited from Colonel Martin, as will be shown later, and – what is more significant – none reveals any knowledge of the existence of his other uncle, Charles Collins. Birkbeck Hill has pointed out what certainly seems to be a contradiction in Johnson's account of Collins. Immediately after describing him as 'doubtful of his dinner, or trembling at a creditor', Johnson proceeds to say that his appearance, when he met him, was 'decent and manly'. 'In what sense', asks Birbeck Hill, 'does Johnson use *decent*?' After citing parallels from Johnson himself and from Goldsmith and Pope, he concludes: 'So Collins's appearance was "becoming" – according to the modern phrase "that of a gentleman" – the reverse of the appearance of Johnson and of many of his brother authors.'

We return to the subject of Mrs. Collin's will, and its effect upon her son's fortunes. It is obvious at a glance that the 'Copyhold or Customary Messuages Lands and Tenements situate lying and being within the Mannor [of Cackham] aforesaid' are identical with the property left to Mrs. Collins by her husband, whose will contains the same words. That it had nothing to do with South-cott Farm can be stated on the best legal authority. A search among the wills of the period reveals that the ownership of Southcott Farm descended from the first Edmund Martin, Mrs. Collins's father, to his elder son, Henry, and that Henry Martin, who died in 1715, left it to his brother Edmund, whom we know as Colonel Martin. That is as far as research along conventional lines will go, but the present owner, Mr. John Goodger, has rendered most valuable help by supplying, through his lawyers, some further information from the title-deeds, which he allows to be published.(2) It is that according to a deed dated the 17th January, 1717, 'Mr. Edmund Martin, described as the eldest son of Edmund Martin and the grandson of Edmund Martin formerly of Appledram in the County of Sussex, sold the property to one John Croucher'. The names of subsequent owners are given, and it can be said with certainty that with the sale to John Croucher the ownership of this estate passed for all time away from the Martin family. It is, therefore, impossible that it should ever have descended to Mrs. Collins, or been secured to her children by her marriage settlement.

When that has been said, however, the fact remains that Mrs. Collins did, by her husband's will, come into possession of land and houses within the Manor of Cackham, and, as we have seen, bequeathed them to her children. The property has not been identified, but seems to have been substantial. Is it true that Collins sold his share 'to his relative Mr. George Payne', subsisted for a time on the proceeds, and 'soon dissipated his small fortune'?

In order to answer that question it will be convenient to leave Collins chatting with his theatrical friends at the end of 1744 and to look several years ahead, so as to ascertain the full effect of Mrs. Collins's will. The settlement of her affairs seems to have been a somewhat dilatory process. Her will was not proved until the 12th August, 1745, more than a year after her death, and it was not for a further two years that the first steps were taken towards the sale of her property in accordance with her intention. A document discovered by Mr. W. L. Wilmshurst in 1933, and bearing Collins's signature, proves that the premises in East Street, Chichester, where Alderman Collins had carried on his business, were sold on 1st May, 1747.(*3*) In the same year, as has been already mentioned, the rights under the lease of the Rectory of St. Bartholomew's were sold for £260.(*4*)

Concerning the Cackham estate it seems probable that there was a difference of opinion, Collins himself being willing to sell it, as his mother had directed, while the two sisters were determined to keep it in the family. For such information as can be found we must look still further ahead to the 8th December, 1750, when the elder of Collins's sisters, Elizabeth, made her will. Elizabeth Collins had by this time become Mrs. Tanner, having been married to Nathaniel Tanner, a Lieutenant in the Buffs, on the 15th October, 1750. Her will is not a simple document like those of others of her family, and we cannot hope to unravel all the details without having access to that 'Tripartite Indenture of Settlement' to which it frequently refers. We learn that this document, dated 16th October, 1749, is concerned not only with Mrs. Tanner's third share of the property left by her mother but also with her third share of certain other 'Copyhold or Customary Lands Tenements and Premises . . . which were purchased by George Payne Esqr. of and from my Brother William Collins Gent in Trust'. It is apparent, then, that Mrs. Tanner and two other persons, probably her sister Anne and George Payne, had agreed to acquire jointly from Collins the property inherited by him from his mother, but in the first instance the whole of the purchase money was provided by George Payne, who must have been, in a modest way, a capitalist. It is unfortunate that there is no mention of the date of the settlement. It was probably later than 1747, as Collins would hardly have sold his share of the Cackham estate, which must have been of greater sentimental value, before disposing of the premises in East Street and his interest in the Rectory of St. Bartholomew.

By the terms of Mrs. Tanner's will the whole of her possessions, including both her original share of the Cackham estate inherited from her mother and the additional share thus acquired from her brother William, were left to her husband; at whose death, provided that she did not have children, it was to revert to her brother William and her sister Anne in equal shares. Collins cannot have benefited by this last provision, as Nathaniel Tanner lived till

47

1767, his death being recorded in the *Gentleman's Magazine* for that year. Mrs. Tanner died some time before the 17th June, 1754, the date when her will was proved, and as she had married late in life it is unlikely that she left children.

From this digression we return to the end of 1744, the time when Collins was moving in theatrical circles, writing a tragedy or attempting to do so, and making regular journeys to Drury Lane; or when, as Moy Thomas chooses to express it, 'he became a frequenter of the leading coffee-houses, and contracted an acquaintance with actors and the theatre'. It must have been about this time that he heard of the death of his uncle Charles. The exact date when this occurred is not known, but the will of Charles Collins was proved on 5th March, 1745. Though he had lived for many years at the Charterhouse, in London, he was the owner of property in Chichester, and as his nephew William Collins was his principal heir, and is named first of the two executors of his will, the other being George Payne, it is very probable that Collins again returned to Chichester early in the year.

Our only information about the career of Charles Collins is derived from official sources, and it will be convenient to bring together here such facts as are available. The date of his baptism, 8th February, 1666, was mentioned in the first chapter. It is almost certain that he was educated at Winchester; for a boy named Collen or Collin(5) was a chorister at the school in 1680,(6) and among the possessions bequeathed by Charles Collins to his nephew were a drawing of Winchester College and a valued collection of church music. On 26th March, 1686, he matriculated at New College, Oxford, as *puer pauper serviens*,(7) but there is no record of his having graduated. On 14th April, 1696, at the Church of St. Peter the Great, Chichester, he married Elizabeth Cardiffe,(8) of whom nothing else is known. On 24th March, 1729, he was admitted a Brother of the Charterhouse, on the nomination of the Duke of Newcastle.(9) His wife must have died before this, as a married man would not have been eligible. In the manuscript list of the electors of Sussex, compiled for the Duke of Newcastle in 1734, he is shown as being resident in London but having a vote in respect of freehold property in the Parish of St. Bartholomew, Chichester.(10) His possession of a

48

vote would have commended him to the Duke, and that may account for his nomination for the Charterhouse; though it is also a possibility that Dean Hargrave, whose son is believed to have been the somewhat disreputable Captain Hargrave known to Collins during his first year in London, used his influence with the Duke on his behalf.

We learn from the document itself that the will of Charles Collins was begun on the 2nd September, 1741, but not completed until the 19th June, 1742. A little further examination reveals that the beginning and end follow the customary legal form, but the main provisions, though clearly explained, are set down in the language which an elderly man might have used in his ordinary correspondence. It may be surmised that the opening lines were written with the help of a lawyer; the lawyer then ascertained by a few questions that William Collins, one of the two persons proposed as executors, was not yet twenty-one; it was decided for this reason to postpone the continuation for the necessary few months, and the old man then took the document home, and, from time to time, went on writing the will in his own way. The following June, we may suppose, realizing that his nephew William was now of age, he took it back to the lawyer for completion and any necessary revision. What is significant, if there is any truth in this conjecture, is that Charles Collins was determined that his nephew William should act as one of his executors, and would not save time by substituting any other name.

After professing his religious faith and giving directions for his funeral, and for the payment of his debts, the testator speaks of 'my Freehold Estate scituate lying and being in the Parish of St. Bartholomews without the Westgate of the City of Chichester Sussex'. This, he says, 'I give and bequeath to my Nephew William Collins of the City and County aforesaid . . . with all Appurtenances belonging to it with all Rents Arrearages and Profits from it arising from one Year after my Decease to be accounted for to him.' Of this estate, which was actually on a more modest scale than the words of the will would seem to imply, more shall be said hereafter.

Collins is also to have the most precious of his personal possessions:

49

Item I give to my Nephew William Collins my Fathers Picture
in a frame and my own picture without a Frame and Alexander
taking Darius in his Tent without a Frame and the Draught of
Winchester Colledge in a black Frame. Also I give to my aforesaid Nephew William Collins my Silver Tankard with my Arms
on it and my Collection of Musick on the Score [;] this collection of Church Musick as well as Songs and other Musick
which if you have no relish of it now, it may be hereafter valuable therefore pray make much of it and keep it for the love the
Family have born to that Faculty.

This appeal shows clearly that the love of music was, as we should
have supposed, a bond of sympathy between uncle and nephew.
It may also be remarked, in passing, that 'Alexander taking
Darius in his Tent' is a picture by Pierre Mignard, apparently
well known.

The other nephew, George Payne, 'Dr. in Physick of Bruton
Street', inherits two separate sums of forty pounds and thirty
guineas, besides pictures of 'King Charles the first and his Queen
in one Frame gilt and King Charles the second and Queen Ann
both in Lacker or Gilt Fram[e]s'. A boy named Charles Richard
Sylvester, probably a godson, the son of Richard and Betty Sylvester, of Golden Square, is to have his silver watch, a framed
picture of himself and one of his wife, his books of arithmetic and a
number of articles of practical use, such as furniture, glassware
and vessels of pewter, brass and copper; and George Payne is
entrusted with ten guineas to have the boy apprenticed to a trade.
'I heartily crave of my nephew Dr. George Payne to do the best
in his power for him which I hope he will punctually and faithfully and God I hope will reward him for so faithfull a discharge
of the Trust repose[d] in him.' George Payne did, in fact, discharge the trust faithfully and punctually by apprenticing the boy
to a goldsmith.(11)

Two provisions of the will stand out in contrast to the kindly
tone pervading the document as a whole, and leave the reader
wondering what motive can have inspired them:

Item I give to my Neice Elizabeth Collins Daughter of Alderman William Collins aforesaid the Sum of one Shilling of good and lawful Money of Great Britain as also my Mother Collins's Wedding Ring. Item I give to Anne Collins my Neice one Shilling of good and lawfull Money of Great Britain.

Had there been a family quarrel? Had the two nieces offended him in some manner which he could not forget, even while contemplating his death, and immediately after professing his Christian faith in no merely formal terms? He may have had an aversion to something in the character of his nieces, but that hardly seems an adequate explanation.

A further mention of the two nieces towards the end of the will creates a new problem without helping to solve the former one. It is in this sentence, which reads as if it might have been inserted in an earlier draft as an afterthought:

As for the Lord Viscount Waymouth and his Sister's Money[,] if there be any likelyhood of it I give [it] to my two Neices Elizabeth and Anne Collins.

We can say at once that whatever likelihood there may have been was not realized. The will of the Lord Weymouth of that day, who died in 1749, contains no mention of any person named Collins. It can also be stated that among the historical papers at Longleat there is no record of any kind to indicate that Charles Collins, his wife, or anyone connected with him had any dealings with Lord Weymouth or any claim upon his estate. With the consent of the Marquess of Bath, Lord Weymouth's descendant, a search was made recently by the librarian at Longleat, Miss Dorothy Carter, but no clue to the mystery was found.

Perhaps at this point it may be possible to account for a curious story attributed by Moy Thomas to the younger Durnford, son of the Rector of Bramdean, who many years later than the time we are now considering became the second husband of Anne Collins. According to Durnford 'the sister of Collins loved money to excess, and evinced so outrageous an aversion to her brother, because he squandered or gave away to the boys in the cloisters whatever money he had, that she destroyed, in a paroxysm of

51

E

resentment, all his papers, and whatever remained of his enthusiasm for poetry, as far as she could'.(12)

That Anne Collins loved money to excess we can believe, but the rest of the story has every mark of improbability. There is not even a rumour of her having exhibited this unnatural hatred of her brother on any other occasion. The traditional belief is that she rescued him from a madhouse and tended him with more than sisterly care in his last illness, and that he died in her arms. Moreover, though it is possible to destroy papers, it would require no ordinary powers of witchcraft or hypnotism or heterosuggestion to destroy another person's enthusiasm for poetry, even to whatever limited extent may be indicated by the phrase 'as far as she could'. Finally, there is nothing in the story to imply that it was not his own money which Collins squandered or gave away. A sister of Anne Collins's temperament might have disapproved of this extravagance, but would she be roused to such fury as to act like a lunatic?

If we assign the paroxysm of resentment to the beginning of 1745 we may arrive at an explanation which, though conjectural, accords rather better with the known facts than the one offered by Durnford. Let us imagine Collins, while engaged on some kind of literary work – probably writing or planning a tragedy – hearing that his uncle Charles had died, that he himself was the principal heir and was now the owner of property in Chichester, and that he was required to act as executor. Let us hope that he did not receive the news with unqualified pleasure, but he was, after all, a young man, and, as his aged uncle had lived at the Charterhouse for sixteen years, he could hardly have met him since he was a small child until he himself settled in London. We should suppose, then, that he returned to Chichester feeling mildly elated. When he arrived he would explain to his sister Anne what had happened, and, perhaps, show her a copy of the will, and she would find to her indignation that she herself was cut off with a shilling. It would be no consolation to her to learn that she was to have half the money of Lord Weymouth and his sisters 'if there be any likelihood of it', as she may have been aware already, and in any case would suspect from the qualifying clause, that there was in fact no likelihood of it whatever. Besides being fond of money she seems to have been something of an egotist, and she may have taken the will as an affront to her dignity as well as an injustice.

If Collins was tactless enough to show any sign of pleasure, and if, soon afterwards, he was seen to be celebrating his good fortune by distributing largesse to the boys in the cloisters, it is easy to believe that Anne's resentment boiled over into a paroxysm. She avenged herself, we are told, by destroying 'all his papers'. It has always been assumed, though Durnford does not say so, that these papers were poems in manuscript, and that literary treasures of unimaginable value were thus lost to the world. We must remember, if the truth is as we have supposed, that the real object of her vindictive fury was not her brother but her deceased uncle, and we must think it most likely that the papers which she destroyed as an act of vengeance were those comprising that 'Collection of Church Musick as well as Songs and other Musick' which had been bequeathed to her brother as an object of special care. We can imagine her, as sheet after sheet went up in flames, murmuring with bitter irony the words of the will: 'Therefore pray make much of it and keep it for the Love the Family have born to that Faculty.'

It is natural to suppose that Collins had left his manuscripts, if he had any, safely locked up in London. In that case Durnford may have been right in saying that Anne destroyed 'all his papers' if by that is meant all the papers that he had with him in Chichester at the time. Legally the sheets of music were, in fact, Collins's property according to the terms of the will, but Anne, if she was really, at the time, bordering on madness, would be incapable of thinking of such technicalities; to her frenzied mind they were her uncle's papers, and her destruction of them was an act of vengeance on the dead. It is a fact of some significance that the name of Charles Collins does not appear on the memorial tablet to the Collins family erected by Anne in St. Andrew's Church, though the name of her maternal uncle, Colonel Edmund Martin, is included.

We have no certain information of Collins's movements for several months after this, and must suppose that he returned from Chichester after a short stay and resumed something like his former routine. He would be likely, in the ordinary course, to pay an occasional visit to his cousin George Payne, the other executor of his uncle's will. We can trust contemporary gossip so far as to believe that two or three conferences did take place, though as to their object and outcome we must form our own conclusions.

At this point we must turn back to that part of Ragsdale's narrative which refers to Collins's career before the time when he came to know him personally. At the beginning he says of William Collins the elder: 'He was pompous in his manner; but at his death he left his affairs rather embarrassed. Colonel Martin, his wife's brother, greatly assisted his family, and supported Mr. William Collins at the University.'

We cannot believe that Ragsdale was told this by Collins, who was consistently reticent about his private affairs, and if it is conjecture it must be described as a most improbable conjecture. There is no evidence that Alderman Collins left his affairs in any degree embarrassed, and his will and that of Mrs. Collins afford positive evidence that he made ample provision for his widow and his family.

What, then, of Colonel Martin? We gather from one of his letters to the Duke of Richmond, already quoted, that he had a poor opinion of the value of an Oxford education, so that his benevolence would be unlikely to take the form of supporting his nephew at the university. That, it is true, is not decisive, because a wealthy and indulgent uncle might have been persuaded to act in such a matter against his better judgment; but we are not altogether without knowledge of the Colonel's financial resources, and it does not appear that he was in a position to exercise the generosity attributed to him, however well disposed he may have been to his sister and her family.

From that very valuable publication *A Duke and his Friends*, to which we have already referred, we learn how Colonel Martin impressed those officers of the Higher Command who knew him intimately on a professional footing. General Hawley, writing to the Duke of Richmond on 16th June, 1746, speaks of Martin's 'ignorance that has appeared in some things and his mean appearance', adding: 'I assure you I have nothing to say against the man but that he is beyonde his sphere and was surely intended by God Almighty, when made, to be only a Capt[ain].'(13) Lord March, in introducing this letter, says that Hawley's 'uncharitable remarks upon poor Colonel Martin denote a tendency to merciless criticism of those whose lack of means precluded them from competing with their better-dressed brother officers'.*(14)* Everyone will agree, but the point of immediate concern is that the Colonel was understood to be a poor man, and that it was on that account that he incurred Hawley's criticism, however unfair and unkind that criticism may have been.

Lord Albemarle, who succeeded Hawley in the command of Fort Augustus, was much more friendly to Colonel Martin, and, as Lord March observes, 'disposed to take a much more charitable view of his failings', but even he admits that 'his forehead is rough, besides being shaby in his dress'.

According to Dr. Johnson Colonel Martin left Collins 'about two thousand pounds', equivalent to something like ten times that sum in the money of today; but the inheritance was to be divided equally between Collins and his two sisters, and from that it follows that the total fortune must have amounted to the equivalent, in the money of today, of sixty thousand pounds or thereabouts. Are we to conclude, then, that the threadbare Colonel was secretly a miser? His open handwriting*(15)* and the breezy tone of his letters to the Duke of Richmond are almost enough in themselves to rule out that possibility.

We find, then, on the one hand, Johnson and Ragsdale, who did not know him, reporting rumours of his opulence, and, on the other hand, General Hawley and Lord Albemarle, who did know him, gossiping about his poverty. The only other evidence available is that of his will, and that must be allowed to settle the question. It is a brief and simple document. He leaves £100 to his niece Elizabeth, the wife of Thomas Napper, his copyhold estates in the Manors of Selsey and Somerly to his nephew Abraham Martin, the youngest son of his late brother Henry, £10 and his wearing apparel to his servant John Kipp, and all the rest of his real and personal estate to be divided equally between his nephew William Collins and his nieces Elizabeth and Anne Collins. Elizabeth Collins is appointed sole executrix.

The mention of copyhold estates at Selsey and Somerly may at first sight suggest the possibility of wealth in the background; but we are able to investigate further, and we find from the will of John Martin, apparently the Colonel's uncle, who died in 1703(16) that the Selsey estate was worth ten pounds a year and the Somerly estate nine pounds a year. Southcott Farm was sold by Colonel Martin in 1717, as has been mentioned already, and we know of a house in Chichester, worth £83, which he sold about the same time, and of which more will be said later. That accounts for the whole of his property of which any record has been found. The phrase 'all the rest of my real and personal estate wheresoever and whatsoever' has the appearance of being designed to account in the usual way for unconsidered trifles, and that is the only part of the will in which Collins is concerned. The will was signed on the 9th April, 1749, and proved on the 30th May. So brief an interval between the date of death and the date of probate can be taken as evidence in itself that the estate was on a small scale.

We must conclude, then, that Johnson was in some way misled or misinformed when he said that Collins's share amounted to about £2,000, and that Ragsdale, partly influenced by Johnson, was also mistaken in supposing that the Collins family, after their father's death, had depended on Colonel Martin's bounty. If either of his uncles supported Collins at Oxford it is more likely to have been Charles Collins, who was an Oxford man himself, though there is no reason to believe that he actually did so.

We return to Ragsdale's narrative. He proceeds to explain, in words already quoted, Collins's reasons for leaving Oxford: that he was disappointed of a Fellowship, that he was in debt, and that he yearned for the dissipation and gaiety of London. The story continues:

Colonel Martin was at this time with his regiment; and Mr. Payne, a near relation, who had the management of the Colonel's affairs, had likewise a commission to supply the Collinses with small sums of money. When Mr. William Collins came from the University, he called on his cousin Payne, gaily dressed, and with a feather in his hat; at which his relation expressed surprise, and told him his appearance was by no means that of a young man who had not a single guinea to call his own. This gave him great offence; but, remembering his sole dependence for subsistence was in the power of Mr. Payne, he concealed his resentment; yet could not refrain from speaking freely behind his back, and saying 'he thought him a d——d dull fellow'; though, indeed, this was an epithet he was pleased to bestow on any who did not think as he would have them. His frequent demands for a supply obliged Mr. Payne to tell him he must pursue some other line of life, for he was sure Colonel Martin would be displeased with him for having done so much. This resource being stopped, forced him to set about some work, of which his 'History of the Revival of Learning' was the first, and for which he printed proposals (one of which I have). The work was begun, but soon stood still.

The whole of this story is vitiated by the false assumption that George Payne was a near relation of Colonel Martin. We know that he was not related to him at all, unless the fact that his maternal uncle had married Colonel Martin's sister can be said to constitute a relationship. There was nothing in common between the veteran soldier and the Bruton Street physician except that they were both natives of Sussex, and neither had lived in Sussex since his youth. Our knowledge of the Colonel's resources is enough in itself to throw doubt on the story that he appointed an agent to manage his affairs and to dole out money to the Collins family; but when we are told that the agent was George Payne, and that Payne was a near relation, the writer is asking too much of our credulity.

Separating the solid facts from the conjectures, so far as may be possible, we should suppose the truth to be something like this. When Collins left Oxford to plunge into the literary life of London he depended, for some months, on an allowance from his mother. Mrs. Collins, it is true, was a strict economist, but that is not incompatible with a certain liberality where her son was concerned. Collins, no doubt, intended to repay the money when he had established himself as an author, and his publications so far afforded some ground for the hope that he would do so within a reasonable time.

If it is true that he called on his cousin Payne immediately after his arrival in London, as Ragsdale seems to simply, that would be merely a courtesy visit. Bruton Street was a fashionable quarter, and Collins would have failed in proper respect for his host if he had not taken care to dress suitably for the occasion. Perhaps he overdid it a little, but he erred on the right side. In wearing a feather in his hat he was not breaking any sumptuary law, written or unwritten; he was adopting the sartorial style of a young man of substance, and by so doing he displayed, in his cousin's opinion, vanity and presumption.

We gather that he met with a rebuff. George Payne had probably by this time received a letter from his brother William, telling him of their young cousin's insolent behaviour at Oxford and his hasty departure. If Payne, as Ragsdale says, remarked on his appearance, and reminded him that he had not a single guinea that he could call his own, he was stretching the privilege of an older relative far beyond its permissible limit, and Collins's resentment was natural. The expression attributed to him, 'a d——d dull fellow', may or may not have been justified, but that or something like it is what ninety-nine out of a hundred young men in his position would have said.

The following July, as we know, his mother died, and that would have the effect, among others, of upsetting his finances. The probability is that he returned to Chichester and had a talk with his sister Elizabeth, the executrix of the will, and that Elizabeth agreed to continue the allowance, perhaps on a reduced scale, on the understanding that the money so advanced should be repaid by instalments out of his share of the property. Collins then returned to London, resumed and then abandoned or postponed his work on the Revival of Learning, toyed with the idea of taking Holy Orders, and finally met Hardham and began to devote himself to the drama.

That would be the state of affairs when, about six months after the death of Mrs. Collins, but while her estate was still, and likely to remain for some time, in the hands of the lawyers, the death of Charles Collins occurred. It may be assumed that Collins's income at this time was only just enough to enable him to live in reasonable comfort in King's Square Court, and was liable to be exceeded. In that case the prospect of a windfall would be, in itself, extremely welcome, but it did not bring any immediate relief to whatever financial strain there may have been. It must have been tantalizing to discover from the will that the inheritance of 'Rents Arrearages and Profits' was not to come into effect until a full year after the testator's death.

We must observe at this point that George Payne, though named by Charles Collins second of his executors, took the lead in completing the formalities, as was, perhaps, natural in view of his settled position and far greater age. To him alone 'Administration was granted of all and singular the Goods Chattels and Credits of the said Deceased', though with 'Power reserved of making the like Grant to William Collins the other Executor named in the said Will when he shall apply for the same'.

A strict economist would have told Collins that there was nothing to gain by asking for any of the money in advance of the final settlement, and that when he did receive it his best plan would be to keep it as a provision for emergencies; but Collins was not a strict economist, and the knowledge that he had such a provision in reserve would tend to create the emergency. Our interpretation of the facts as Ragsdale has recorded them must be that Collins went to Bruton Street again, however reluctantly, to interview George Payne; this time not for the purpose of paying a social call, but strictly on business. He asked for and was given a small loan in advance, accompanied, no doubt, by a stern lecture on the evil of extravagance. After an interval he asked for more, and that application, or possibly a third, was refused. That seems to be the true foundation of Ragsdale's story of Collins's 'sole dependence' on George Payne as the dispenser of Colonel Martin's bounty, of the 'frequent demands for a supply', and of the final warning that 'Colonel Martin would be displeased with him for having done so much'.

A recent and important discovery enables us to say more about Collins's inheritance from his uncle Charles. In 1953 Mrs. Phyllis Heseltine, who had purchased the house now 13, Westgate, Chichester, was handed by her lawyer 'a "bundle of old Deeds and documents" – yellowed with age and not at once decipherable, which had accompanied the Deed of Conveyance of the freehold'. Fortunately Mrs. Heseltine did not ask the lawyer to keep the bundle himself or to send it to the bank, which is what most purchasers would have done; feeling that the documents might turn out to have an antiquarian interest of their own she took them home, and, with the help of her sister, Miss Audrey Jennings, who, by extreme good fortune, was an experienced worker in the field of genealogical research, examined them at her leisure. She found to her surprise that one of her early predecessors in the ownership of the house was William Collins. A copy of the will of Charles Collins, from which some extracts have been given already in this chapter, was among the deeds, and further investigation established beyond doubt that this was the 'Freehold Estate scituate lying and being in the Parish of Saint Bartholomews without the Westgate of the City of Chichester' which Collins had inherited in 1745.

Mrs. Heseltine published a very interesting account of her discovery in the *Sussex County Magazine* for November, 1955, illustrated with a full-page photograph of the house and with views of Westgate in Collins's time and today. An even more informative article, on more technical lines, had already been published in *Notes and Queries* for February, 1954, by Miss Jennings, and it is mainly from that article that the information now to be given is extracted.

It appears from the earliest deed in Mrs. Heseltine's collection that the house had been purchased by Charles Collins on the 7th October, 1720, from one William Grigg; but Grigg could not have owned it for long, it having been 'lately' purchased by him 'of Edmund Martin gent'. This Edmund Martin must be identical with the Colonel Martin of later years whom we know as Collins's uncle, as his father, also Edmund Martin, had died in 1704. The possibility that he was a different person who happened to be a namesake is hardly worth considering in view of some further facts now to be mentioned. One of the witnesses to the transaction was William Collins, 'presumably', as Miss Jennings says, 'the poet's father', and therefore, if he and Edmund Martin have been correctly identified, the brother-in-law of the former owner and brother of the purchaser. The house is described as 'now in the tenure or occupation of John Scott gent.', and we remember that a man of that name, then living in Kent, married Judith Collins, the sister of Charles and William, on 21st January, 1707, and soon afterwards removed to Chichester.(*17*) Colonel Martin, we may recall, had sold Southcott Farm to John Croucher in January, 1717, and it was probably about the same time that he sold the house in Chichester.

The price paid by Charles Collins to Grigg was £83, equivalent to something approaching a thousand pounds in the money of to-day. It appears, then, that when Collins acquired the house in 1745 he did not inherit a fortune, and the mention in his uncle's will of a 'Freehold Estate ... with all Rents Arrearages and Profits from it arising' could, at first sight, give a false impression.

That by no means exhausts the interest of the bundle of deeds, to which we shall return. In the meantime we must record the only certain information that we have of Collins's movements during the remainder of 1745. On 7th September of that year Mulso writes to Gilbert White:

Collins has been some Time return'd from Flanders, in order to put on ye Gown as I hear, & get a chaplaincy in a Regiment. Don't laugh, indeed I don't on these occasions: This will be ye second acquaintance of mine who becomes ye Thing he most derides.(*18*)

The phrase 'as I hear' seems to indicate that Mulso on this occasion was reporting what he had been told by some third person, and that would account for his being well informed about Collins's actions without professing to understand their motives. It is safe to assume, in the first place, that Collins's immediate object in going abroad was to consult with his military uncle, Colonel Martin. We know from his correspondence with the Duke of Richmond that the Colonel was still, on 14th May, 1745, at Fort William, where he had been for some eighteen months; but the King's Regiment, to which he had been transferred on 1st May, was in Flanders, and he must have joined it in that country long before September.

What, then, was the object of the consultation? The answer is suggested by the fact that 'some time' before the date of Mulso's letter – actually on 25th July, 1745 – the Young Pretender had landed in Scotland. The Government of King George the Second was in far greater danger than is commonly realized by people who allow their view of the rebellion to be obscured by Culloden. Military historians have found much to admire in the Prince's strategy, and in the tactics to which he owed his victories of Prestonpans and Falkirk. His one major error was to spend time in raising the Highlands instead of taking the tide in his affairs at the flood and marching straight to London; had he had the iron nerve of Edward the Fourth, whom in some of his qualities he resembled, he might have won an easier victory in a second Battle of Barnet.

Although, temperamentally, Collins may have resembled his grandfather rather than his father, we must think of him as in matters of politics the son of the Whig Alderman rather than the grandson of the Royalist Vicar Choral. He was, moreover, by this time a Londoner, and the dread of seeing a Jacobite army marching through London may well have roused him to action. If he thought of offering himself as a volunteer his uncle was obviously the person to advise him, and it would be easier to cross the water and to see Colonel Martin while he was still in Flanders than to wait for his return to Scotland, which was now the scene of a civil war. An officer of Colonel Martin's experience would not take long to decide that the young man who presented himself, and whom possibly he had never seen before, would be no acquisition to the Army, but he would remember that the same young man had caused him some embarrassment the previous year by applying to the Duke of Richmond for help in finding a curacy, and that would suggest the idea that, if he wished to serve his King and country he should join as a Chaplain. That we must suppose to be the true origin of the story that Collins went straight from Oxford to Flanders 'at the desire' of Colonel Martin, that the Colonel 'would have provided for him in the army, but found him too indolent', and that it was 'by the Colonel's desire' that he applied to Mr. Green for the Curacy of Birdham. The interview with Colonel Martin in Flanders, in the summer of 1745, has been confused with the application to the Duke of Richmond in the previous year, in which Colonel Martin was not directly concerned.

It is probable that Mulso was reporting the uncle's advice rather than the nephew's intention when he said that Collins had returned 'in order to . . . get a chaplaincy in a Regiment'. Collins did not, as far as we know, take any further steps towards ordination. He returned to King's Square Court, and resumed his former life as well as he could in an atmosphere of excitement.

There is no indication that up to this time he had had any serious financial worries, and we have surmised that from the time of his mother's death to the final settlement of her affairs he was allowed a small income from his share of the property. After the 12th August, 1745, when Mrs. Collins's will was proved, he would be free to take possession of his inheritance. The feeling of independence and comparative opulence thus induced might well have led him into extravagance, and there is reason to believe that that is what happened.

He had already, as we have seen, tried without success, or with very little success, to raise a loan on the house in Chichester inherited from his uncle Charles, and had been thwarted by George Payne. Payne, no doubt, had the instinct of an economist, like his uncle the Alderman and his cousin Anne Collins, and, however ungracious his manner, is entitled to credit for good intentions in keeping a check on his young cousin's prodigality. The strength of his position as executor lay in the fact that Collins could not, by the terms of the will, enter into his inheritance until a year after his uncle's death. The year would expire at some time about the beginning of 1746.

It is a relief at this point to be able to return to Mrs. Heseltine's deeds and to state two facts which are entirely beyond the region of conjecture, being supported by documentary proof. The first is that on the 10th April, 1746, Collins raised a mortgage of fifty pounds on the house in Westgate from Thomas Sefton, husbandman, of Halnaker in the Parish of Boxgrove, Sussex. In the indenture William Collins is described as 'of Chichester, gent.', and as the 'only son and heir of William Collins, citizen and alderman of Chichester, decd. and also nephew and heir at law as well as devisee of Charles Collins, . . . who was the only brother of the said William Collins decd'. The endorsement has Collins's signature, and Miss Jennings observes that 'in all, there are seven autographs of the poet on these documents'.

The second of the two facts just mentioned is that on the 30th

May, 1746, Collins sold the freehold outright to William Milton, of Chichester, for sixty-two pounds, of which fifty pounds went to Thomas Sefton to pay off the mortgage and the balance of twelve pounds to Collins. It was a bad bargain, for his uncle had paid eighty-three pounds for the house in 1720, and we learn that since then the premises had been improved by some small additions.

Mulso, writing to Gilbert White on 28th May, 1746, gives an indication of the direction which Collins's extravagance was taking, and the kind of difficulty in which he had involved himself:

> I can't help telling You, tho' 'tis a little uncharitable, that Collins appears in good cloaths & a wretched carcass, at all ye gay Places, tho' it was with ye utmost Difficulty that He scrap'd together 5 pound for Miss Bundy at whose Suit He was arrested & whom by his own confession He never intended to pay. I don't believe He will tell ye Story in Verse, tho' some circumstances of his taking would be burlesque enough. The Bailiff introduc'd himself with 4 Gentlemen who came to drink Tea, & who all together could raise but one Guinea. The ἀναγνώρισις (a word He is fond of) was quite striking & ye catastrophe quite poetical & interesting.(19)

That is all very much as we should expect. It is not a story of poverty; it is a story of financial embarrassment of the kind which would have appealed to Sheridan, complete with the touch of humour common to such stories in the eighteenth century. There must have been dozens of young men accustomed to appear 'at all ye gay Places' who at some time had had a similar experience. It may have been partly to teach her lodger a lesson that Miss Bundy went through the form of having him arrested, for Mr. H. O. White has done some research into the lady's family history, and has discovered that she was the daughter of a deceased clergyman whose sermons had been published.(20) If it was by her stage-management that the bailiff arrived at the same moment as the four gentlemen who had come to drink tea she must have had a fine sense of dramatic effect.

64

The probability is that Collins had spent in advance, by living on credit, a substantial part of the sum which he raised ultimately by mortgaging the house in Westgate, and that when, some time after the 10th April, he returned from Chichester with the affluent look of a person having fifty pounds – or what remained of it – in his possession, he thought first of entertaining his friends instead of paying his debts. That is understandable, but we cannot believe on Mulso's unsupported testimony that he never intended to pay Miss Bundy, as Mulso does not say or imply that the confession was made to him or in his presence. We do not hear of Miss Bundy again. It was two days after the date of Mulso's letter that the sale of the house in Chichester was completed, and it must have been very soon after that – though we have no knowledge of the exact date – that Collins left London and settled at Richmond.

It is regrettable that we do not know the names of the four guests who were present at the tea party. Some of them may be known to literary history, and it is a pleasing fancy, though nothing more, that it was one of these friends who brought Dr. Johnson on to the scene. We know that it was by Johnson's help and at his suggestion that Collins left London. After describing Collins's appearance as 'decent and manly', and adding that his knowledge was 'considerable, his views extensive, his conversation elegant, and his disposition chearful', he continues by relating an incident strongly reminiscent of the occasion when he helped Goldsmith to find a publisher for *The Vicar of Wakefield*:

> By degrees I gained his confidence; and one day was admitted to him when he was immured by a bailiff that was prowling in the street. On this occasion recourse was had to the booksellers, who, on the credit of a translation of Aristotle's *Poeticks*, which he engaged to write with a large commentary, advanced as much money as enabled him to escape into the country. He showed me the guineas safe in his hand.

This prepares us for our next news of Collins, which is that he was settled at Richmond, was engaged on his translation of Aristotle and had formed a friendship with Ragsdale. We have found reason to reject Ragsdale's story of Collins's dependence on small sums of money doled out by George Payne as the agent of Colonel Martin, but it is easy to detect the change of tone, and the sudden access of confidence, when he comes to the time of his personal acquaintance with Collins and could speak with apostolic certainty of the things which he had seen and heard. After referring to the 'History of the Revival of Learning', which 'was begun, but soon stood still', he continues:

> Both Dr. Johnson and Mr. Langhorne are mistaken when they say the 'Translation of Aristotle' was never begun. I know the contrary, for some progress was made in both, but most in the latter. From the freedom subsisting between us, we took the liberty of saying anything to each other. I one day reproached him with idleness; to convince me my censure was unjust, he showed me many sheets of his 'Translation of Aristotle', which he said he had so fully employed himself about, as to prevent him calling on many of his friends so frequently as he used to do.

That is convincing, and so is Ragsdale's next recollection:

> Soon after this he engaged with Mr. Manby, a bookseller on Ludgate Hill, to furnish him with some Lives for the 'Biographica Britannica', which Manby was then publishing. He showed me some of the Lives in embryo; but I do not recollect that any of them came to perfection.

We know something of the *Biographica Britannica,* which may now be regarded as an early forerunner of the *Dictionary of National Biography.* A royal Patent dated 26th September, 1744, acknowledges that the projectors of the work

> have, by their Petition, humbly represented unto Us, that they have for several Years past been at great Pains, and a very large Expence, in procuring and furnishing Books, and other Materials, to Gentlemen of Learning, who have employed their utmost Attention and Diligence in compiling a very useful and extensive Work, intituled *Biographia Britannica*: Or, The

Lives of the most Eminent Persons who have flourished in Great
Britain and Ireland, from the earliest Ages down to the present
Times.

Richard Manby, whom Ragsdale mentions, was one of a group of
publishers concerned in the enterprise. Another was Mrs. Mary
Cooper, the publisher of Collins's 'Epistle to Hanmer'. It is possible
that the first volume may contain unrecognized contributions by
Collins, though there is nothing that proclaims his authorship.

Ragsdale's next statement must be considered as another example of his habit of mixing fact with conjecture: 'To raise a present subsistence, he set about writing his Odes.' The continuation,
describing how his guest frequently wrote poems in his presence
and afterwards thrust them into the fire, leaves no room for doubt
that he could speak from actual observation, but how did he know,
unless Collins told him, that the motive was 'to raise a present
subsistence'? Perhaps we may feel that in this matter Sir Egerton
Brydges was right, even though we do not, in a democratic age,
profess his scorn for the man of commerce: 'That he wrote the
Odes to gain a present subsistence is but the tradesman's mistaken
comment.'

Ragsdale concludes in a tone which tends to spoil the impression
of helpfulness and generosity which he seems anxious to convey:
'In this manner he lived, with and upon his friends, until the death
of Colonel Martin, who left what fortune he died possessed of unto
him and his two sisters.' We have just been told that Collins had
'a general invitation to my house', and he may have taken it a
little too literally when he 'frequently spent whole days there';
but a misunderstanding of that kind hardly deserves the reproach
implied by the words 'with and upon his friends'. Possibly the
meaning intended is nothing more than that Collins sometimes
called at times domestically inconvenient, or that he sometimes
overstayed his welcome. In matters of that kind a poet can be
strangely unimaginative.

According to Murdoch, the biographer of Thomson, Collins
had lived for 'some time' at Richmond when Thomson died in
August, 1748, and by 'some time', calculating from the affair of
the bailiff at King's Square Court, we should suppose that he

F

meant rather more than two years. It is to be hoped that when, in 1747, he sold his father's old premises in East Street and his financial interest in the Rectory of St. Bartholomew, as his mother's will directed, he acted more wisely in his use of the proceeds than he had done in the matter of the inheritance from his uncle Charles. He may well have learned from experience what he had failed to learn from the admonitions of George Payne. He was, after all, on friendly terms with Thomson, and moving as an equal in the Thomson circle, and that was not a company of beggars.

Dr. Johnson's words, 'doubtful of his dinner, or trembling at a creditor', which some later writers have elaborated into a harrowing tale of privation and misery, seem to have been suggested by a single incident, which Johnson's readiness to sympathize with a struggling author would easily lead him to misunderstand. Ragsdale's recollections, apart from the phrase 'with and upon his friends', give a general impression of literary labour sustained with difficulty against incursions of cheerfulness, and that is hardly compatible with the haunting presence of worry about the means of subsistence. It is noticeable also that Ragsdale does not repeat Dr. Johnson's estimate of the amount of the legacy from Colonel Martin, but prefers to speak cautiously of 'such fortune as he died possessed of'. These words may have been intended to conceal more precise information which he did not care to bring into the open. If we knew the date of the sale of the Cackham property to George Payne, mentioned in Mrs. Tanner's will, it might turn out that it was that transaction, and not Colonel Martin's bequest, which brought Collins a sudden access of wealth in 1749. Some problems must remain, but the facts available lead us to conclude that both Collins's poverty before the death of Colonel Martin and his affluence after that event have been exaggerated.

NOTES TO CHAPTER V

1. *Poetical Works of William Collins,* pp. xvii-xviii.
2. I am very grateful to Mr. Goodger for this permission, and to Messrs. Pink, Marston and Birch, Solicitors, of Portsmouth, for furnishing the information at his request.
3. See Mr. Wilmshurst's letter to the *Times* Literary Supplement for 9th February, 1933.
4. See p. 8, above.
5. Either is a possible variant of the name of the Essex family of Collins.
6. *Winchester Long Rolls,* ed. C. W. Holgate, pp. 36, 40.
7. Foster, *Alumni Oxonienses* (Early Series), Vol. I, p. 308. His name is given alternatively as 'Colling', but his identity is clear from his father's name, Roger, and his being 'of Chichester'.
8. B.M. Add. MS. 5699, f. 184.
9. Private information kindly furnished from the records of the Charterhouse by Captain E. R. Wilson. It may be added that although, generally speaking, the inmates were gentlemen by birth who had fallen into poverty, the latter condition was subject to many exceptions. Smythe (*Historical Account of Charterhouse,* pp. 256-260) gives an impressive list of doctors, scientists and scholars who chose to live there for the sake of peace and freedom for study, concluding, 'And very recently, Sir Henry Mackworth, Bart., here terminated an existence the latter part of which was spent in great comfort in this peaceful spot'.
10. B.M. Add. MS. 33059 B.
11. Manuscript list of 'Eighteenth Century Apprentices' in the Library of the Society of Genealogists.
12. Moy Thomas, *Poetical Works of William Collins,* p. lxiii.
13. *A Duke and His Friends,* p. 511.
14. Ibid., p. 524.
15. The originals of the letters printed in 'A Duke and His Friends' are in the possession of the Duke of Richmond and Gordon at Goodwood, and I have been privileged to see them.
16. Among the old Chichester wills in the District Probate Registry, Winchester.
17. See p. 4, above.
18. *Letters to Gilbert White,* p. 9.
19. Ibid., p. 14.
20. *Review of English Studies,* Vol. VI (1930), p. 439 etc.

VI

The Odes Begun

THE disastrous Battle of Fontenoy was fought on 11th May, 1745. Collins was then, to the best of our information, living at King's Square Court. Colonel Martin, as we know from one of his letters to the Duke of Richmond, was still at Fort William on 14th May, though the King's Regiment, which he was soon to join, was engaged in the action. 'It is noteworthy,' as Lord March observes, 'that he dates his letter three days after Fontenoy had been fought; but the news of that disaster cannot have reached him at the time of writing, as he makes no allusion to it.'*(1)*

There is reason to believe, however, that Collins, besides experiencing his full share of the gloom which overspread London, was in some way personally affected by the death of a young officer with whom he may have been distantly acquainted, or whom he may have known only by name. At some time within a year of the battle he wrote his *Ode to a Lady on the Death of Colonel Ross in the Action of Fontenoy*. The date of composition is uncertain. Dodsley, who published it in his *Museum* in June, 1746, and again in his *Collection* in 1748, added a note below the title, 'Written May, 1745'. That may well be an assumption from the known date of the battle, and in any case it is contradicted by a note reading 'Written in the same Year' at the head of the ode *Written in the Beginning of the Year 1746*, which dates itself by the title. Between the two appearances for which Dodsley was responsible Collins included the poem in his volume of Odes, with some verbal changes and with two additional stanzas which, except

70

by a miracle of foresight, he could not have written earlier than 16th April, 1746, the date of the Battle of Culloden.

The two stanzas, numbered 7 and 8 in the poem as we have it, have given some trouble to Collins's editors, who usually either exclude them or admit them reluctantly, remarking on their absence from the version of the poem printed by Dodsley and generally conveying the opinion that Dodsley's judgment was correct. Bronson supposed that Collins himself was responsible for their omission from the text of 1748, as he realized that they 'lessen the unity of the ode by drawing attention from the death of Ross and the sorrow of the lady to the state of the nation'. That would be more convincing if the remainder of the poem were concerned less with the state of the nation and more with the death of Ross and the sorrow of the lady. The reader does not notice the digression which Bronson's criticism leads us to expect. He is more likely to feel that the 'blest youth' is a symbolic figure like Milton's Lycidas, and that his death was to Collins what the death of Edward King was to Milton: the pretext rather than the occasion of the poem.

If Bronson's criticism has any validity, it is only on the assumption that the poem was written immediately after the battle, and was designed strictly as an elegy on the death of Ross; but it did not appear in print, as we have seen, until June, 1746, and there is no apparent reason why Collins should have kept it in manuscript for thirteen months. Dodsley, always a good judge of a saleable product, would certainly have wished to publish it while the country was ringing with the name of Fontenoy if it had been shown to him at that time.

The internal evidence, if the additional stanzas are taken into account, points to the same conclusion. Freedom at present lies with 'matted tresses madly spread', and 'turns her joyless Eyes' upon the desolate scene, but will do so only

> Till Notes of Triumph bursting round
> Proclaim her Reign restor'd:
> Till *William* seek the sad Retreat,
> And bleeding at her sacred **Feet,**
> Present the sated Sword.

71

It would not be natural to urge William (better remembered as the Duke of Cumberland) to return as an avenging hero to the scene of Fontenoy immediately after the battle, when he was so little anxious to 'seek the sad Retreat' that his dearest wish was to extricate himself from it without further disaster. The kind of emotion to which the words would be appropriate is that which swept the country during the second half of April, 1746, immediately after Culloden. It is that emotion which Handel has recorded for all time in *Judas Maccabaeus*, and which reaches its climax in the aria 'See the Conquering Hero Comes'. It is said that the victorious army, drawn up on the field of Culloden after the battle, called out to the Duke as he rode by, 'Now, Billy, for Flanders'.(2) That cry was soon to be echoed by the whole nation; for it was felt that Cumberland, having saved the country from invasion, would yet beat Marshall Saxe on his own ground, and wipe out the memory of Fontenoy. To say, therefore, that the exhortation to 'seek the sad Retreat' impairs the unity of a poem on Fontenoy is to lose sight of the historical background. The present generation can remember a similar situation on a grander scale, when a greater disaster than Fontenoy was retrieved by a greater victory than Culloden. After the landing on the coast of Normandy in April, 1944, the question was heard on all sides, 'When do we return to Dunkirk?'

The ode *To a Lady* is not among the best of Collins's poems, and may deserve all the disparagement which Professor Garrod has heaped upon it, but in its biographical setting it has an interest not related to its intrinsic merit, and for that reason it is necessary to speak of it at somewhat disproportionate length. It throws a faint light on an episode on Collins's career which has not been, and perhaps never will be, fully understood. We first hear of it from a letter written by Joseph Warton to his brother Thomas, and happily preserved by the former's biographer:

You will wonder to see my name in an advertisement next week, so I thought I would apprize you of it. The case was this. Collins met me in Surrey, at Guildford Races, when I wrote out for him my Odes, and he likewise communicated some of his to me: and being both in very high spirits we took courage, resolved to join our forces, and to publish them immediately. I flatter myself that I shall lose no honour by this publication, because I believe these Odes, as they now stand, are infinitely the best things I ever wrote. You will see a very pretty one of Collins's on the death of Colonel Ross before Tournay. It is addressed to a lady who was Ross's intimate acquaintance, and who by the way is Miss Bett Goddard. Collins is not to publish the Odes unless he gets ten guineas for them.

I returned from Milford last night where I left Collins with my mother and sister, and he sets out to-day for London . . .(3)

This letter, we are told, is 'without a date of time or place', but, assuming that the poem had at the time been only recently composed, we should suppose the encounter with Warton to have taken place in late April or early May. It probably occurred before the affair of the interrupted tea-party and the migration to Richmond; for Collins would hardly be in the mood, after that incident and after he had settled down to the pleasures of a tranquil life in the country, to make the considerable journey from Richmond to Guildford for the sake of a few hours' excitement at the races.

From Warton's letter has sprung the legend that Ross was not the only young man who was attracted to Elizabeth Goddard, another being Collins himself. William Seward, writing in 1797, says that 'Collins was extremely attached to a young lady who was born on the day before him, and did not return his passion with equal ardour. He said, on that occasion, "that he came into the world a day after the fair".' 'The young lady, in fact,' says Mr. Garrod, rounding off the story, 'preferred soldiers to scholars. There were wars to be won; and she engaged herself to a Colonel Ross, a gallant soldier who fell in the battle of Fontenoy. It was to the memory of this Colonel Ross that Collins, with a poet's generosity, dedicated the Ode which bears Ross' name in its title.'

The only other fact about Miss Goddard which is usually taken as established is that she belonged to the Sussex village of Harting, where Collins might well have met her. The evidence is said to be found in the concluding lines of the poem –

73

Ev'n humble *Harting's* cottag'd Vale
Shall learn the sad repeated Tale,
And bid her Shepherds weep –

but to one reader at least these lines seem to admit of, and even to demand, a different interpretation. Why should it be remarkable that *even* Harting should learn the tale of Ross if its small population included the lady to whom he was engaged? May we not explain the mention of Harting by its being a place well known to Collins himself, and may we not read the three lines as meaning that the hero's fame should spread through the whole country, from the north of Scotland, where his home was, to a small village on the south coast of England?

Many enquirers have searched the records of Harting and other likely places for an entry concerning Elizabeth Goddard, but none has been rewarded. That is disappointing, because, if Seward's information is correct, and if Miss Goddard is the person to whom he refers, we know the exact date of her birth. Our hopes were raised momentarily in 1956, when Mr. J. S. Cunningham published his *Drafts and Fragments*. In his Introduction Mr. Cunningham says of his Fragment 2, as we must call it, a poem in stanza form beginning 'No longer ask me Gentle Friends', that it 'was evidently written with Elizabeth Goddard, the niece of Colonel Ross, in mind', and adds: 'To her Collins addressed his Ode on the occasion of Ross's death at Fontenoy.'

This is elaborated by Mr. Cunningham in his notes:

We may identify the 'Delia' ('my Laura' at 1. 60) to whom the poem is addressed as Elizabeth Goddard, for whom in May 1745 Collins wrote his Ode on the death of Colonel Ross, her uncle. He makes oblique reference to her home at Harting, in Sussex, in his mention of Thomas Otway . . .

Miss Goddard emerges as the 'Young Lady' who, in one account, was loved by Collins, but 'did not return his passion with equal ardour'.

The repeated statement that Ross and Miss Goddard were related as uncle and niece – a strange departure from the accepted belief for which no authority is cited – must be received with scepticism. That Miss Goddard's home was at Harting we have already found reason to doubt, and this assumption is not confirmed by the only lines relevant to the problem:

> Now tell me you who hear me sing
> and prompt the tender Theme
> How far is Lavant's little Spring
> From Medway's mightier stream!
> Confined within my Native dells
> The world I little know
> But in some Tufted Mead she dwells
> Where'er those waters flow.

By 'those waters' does not Collins mean the waters of the Medway, which otherwise he would have no occasion to mention, and does he not convey that Delia, whether identical with Miss Goddard or not, lived somewhere in Kent? Perhaps some day further discoveries will be made, and we shall know whether, if the traditional story is true, Miss Goddard found better consolation than the verses of an unwelcome admirer.

However that may be, there is no reason why Captain Ross – for he never attained the rank of Colonel – should continue to be the elusive and shadowy figure who has haunted the pages of Collins's editors. There are sources of information from which we can trace the outline, at least, of his brief career. He was born on 9th February, 1721, and in 1732 succeeded his great-uncle, General Charles Ross, as owner of the estate of Balnagown.(5) At the age of eighteen or nineteen he was commissioned in the Scots Guards. According to Sir Frederick Maurice this was in 1741,(6) but the true date seems to have been somewhat earlier, as we find the young man's father writing on 18th September, 1740: 'I wish ye town election in Tayn may not keep Charles too long in ye country since he is oblidge to be with ye regiment next month and they are at Bristoll.'(7)

In the election at Tain Ross was the successful candidate,(8) and thereafter represented the County of Ross in Parliament. In spite of his military duties he must have taken his seat and attended the House with some sort of regularity for a few months, as he incurred criticism at home by his 'constant way of voting with ye Opposition'.(9) A fragment of one of his letters, dated 25th February, 1742, has survived, and includes the fateful sentence: 'I set out for Flanders very soon, what to do the Lord knows.'(10) That accords with the fact that, after an unforeseen delay, the Guards embarked at Woolwich for Ostend on 26th May, 1742,(11) and did not return home until after the engagement in which Ross lost his life. 'Altogether,' says the editor of the family papers, 'we see a brave and generous youth, more inclined for soldiering than business, yet in politics with a mind of his own, and no time-server.'(12)

We may conclude, then, that Ross was either living in London or spending some part of his time there at intervals between the autumn of 1740 and the spring of 1742, and it is possible that during that period he met Miss Goddard and was thereafter, as Warton expresses it, devoted to her. It seems unlikely, however, that there was any formal engagement. In none of the several letters included in 'Old Ross-shire and Scotland' which speak of Ross before and after his death is there any sign of awareness that Miss Goddard or any other lady had entered his life.

Collins, as we have seen, did not settle down as a Londoner until the beginning of 1744, and it follows that he could not, in the ordinary course, have been personally acquainted with the hero whose memory he celebrates. Ross, as we know, was twenty-three years of age and a Captain in 1745, so that by speaking of him as a 'youth' in the poem and as 'Colonel' Ross in the title Collins reveals that his information was somewhat vague. That may help to explain a peculiarity which Mr. Garrod has observed with strong disapproval: 'The lines on Colonel Ross commemorate, we must suppose, a man whom Collins knew; in any case, they are a *consolatio* addressed to a person very dear to Collins, and to whom Ross had been very dear. Yet they want, for the most part, precisely that out of which it is reasonable to think they sprang – personal feeling.'(13)

It is possible that Collins first heard the name of Ross from Miss Goddard or some of her friends, but there are other persons who might have mentioned it in his presence. One such person

76

is John Forbes. It is probable that Forbes and Ross were in some degree cousins, as their families, both of high distinction in Scotland, were neighbours and friends, and there had been marriages between them.(14) Whether related or not the two young men were about the same age, and had been commissioned about the same time. It is in an undated letter addressed by Colonel Munro to John Forbes's father, Duncan Forbes of Culloden, the famous Lord President of the Court of Session, that we find the earliest intimation, so far as is known, of Ross's death. The writer begins with the assurance 'that your Son is in good Health, and suffered nothing but the loss of his horse, who was shot in our retreat'. He then relates how 'poor Charles Ross of Balnagown was shot with a musket-ball early in the action, and died the same night at Headquarters'.(15)

John Forbes's regiment was the Royal Regiment of Horse Guards, which, during the crisis of the Jacobite rebellion, was one of those held in reserve in case it should be necessary to defend London. Forbes may well have been one of the 'club of officers, mostly Scotch', with whom Alexander Carlyle often dined at this time, as he tells us, at a coffeehouse in the Strand, and who included many 'who had been spared at the fatal battle of Fontenoy'.(16) After Culloden a detachment of the Horse Guards was stationed at Kingston-on-Thames.(17) From there it would be, for a cavalry officer, an easy ride to Richmond, and John Forbes would be likely to make the journey, for his father, described in the *Seasons* as 'truly generous, and in silence great', was one of the most helpful of Thomson's friends in high places, and had done much to advance his reputation. For the younger Forbes Richmond would have a further attraction in the presence there of Patrick Murdoch, his old tutor, destined ultimately to be Thomson's biographer.

The conversation of John Forbes, then, is one channel by which Collins might, in the spring of 1746, have learned fresh details of the Battle of Fontenoy, and been moved to address his appeal to the victor of Culloden to 'seek the sad Retreat'. But, closely connected with this, there is another possibility, and one that opens out a wider field of enquiry.

We are accustomed to think of Alexander Carlyle as a portly

77

and magnificent veteran, partly, perhaps, because of Scott's description of him as 'the grandest demigod I ever saw, . . . commonly called "Jupiter Carlyle",'(8) and partly because, being 'no more a poet than his precentor',(19) as Scott unkindly adds, he did not make a name for himself in literary history till late in life, when he found himself in possession of the manuscript of one of Collins's lost poems. But, however Olympian in his later years, he was young in 1746, being younger than Collins by rather more than a year. He seems to have had a remarkable talent for being in the right place at the right time to witness events that were to make history, and, though he was exploring London for the first time, it was inevitable that he should be 'in the coffeehouse with Smollett when the news of the battle of Culloden arrived, and when London all over was in a perfect uproar of joy'.(20)

He had arrived in London, as we learn from his *Autobiography*, at the end of February or the beginning of March, and stayed till the middle of May.(21) During that time, besides the group of officers who were survivors of Fontenoy, he met several 'literary people', among whom, he says, 'I must not forget Thomson the poet and Dr. Armstrong'. Immediately afterwards he speaks of a party at the Ducie Tavern, 'where the company were Armstrong, Dickson, and Andrew Millar, with Murdoch his friend'.(22) All these, with the single exception of Dickson, were or had been on intimate terms with Collins, and the suspicion arises that Collins may have been one of the 'literary people' not mentioned by name. Armstrong was one of the authors who, according to Ragsdale, 'frequently took his opinion on their pieces before they were seen by the public'. Andrew Millar was Thomson's publisher, and a few months later was to be the publisher of Collins's Odes. Murdoch, already mentioned, was another of Thomson's retinue in the Castle of Indolence.

So far it will seem probable, though not certain, that Collins and Carlyle met at some time during this period. From here we must turn to two poems which suggest the interesting possibility that they not only met but actually collaborated. Both are found in the *British Magazine*, an Edinburgh periodical, for February, 1747.

The first of the two poems commemorates Colonel Gardiner,

who had lost his life in the Battle of Prestonpans in September, 1745. The fame of Colonel Gardiner lives today in the pages of *Waverley*, where Scott has placed him in command of the regiment which the hero left in order to join the rebels, and, as he was becoming a legendary figure even in his own time, it is fitting that his earthly renown should have been immortalized in fiction before he had faded out of history. After a dissolute youth he had undergone a strange conversion, which Dodderidge, in *Remarkable Passages in the Life of Colonel Gardiner,* attributes to a miraculous vision, though Alexander Carlyle preferred to believe that a book by a Suffolk clergyman, *The Christian in Complete Armour,* supplied the motive force.(*23*) There can be no doubt that the conversion, however accomplished, was genuine and lasting, and in the course of time Colonel Gardiner, combining the qualities of a brave soldier and a fervent evangelist, appealed to the popular imagination in much the same way as did General Gordon in a later generation.

Carlyle in his youth must have known the Colonel Gardiner of real life even better than Edward Waverley knew the Colonel Gardiner of the novel. His father was the Parish Minister of Prestonpans, and Colonel Gardiner was one of his parishioners, having bought the considerable estate of Banktown in 1733. His worldly wealth did not escape the unfavourable notice of Collins's military uncle, Colonel Martin, who wrote to the Duke of Richmond on 14th May, 1745: 'Col. Gardiner, since he is grown rich and lazy, is ye most altered man I have seen in so short a time; he stoops, pockes out his head, and has ye appearance of a Very Old Man.'(*24*)

The following September the Battle of Prestonpans was fought immediately in front of Carlyle's home, and it appears from his account of it that he must have been the last to speak to Colonel Gardiner as he was riding out to his death.(*25*) He expressed his grief in a poem entitled *Fannie Weeping* (Fannie being Colonel Gardiner's daughter), which, after 1790, when it appeared in the *Scots Musical Museum,* was wrongly attributed to Sir Gilbert Elliot.(*26*) Whatever may be its merits as poetry, it displays genuine personal feeling besides conveying a true sense of the dismay which overspread the country after Prestonpans. We can

79

understand what Smollett meant when he told the author in a
private letter that it 'has a good deal of nature in it, though, in my
opinion, it might be bettered'.(27)

Did Carlyle attempt to 'better' his tribute to Colonel Gardiner,
and was he in some way assisted by Collins? That question is suggested by the first of the two poems already mentioned, which
shall now be given in full.

An Ode,

To the Memory of Colonel Gardiner,
In Imitation of Milton.

Weep! 'tis Gard'ner's flow'ry rest,
With Violets and Rosemary drest;
Which spring, with dewy fingers cold
Thick, sprinkles on his hallow'd mold.
Next, *Autumn's* eve, the fairy throng
Meet here; at one his knell is rung;
Then *honour* comes, a pilgrim grey,
To bless the turf that wraps his clay;
And *freedom*, in her hermit wear,
From woods and wilds will saunter here;
Religion pure, a heavenly guest,
To glad the meeting, down will haste;
And *love*, with all his smiling train,
Comes here from fair *Arcadia's* plain;
True *friendship* comes, a stranger rare,
And *sorrow* with dishevel'd hair;
A mourning wife, but *beauty* too,
My Fanny comes and comes with you.
From *Falkirk's* Field, and healthy tomb,
Monro and Whitney both will come,
And Ker, beloved youth, will leave
His rest in fam'd Culloden's grave.
Assemblage high! ten thousand more
Will croud from* Schelda's bloody shoar;
With these a *matron,* sad, yet great,

80

> The *genius* of our sinking state,
> With thistles crown'd, they faded all
> The morn of noble Gard'ner's fall.
> Last *silence, darkness,* sisters twin,
> At one his obsequies begin:
> The meeting's set, betimes attend,
> Just as the first cock crows, they end.

*Fontenoy [author's note].

Edinburgh, Feb. 10, 1747.   X.

It is hardly necessary to point out that we have here, from the third to the tenth line, an imitation of Collins's 'How sleep the brave': so close an imitation that it might well be an exact copy of Collins's lines as they appeared in some earlier draft. But is it only up to the tenth line that we recognize the hand of Collins? The personification of religion, love, friendship and sorrow follows naturally upon that of freedom, and is in Collins's manner. That would clearly not be true of the lines immediately following, which, if internal evidence counts for anything, are the work of Alexander Carlyle. The 'mourning wife, but beauty too' is Colonel Gardiner's daughter, commemorated in *Fannie Weeping*, and there must have been few persons in a position to speak of her familiarly as 'my Fanny'. Carlyle, who had known her since he was a boy, and whose father was the minister of the parish in which she lived, was one of that small number. He was also if not a poet, at least capable of writing verse, and verse very much in this style.

Of the three soldiers mentioned in the subsequent lines, Monro was, presumably, the officer who had written to Duncan Forbes after Fontenoy, informing him of Ross's death.(28) Whitney and Ker (or Kerr) would be remembered by Carlyle as long as he remembered Prestonpans. In his *Autobiography* he describes how Colonel Whitney, though wounded, attempted to rally his men for a last charge, and how Kerr, a young Cornet, stood by Colonel Gardiner to the last, when the main body of the army was in flight.(29) He had dined with Kerr the evening before the battle, and had admired his coolness and confidence,(30) so that the epithet 'beloved' might well express genuine personal feeling. The heroes of 'Schelda's bloody shoar' follow naturally, for Carlyle, as we remember, had met a number of officers who had returned from Fontenoy.

Of one thing we may be certain if we assume Carlyle's authorship of the lines not contributed by Collins. This is not a simple case of plagiarism, although the interval between the publication of Collins's Odes at the end of 1746 and the appearance of the lines on Colonel Gardiner might, at first sight, seem to suggest that possibility. Our knowledge of Carlyle's character forbids us to believe that he read Collins's poem in print some seven months after his return to Scotland, dressed it up as a spurious tribute to Colonel Gardiner by adding some lines of his own, and published it in an Edinburgh periodical which Collins was not likely to see. Such an action would be to Carlyle morally impossible. His severest critics – and he had his critics, and even enemies – would not have denied that his honesty was above suspicion.

The other poem now to be considered has even more evident signs of composite authorship. Here it is in full:

An Ode to Evening,
In Imitation of Milton

I.

Evening, thou Nymph divine and holy,
Devout, demure, and melancholy;
Oh teach me, gentle maid,
In pensive strains to tell my tale,
Soft as the breathings of the gale
That fans thy sleeping shade.

II.

Full on yon heaving billow's breast
His head reclin'd, eyes sunk in rest:
I view the falling light.
With him, the wakeful pleasures fly
To chimes, where day ne'er shuts his eye,
Nor dreads the sullen night.

III.

But now, thy folding dewy star,
Its paley circlet shews from far,
To warn the dapper elves
That slept in rose-buds all day long
Or lurk'd amidst the sun-beams throng,
To haunt the lawns and shelves.

IV.

And many a nymph who sheds her brows
With Sedge-leaves dipt in freshning dews,
Now leave their wet abode.
But church-yards drear, and lonely shores,
The lated traveller abhors,
And takes a safer road.

V.

Then let me rove some healthy scene,
Where glaring ruin sits between,
And tomb-stones shew their head;
Where o'er a grave, some plaintive ghost
Bewails a life untimely lost,
And charms the list'ning dead.

VI.

In days now past, sure days of yore,
When mankind own'd religion's pow'r,
Nor scorn'd a Saviour's sway;
God's praise, with morning light begun,
And when the ev'ning bell was rung,
It sooth'd the twilight gray.

VII.

But now, forgotten and forlorn,
With eyes enflam'd, the flushed morn
Sees rebel mortals rise.
Nor Night, in all her brown array,
Can bend the stubborn heart to pray,
Or learn them to be wise.

G

VIII.

But soon a midnight trump shall blow,
And bid the sheeted dead, below,
Awake and meet their doom:
A midnight, ah! how blank and drear,
To him who never pour'd a pray'r,
Nor begg'd a Saviour's boon.

Edin. Feb. 10, 1647 (*sic*).   X.

The first five stanzas are obviously the work of Collins, or strongly influenced by him. That the last three are by Carlyle does not admit of proof, but if we recognize his hand in the ode on Colonel Gardiner we can hardly doubt that he was the collaborator in this poem also, as the style and sentiments are characteristically his. At the beginning of 1747 Carlyle was back in his father's house at Prestonpans, preparing for his ordination in the Presbyterian ministry, and as Prestonpans is not more than fifteen miles from Edinburgh it would be natural to him, if he wished to go into print, to entrust his manuscript to an Edinburgh journal rather than send it to London. There is evidence that he did this on a later occasion, for his *Fannie Weeping* was first printed in the July number of the *British Magazine*, though according to an introductory note it was composed on the day of the battle, 21st September, 1745.

It is well known that Collins in his ode *To Evening* borrowed some phrases from Milton, but we should not think of describing the poem, taken as a whole, as 'in imitation of Milton'. The rhymed ode is so described, and not unfairly. The first stanza is taken from the invocation to Melancholy at the beginning of *Il Penseroso*. The next three are indebted to the speech in which Comus addresses his 'rout of monsters', but the moral to be drawn is, as we should expect, the opposite of that of Comus. Whereas Comus welcomes the setting of the sun because it ushers in the time of

joy and feast,
Midnight shout and revelry,
Tipsy dance and jollity,

the anonymous poet wishes that he could follow the sun on his journey, because 'the wakeful pleasures' are what he wishes to avoid. He knows that the 'folding dewy star' (Milton's 'star that bids the shepherd fold') will bring out the 'dapper elves' and wood-nymphs, so he chooses his direction to keep them at a distance. He calculates that Comus and his retinue will not be looking for their victims among 'church-yards drear, and lonely shores', knowing that 'the lated traveller' abhors such places, and for that reason he prefers to 'rove some healthy scene', where there is 'glaring ruin', among tomb-stones, graves and ghosts. This leads naturally to the denunciation of midnight revelry in the last three stanzas, which obviously owe nothing to Collins or to Milton. The design of the poem, though we do not realize it at the beginning, is that of a sermon: in substance, no doubt, just such a sermon as Carlyle was soon to preach to his congregations at Cockburnspath and Inveresk.

There is thus, in the rhymed ode, an unbroken sequence of thought. The elves and wood-nymphs present a danger, and it is to avoid that danger that the poet seeks the healthy scene, the ruin and the tomb-stones. In Collins's familiar lines there is an abrupt transition which cannot be explained except by reference to the earlier version; for that is what we must suppose the rhymed ode to be. To Collins the Hours, the elves and the nymphs are attractive and delightful; the 'Pensive Pleasures', now personified, are even 'lovelier still', though as the 'wakeful pleasures', before their transmigration, they had been to the moralist objects of dread. There is no apparent reason, therefore, why, in Collins's ode, the speaker should turn his back upon these alluring creatures of his (or Milton's) imagination and prefer to roam in places where he will not encounter them.

This inconsistency gives rise to a defect which has not escaped the critical penetration of Mr. Garrod, who remarks that in the first twenty lines, comprising the first main division, 'the poet has in a sense said all he had to say. At least, few readers, I fancy, can fail to feel that the connexion of these twenty lines with the twenty lines which make the second division of the poem is ill managed.' The second division begins with the rising of the evening star, and that is the time when Collins is moved to

> rove some wild and heathy Scene,
> Or find some Ruin 'midst its dreary Dells.

Mr. Garrod feels that in these and the following lines the poet has 'failed to achieve . . . true harmony between what he is saying and what he has already said'.(*31*)

The explanation which must occur to us if we take the rhymed ode into account is that Collins was re-writing as a poem what had been a versified sermon, though with his own embellishments. Some components of the sermon remain, and have not been perfectly assimilated to the new design. That must have been apparent to Collins himself, for when he came to revise the poem for Dodsley's *Collection* in 1748 he showed himself aware of the existence of some jagged edges. He had already modified the terror of the 'healthy scene' – a scene gloomy enough as described in the rhymed ode, but healthy in a moral sense, by comparison with the domain of Comus – into a 'wild and *heathy* Scene'; but he must have realized on second thoughts that the substitution of *heathy* for *healthy*, ingenious though it might be, was a poor device for effecting the change of meaning which he intended, and in the revision he transforms the scene into something too remote and enchanting to be described as either *healthy* or *heathy*. The earlier wildness is relieved by dancing ripples on the surface of a lake; and the ruin – a 'glaring ruin' originally, then, in Collins's first version, 'some Ruin' of unqualified bleakness – is seen in the distance as a symbol of the ageless human instinct for worship:

> Then lead, calm Vot'ress, where some sheety lake
> Cheers the lone heath, or some time-hallow'd pile,
> Or up-land fallows grey
> Reflect it's last cool gleam.

It is as if Collins had foreseen Mr. Garrod's criticism and had attempted to meet it, with the result, in the critic's view, that he has made matters worse. Not every reader will agree that the substituted stanza illustrates Collins's habit of moving 'from a less to a greater carelessness'.(*32*)

NOTES TO CHAPTER VI

1. *A Duke and His Friends,* p. 460.
2. See the *D.N.B.* under 'William Augustus, Duke of Cumberland'.
3. John Wooll, *Biographical Memoirs of the Late Revd. Joseph Warton, D.D.* (1806), pp. 14-15, note.
4. *Collins,* pp. 52-3.
5. Ross Pedigree, quoted by Robertson (continuation of Crawford's *Description of the Shire of Renfrew* (1818), p. 519).
6. *History of the Scots Guards,* Vol. II, p. 354.
7. William MacGill, *Old Ross-shire and Scotland from Tain and Balnagown Documents,* No. 207.
8. Ibid., No. 266.
9. Ibid. No. 268.
10. Ibid., No. 723.
11. Sir Frederick Maurice, *History of the Scots Guards,* Vol. I, pp. 117-8.
12. William MacGill, op. cit. No. 724.
13. *Collins,* p. 81.
14. See *Some Kindeace Letters,* p. 1.
15. *Culloden Papers,* p. 200.
16. *Autobiography,* ed. J. H. Burton, p. 204-5.
17. Packe, *An Historical Record of the Royal Regiment of Horse Guards, or Oxford Blues,* pp. 90-1.
18. Quoted by John Hill Burton, Carlyle's *Autobiography,* p. 595.
19. Ibid. p. 592.
20. *Autobiography,* pp. 198-9.
21. Ibid., pp. 191-207.
22. Ibid., pp. 205-6.
23. Ibid., p. 19 etc.
24. Lord March, *A Duke and His Friends,* p. 461.
25. *Autobiography,* ed. Burton, p. 148 et seq. The whole of this chapter is very interesting as a vivid description of the battle by an eye-witness.
26. The case for Carlyle's authorship of *Fannie Weeping* was stated in an article ('Collins and Alexander Carlyle') in the *Review of English Studies* for January, 1939; but the decisive fact is that it is attested by Carlyle's nephew and heir, the first Carlyle Bell, in a note among Carlyle's unpublished papers now in the possession of Mrs. Carlyle Bell, of Cowden, Kent. See next note.
27. Smollett's *Letters,* ed. Noyes, p. 7. The original is among Carlyle's papers in the possession of Mrs. Carlyle Bell, and attached to it is a copy of *Fannie Weeping* and the note by the first Carlyle Bell mentioned in the previous note.

28. See note 15, above.
29. *Autobiography,* ed. Burton, p. 153.
30. Ibid., pp. 141-2.
31. *Collins.* pp. 75-6.
32. *Collins,* p. 48.

VII

The Odes Continued

IN the absence of such external evidence as would settle the question conclusively, we must be content with the probability that Collins and Alexander Carlyle met and collaborated at some time in the spring of 1746. Proceeding on that assumption from the point reached in the last chapter, we must suppose that Carlyle, when he left London in May, took with him the manuscripts of the ode on Colonel Gardiner and the rhymed *Ode to Evening*, and that early the next year, after he had returned to Prestonpans, he sent them to the *British Magazine*, probably with no extensive revision. It would be natural to him to think of both poems as his own, though he would probably have acknowledged that he had received some help in points of detail.

Both poems, as published in the *British Magazine*, are signed 'X'. From beginning to end of his *Autobiography* Carlyle never reveals that he had at any time written poetry, but *Fannie Weeping* is evidence that he was a poet at least by aspiration, and Scott must have known of some attempts when he used the words, 'no more a poet than his precentor'. It is easy to understand his reticence, particularly at the beginning of 1747. He was at that time about to be presented to Inveresk, the parish with which his name was to be associated for the rest of his life, but there were prejudices to be overcome. 'There arose,' he says, 'much murmuring in the parish against me, as too young, too full of levity, and too much addicted to the company of my superiors, to be fit for so important a charge, together with many doubts about my having the grace of God.'(*1*) The fact that he had written poetry might well have been cited as evidence of his levity. Throughout his career he was, by the standards of his age and country, a man of remarkably broad views. In 1757, when his friend John Home produced *Douglas*, he was prosecuted before the Presbytery for attending a stage-play, though on that occasion, as formerly by his appointment to Inveresk, he achieved a notable victory over the straiter sect.(*21*) In Scotland, where he was to become known as a popular preacher and a pillar of his Church, we may leave him for the present. It is unlikely that he ever met Collins again, though he must have heard of him in later years from some of his friends.

From all the evidence available we should suppose that Collins's encounter with the bailiff, when Johnson came to his rescue and helped him 'to escape into the country', occurred about the same time as Carlyle's return to Scotland. It is an interesting possibility that Collins at this time had already formed the beginning of a friendship with Thomson, and that it was the wish to be near Thomson that drew him to Richmond. We have already noticed Carlyle's account of how he met several 'literary people', some of them known to Collins, at a party at the Ducie Tavern. Thomson was one of those present, though he arrived late and did not show to advantage. 'Armstrong bore him down,' says Carlyle, 'having got into his sarcastical vein by the wine he had drunk before Thomson joined us.'(*3*) On this Mr. Douglas Grant comments: 'The poet, however, had never shone in general company, and his quietness on this occasion would be increased not only by Armstrong's sarcasm but by dislike of visiting London. He no longer left Richmond willingly, and particularly objected to meeting his friends in London taverns.'(*4*) Collins, therefore, could not have had many opportunities of meeting him before he settled at Richmond, and, if he was already on friendly terms with him at that time, it is very likely that Thomson's short and reluctant visit to London on this occasion was the beginning of their acquaintance.

The exact date is of no great importance, but we are led to suppose that it was during the late spring, when man and nature are on the friendliest terms, that he first saw the woods, the meadows, the stream and the church with its whitening spire. Collins, though he must have roamed about the Sussex Downs, had never before lived in the country, and he would be likely to find Richmond enchanting. If it is true, as Ragsdale says, that he had left Oxford with 'a desire to partake of the dissipation and gaiety of London', we may be certain that he had not found half the pleasure in gratifying that wish that he now found among his new friends at Richmond.

The third of the fragments in Mr. Cunningham's collection deserves to rank among Collins's best poems, and may be assigned with extreme probability to the beginning of his life at Richmond. It anticipates, in reverse, Browning's *Up at a Villa – Down in the City*. It breathes the spirit of a young poet, fresh from the town, who is discovering the delights of nature for the first time:

> Ye Genii who in secret state
>   Far from the wheaten field
> At some throng'd Citie's antique Gate
>   Your unseen sceptres wield
>
> Ye Pow'rs that such high Office share
>   Oer all the restless Earth
> Who see Each day descend with care
>   Or lost in senseless Mirth
>
> Take Them who know not how to prize
>   The walks to Wisdom dear
> The Gradual Fruits and varying skies
>   That paint the gradual Year
>
> Take all that to the silent Sod
>   Prefer the sounding street
> And Let your echoing squares be trod
>   By their unresting feet
>
> But me by [. . . .] Springlets laid
>   That thro' the Woodland chide
> Let Elms and Oaks that lent their Shade
>   To hoary Druids hide

It may be permissible at this point to make a slight digression in order to say something of this early mention of the 'hoary Druids'. It has an interest which might not have been apparent a few years ago, for some considerable research has been devoted to the question what Collins meant by his allusion to the Druids in the ode *On Liberty*, and, later, by his description of Thomson as a Druid. Here it will hardly be disputed that he adopts with uncritical faith what may be called the popular view. Most people retain somewhere in their minds an idea of the Druids derived from their earliest lessons in history. They remember a picture showing a group of patriarchal men in white robes walking in procession among the oak-trees, while the leader is just about to cut the mistletoe with a golden sickle. It may be as unhistorical as the succeeding pictures of Alfred the Great, also a patriarchal figure, watching the cakes burn in the widow's hut, and of Drake playing bowls on Plymouth Hoe, with the Spanish Armada visible in the background, but because it makes a deep impression on the young imagination it is never completely erased from the memory. It is, in fact, what people of all ages and all degrees of knowledge call to mind when the Druids are mentioned in casual conversation. Collins, we may be sure, had learnt to think of the Druids as hoary figures moving in the shade of oak-trees even before he went to Winchester, though the elms are his own addition. According to Dr. Johnson 'he loved fairies, genii, giants, and monsters; he delighted to rove through the meanders of enchantment, to gaze on the magnificence of golden palaces, to repose by the waterfalls of Elysian gardens'. A person of whom that can be said would be certain to feel an affection for the Druids, but they must be the unreal Druids of romance, not the despotic and terrifying Druids of authentic history.

That is all that needs to be said about the Druids in connection with this poem, though we shall have occasion to return to them. In the continuation we notice another point of interest which, besides being important in itself, helps to strengthen the impression that Collins was writing while living at Richmond and on friendly terms with Thomson, and that Fragment 3 is, therefore, a later composition than the 'Epistle to Hanmer'. There are signs that since writing the 'Epistle', in which Raphael is the only painter considered, Collins had enlarged his knowledge of pictorial art. For his broader outlook he may well have been indebted to conversations with Thomson, whose 'influence on art', says Mr. Grant,

> was only less important than on poetry. His imagination was primarily pictorial. His boyhood among the Borders had trained him to see Nature as landscape, and whether the scenery in his poems was English or foreign, known or imaginary, it was deliberately arranged to conform to his early vision. His descriptions are built up as formally as though they were intended to be transferred on to canvas. His broad descriptions of landscape and his meticulous observation of all effects of light and shade appealed to painters, and it would be a long task to catalogue the pictures whose titles had appended to them quotations from *The Seasons*.(5)

Mr. Hagstrum, while noticing that the 'wild and heathy Scene' of the ode *To Evening* is 'at once Salvatorian and Claudian', adds that this is 'one of the very few occasions on which Collins invokes scenes characteristic of these painters'. Generally speaking, he thinks, 'Salvator Rosa and Claude are subordinate to Guido Reni in Collins' poetry'.(6) Collins himself in Fragment 3 acknowledges that he is reminded of Claude Lorrain and Salvator Rosa, as well as of Ruisdael:

> Some times when Morning oer Plain
>   Her radiant Mantle throws
> I'll mark the Clouds where sweet Lorrain
>   His orient Colours chose
>
> Or when the Sun to Noon tide climbs
>   I'll hide me from his view
> By such green Plats and cheerfull Limes
>   As [——] Rysdale drew
>
> Then on some Heath all wild and bare
>   With more delight Ill stand
> Than He who sees with wondring air
>   The works of Rosa's hand

Guido Reni is not mentioned, but we know that he was one of the artists represented in Thomson's collection. Thomson's effects were sold by auction in 1749, and Mr. Grant has observed that 'there were many engravings after famous painters, and the names of Raphael, Carlo Maratti, Guido Reni, Nicholas Poussin, and Veronese often recur in the catalogue'.(7)

But in comparing Fragment 3 with the 'Epistle to Hanmer' we notice a difference immensely more important than a wider acquaintance with the work of artists. There had come to Collins the realization of a truth of which he had given no hint in the earlier poem, and to which, perhaps, he could never have attained if he had remained in London. It is that neither painting nor poetry can rival the glories of the supreme artist, nature. He delights in the clouds of Claude Lorrain, the trees of Ruisdael, the landscapes of Salvator Rosa, but compared with the light of the moon, peeping above some eastern hill,

> All Tints that ever Picture us'd
> Are lifeless dull and mean.

It is regrettable that a number of words, and one whole line, are missing, but the last two stanzas are happily complete, and sum up the whole matter:

> What Art can paint the modest ray
> So sober chaste and cool
> As round yon Cliffs it seems to play
> Or skirts yon glimering Pool,
>
> The tender gleam her Orb affords
> No Poet can declare
> Altho' he chuse the softest words
> That e'er were sigh'd in air.

It would not be true to say that he had learnt this from Thomson, for he had no need of an instructor; but Thomson could have made the words his own, and it is easy to believe that each responded to the other's feeling and helped to intensify it. The sentiment expressed by Collins in the last stanza just quoted is found in the *Seasons*:

> Behold yon breathing prospect bids the Muse
> Throw all her beauty forth. But who can paint
> Like Nature? Can imagination boast,
> Amid its gay creation, hues like hers?
> Or can it mix them with that matchless skill,
> And lose them in each other, as appears
> In every bud that blows? If fancy then
> Unequal fails beneath the pleasing task,
> Ah, what shall language do?(8)

For Thomson, so far as we know, these rhetorical questions were the end of the matter, and he was content to excuse the persistence of art in its hopeless competition with nature by adding, 'Yet, though successless, will the toil delight'. That somewhat dispiriting conclusion would also, we must suppose, have satisfied Collins at the time to which we have assigned Fragment 3: the time when he first settled at Richmond, formed or renewed an intimate friendship with Thomson and made his first real acquaintance with the delights of nature. Would it have satisfied him at the later period when he composed the poem by which he is best remembered?

To ask that question is to answer it. In the ode *To Evening* Collins is not troubled by the thought that the light of the moon is something which 'no Poet can declare'. He does not lament the powerlessness of language to describe the indescribable; he appeals for inspiration to compose a work of literary art which shall harmonize with the spirit of nature made manifest by the visible creation. In his own words, addressing the personified Evening:

> Now teach me, *Maid* compos'd,
> To breathe some soften'd Strain,
> Whose Numbers stealing thro' thy darkning Vale,
> May not unseemly with its Stillness suit,
> As musing slow, I hail
> Thy genial lov'd Return!

It appears, then, that since writing Fragment 3, probably only a few months earlier, Collins had adopted a new view of the function of poetry, and it is a reasonable supposition that the change had been brought about by that close study of Aristotle which the attempt at a translation must have involved. That is not incompatible with the evident fact that the translation itself was found to be a disagreeable task.

The ode *To Evening* might have been used by Coleridge to illustrate the argument of his essay *On Poesy or Art*, which may be taken to be the expression of his maturest thought on the subject.(9) The function of art, he contends, is to *imitate* nature in the Aristotelian sense: not mechanically to copy the finished product but to imitate, or express, or manifest, the soul of nature in its creative activity. He mentions 'waxwork figures of men and women' as an example of copying as opposed to true imitation. 'If there be likeness to nature without any check of difference, the result is disgusting, and the more complete the delusion, the more loathsome the effect.' The artist, he continues,

must out of his own mind create forms according to the severe laws of the intellect, in order to generate in himself that co-ordination of freedom and law, that involution of obedience in the prescript, and of the prescript in the impulse to obey, which assimilates him to nature, and enables him to understand her. He merely absents himself for a season from her, that his own spirit, which has the same ground with nature, may learn her unspoken language in its main radicals, before he approaches to her endless compositions of them.

The eloquence is Coleridge's, but the doctrine is that of Aristotle, and it is that doctrine which Collins exemplifies in the ode *To Evening*.

The ode, then, seems to have evolved through three stages of Collins's experience. The rhymed ode, which marks the first stage, and which we suppose to have been written partly by Alexander Carlyle while he and Collins were still in London, expresses what may be called the *literary* view of nature; it might have been composed by a moralist with a taste for poetry who had never moved out of his library. To recognize the second stage we must turn aside to Fragment 3, where we find Collins seeing nature not as reflected from the pages of *Il Penseroso* and *Comus* but as it really is, and discovering, in sympathy with Thomson, that its mysterious beauty excels to an infinite degree anything that the art of man can invent or that words can describe. The enthusiasm apparent in these verses may well have been prompted by his feeling on first arriving at Richmond. At the third stage, before which he had devoted some time, however reluctantly, to the study of the *Poetics,* he writes as if he were applying the rule to be expounded to a later generation by Coleridge, who had also learnt it from Aristotle. 'If the artist,' to quote Coleridge again,

> copies the mere nature, the *natura naturata,* what idle rivalry! If he proceeds only from a given form, which is supposed to answer to the notion of beauty, what an emptiness, what an unreality there always is in his productions, as in Cipriani's pictures! Believe me, you must master the essence, the *natura naturans,* which presupposes a bond between nature in the higher sense and the soul of man.

In the ode *To Evening* we find that there is, after all, an answer to Thomson's despairing question,

> If fancy then
> Unequal fails beneath the pleasing task,
> Ah, what shall language do?

The answer is that language can 'breathe some soften'd Strain' so as to make articulate the sense of divinity which is the 'bond', in Coleridge's words, 'between nature in the higher sense and the soul of man'. We have not here a verbal copy of nature but a vision of the reality which nature shadows forth, and a vision implies a beholder. The effect upon the beholder is not to make him feel helpless and insignificant in the presence of inanimate things; it is to make him conscious at the same time of the imperfection which he shares with the whole creation and of the privilege which he still has of seeing, of reflecting upon what he sees and of giving expression to his thoughts.

The rhymed ode *To Evening* must have been associated in Collins's mind with the ode *To the Memory of Colonel Gardiner,* and in that poem also Collins must have seen greater possibilities than Alexander Carlyle could have realized. The fame of Colonel Gardiner was secure, and the needless exhortation to weep at his flowery rest was changed into a tribute to

> the Brave, who sink to Rest,
> By all their Country's Wishes blest.

The spring, in the earlier version, had merely sprinkled flowers, which must have died with the approach of autumn; in the revision it *returns*, and that single word penetrates to the deep human instinct which has from the beginning seen the spring as the bringer of new life. In the earlier version there is no necessary connection between the assembly of the fairies, who meet without accomplishing anything, and the ringing of the knell, which is done by a real bell at a precise moment; in the revision a mystical bell is rung by fairy hands, and the dirge is sung by forms not of this earth. These 'Forms unseen' are substituted for the 'religion' of the earlier version, and rightly so; for 'religion', hastening down 'to glad the meeting', and placed between freedom and love, reminds us of a jovial Bishop at the Athenaeum, or of the more sociable of those Presbyterian dignitaries with whom Carlyle's *Autobiography* has made us acquainted.

'How sleep the Brave' is the shortest of the poems by which Collins is remembered, and many critics have considered it the gem of the collection. If the reader feels that it might with advantage have been expanded to somewhat greater length that is a tribute to its merit. Its brevity seems to be due to Collins's determination to speak of 'the Brave' collectively rather than to celebrate the memory of a particular hero.

In a former chapter it was found convenient to take a comprehensive view of Collins's financial problems up to the year 1749, after which they cease to have any significance. That involved some overlapping with the period which we are now considering, and we have already seen Collins, as the frequent and not always welcome guest of Ragsdale, making a serious beginning at his translation of the *Poetics* as well as helping, or engaging to help, with the *Biographia Britannica*. The writing of short biographies for the general reader would be mere hack work. The translation of Aristotle was believed or assumed by Johnson to be still in progress in 1748,(*10*) but if it ever came within measurable distance of completion we can only regret that no trace of it has been found. The probability is that Collins abandoned it soon after he had written the 'many pages' which he showed to Ragsdale. He could have returned the ten guineas advanced by the publisher, if he had no other means of doing so, out of the twelve pounds received on 30th May, when he relinquished his nominal possession of the house in Westgate, and so regained his freedom. It is not unlikely that the task of translation had proved difficult as well as irksome. The *Poetics* present some formidable problems to a commentator even today, and it would hardly be an overstatement to say that all the serious work toward the solution of those problems has been done within the last hundred years. We can hardly believe that even the best classical scholar of the age, which Collins certainly was not, could have taken them in his stride in 1746.

However that may be, there is one of Collins's poems which proclaims clearly that he had freed himself from some kind of intellectual bondage, and rejoiced in his freedom. That poem is *The Manners,* which critics generally have assigned to the time when he left Oxford. 'The closing lines, in particular,' says Bronson, 'are full of the exaltation which a man of Collins's temperament would feel upon plunging, with a sense of newly acquired freedom, into the varied life of a great city.' To one reader, at least, it seems that Bronson has read into these lines what he expected to find rather than what is actually expressed, and that it is the prospect of enjoying his newly acquired freedom in the country, far from the varied life of a great city, which moves the poet to exaltation:

> O Nature boon, from whom proceed
> Each forceful Thought, each prompted Deed
> If but from Thee I hope to feel,

On all my Heart imprint they Seal!
Let some retreating Cynic find,
Those oft-turn'd Scrolls I leave behind,
The *Sports* and I this Hour agree,
To rove thy Scene-full World with Thee!

Mr. Garrod also considers that 'the Ode entitled *The Manners*
is, on the face of it, a farewell to university studies by an undergraduate just "going down" ... In it Collins bids farewell to
Oxford and Oxford philosophy.'(*11*) That is thought to be so obvious that the writer does not mention the difficulty presented by
the footnote referring to 'Him, whom *Seine's* blue Nymphs de-
plore'. Collins left Oxford at the end of 1743, and the footnote
reads: 'Monsieur *Le Sage,* Author of the incomparable Adven-
tures of *Gil Blas de Santillane,* who died in *Paris* in the Year
1745.' Actually Collins was misinformed; Le Sage died at Bou-
logne, and not till November, 1747, so that he was still living
when the poem was written; but the point is that Collins could not
in 1743 have believed, correctly or otherwise, that Le Sage or
anyone else died in 1745.

Bronson proposed to remove the difficulty by suggesting that
'lines 67-70, with the footnote about Le Sage's death in 1745,
could easily have been inserted later, upon a report of his decease'.
That is possible, but if we suppose that Collins was writing in
1746, and that the 'oft-turn'd Scrolls' which he now leaves behind are the works of Aristotle, there is no difficulty to remove.
The poet has renounced philosophy in favour of a life of 'ampler
Range', which would include, for him, the freedom of original
composition; he looks forward to human society and lively conversation, and he hopes to acquire the kind of knowledge to be
gained from 'Life's wide Prospects' and her 'mingling Sons'. At
Richmond, with Thomson and his friends, he would have found
just the life that he desired, and in the perfect setting.

It must be to this period that Ragsdale refers when he says that
Collins 'set about writing his odes'. That, no doubt, he could report from actual observation, though his assumption that the
motive was 'to earn a present subsistence' must be considered as
open to doubt. Perhaps in one of those conversations in which

they 'took the liberty of saying anything to each other' Collins may have been reminded of his duty to work at his translation, and may have replied that poets as well as translators had been known to make a living.

Ragsdale continues by saying that, 'having a general invitation to my house, he frequently passed whole days there, which he employed in writing them, and as frequently burning what he had written, after reading them to me. Many of them which pleased me I struggled to preserve, but without effect, for pretending he would alter them, he got them from me and thrust them into the fire'. This, in conjunction with the next statement, 'He was an acceptable companion everywhere', indicates a state of mild elation rather than grim devotion to the literary grindstone. Collins would be in just such a mood when he put away his work on Aristotle – perhaps with a vague intention to resume it in some indefinite future – and began to indulge freely in the social and intellectual pleasures of the life around him. It seems probable that *The Manners* was the first, or one of the first, of the productions of this happy season, and that the ode *To Evening* and 'How sleep the Brave' were among the others.

It remains true, however, that problems which had made heavy demands on his time, so as to prevent him, as he told Ragsdale, from seeing his friends as often as he would have wished, would still leave an impression on his mind after he had turned away from them. No one who had attempted to translate the *Poetics,* even unsuccessfully, could fail to have the phrase 'pity and fear' imprinted on his memory, and it is reasonable to suppose, therefore, that the choice of the subjects of the odes *To Pity* and *To Fear* was due in some degree to the recollection of Aristotle. It is overstating the case, however, to say that 'Collins' Pity and Fear are . . . the Pity and Fear of Aristotle'.(*12*) The ode *To Pity* has a strongly personal note, in which we may detect the poet's relief at returning from Greece to southern England, from Euripides to Otway, from the task of interpreting abstract ideas not his own to the joy of free expression:

> But wherefore need I wander wide
> To old *Ilissus'* distant Side

101

Deserted Stream, and mute?
Wild *Arun* too has heard thy Strains,
And Echo, 'midst my native Plains,
Been sooth'd by *Pity's* Lute.

There first the Wren thy Myrtles shed
On gentlest Otway's infant head,
To Him thy Cell was shown;
And while He sung the Female Heart,
With Youth's soft Notes unspoil'd by Art,
Thy Turtles mix'd their own.

The lines on Otway are the heart of the poem. They express an affection which Collins displayed by word and deed at several stages of his life, and which those critics who have thought him deficient in ordinary human feeling would do well to ponder. We may recall that before leaving Winchester he had joined with Warton in erecting a 'marble' to Otway's memory. In Mr. Cunningham's Fragment 8, which we have supposed to belong to an earlier version of the 'Epistle to Hanmer', there is some veiled disparagement of Davenant, and a footnote reads: 'Otway despis'd as a Writer while Dav'nant was in repute.' There is a further tribute in Fragment 2, which is probably, as we shall see, a comparatively late composition:

To Resnel's Banks, again to greet
Her Gentle Eyes I strayd
Where once a Bard with Infant Feet
Among the Willows play'd
His tender thoughts subdue the Fair
And melt the Soft and Young
But mine I know were softer there
Than ever Poet sung.

That the allusion is to Otway is proved by the manuscript, in which the word 'once a Bard' have been substituted for 'Otway first'.

If Collins's 'Pity' is not derived from Aristotle that must be true also of his 'Fear', for in Aristotle's theory pity and fear so

102

interact with each other that the reader sometimes feels the need of a single word to express the combination of the two. The fact, therefore, that Collins makes each of them the subject of a separate poem, unconnected with the other, is itself an indication that he was not guided by the *Poetics*. There is another and more obvious reason, however, which compels us to think of his treatment of Fear as peculiarly his own. We remember Johnson's observation that Collins was 'eminently delighted with those flights of imagination which pass the bounds of nature'. Fear is the subject of all others which allows the poet legitimately to 'pass the bounds of nature', for it may, in an extreme form, call up visions of monsters, fiends, phantoms and every kind of threatening evil; of ghosts which

> as Cottage-Maids believe,
> Their pebbled Beds permitted leave,

and of goblins which

> haunt from Fire, or Fen,
> Or Mine, or Food, the Walks of Men!

Throughout the poem he avails himself freely of the licence allowed by the subject to indulge his imagination.

When that has been said, however, it is important to add that Collins never loses his mastery of the characters and situations which he creates. Every detail contributes to the architecture of the whole, and it is in that sense, but only in that sense, that the poem is truly Aristotelian. It follows the rule of Hamlet in his advice to the players: 'In the very torrent, tempest, and (as I may say) the whirlwind of passion, you must acquire and beget a temperance that may give it smoothness.' Mr. Woodhouse is right when he dismisses as 'wrong-headed' Watts-Dunton's misguided tribute to Collins's 'imaginative power of seeing a man asleep on a loose hanging rock, and of actualizing in a dramatic way the peril of the situation'. We must agree that 'Collins's Danger is not a man, but a giant being whom "no mortal Eye can fix'd behold"; ... Danger is a figure of ideal wonder touched with terror, the

103

creature of a shadowy spirit world, revealed to the poet in a sort of vision, while "Fancy lifts the Veil between".'(13)

Mr. Hagstrum more recently has made the same point, though he arrives at it by a different approach. He contrasts Collins's power of imaginative description with Thomson's, and says: 'Although fundamentally related, there is this difference between Thomson's and Collins's imagery. Thomson's at its best arises from the vivid personification of *natural* detail, and the organization of the scene around that personification, but Collins at his most typical personifies the *moral* and psychological abstraction and makes that personification central to the entire poem.'(14) These last words express a truth which the reader of the ode *To Fear* must perceive for himself if the unity of the poem is to be apparent to him, as it could not have been to Watts-Dunton.

In the ode *To Simplicity* the influence of Aristotle is more easily discernible. The text is obviously inaccurate, but what Collins seems to say, in the first four and the sixth and seventh stanzas, is that Simplicity was first seen to perfection in Athens, but departed, when the city lost its liberty; it then fled to Rome, and was happy in the days of the Republic, but remained to see only the beginning of the Empire under Caesar Augustus; it was next observed 'in Hall or Bow'r', perhaps in Italy in the time of Petrarch, but the passions, which expressed themselves in love poetry, would not submit to its control. This brief historical sketch, if it may be so called, is interrupted by the fifth stanza. The possibility suggests itself that that stanza has been somehow misplaced by the printer, and that it ought to follow the seventh as we know it. We should then proceed straight from Athens to Rome and from Rome to the Middle Ages, after which the poet would address himself to Simplicity in lines which, though defective in some points of detail, would at least display continuity of thought. Thus:

> O Sister meek of Truth,
> To my admiring Youth,
> Thy sober Aid and native Charms infuse!
> The Flow'rs that sweetest breathe,
> Tho' Beauty cull'd the Wreath,
> Still ask thy Hand to range their order'd Hues.

Tho' Taste, tho' Genius bless,
To some divine Excess,
Faints the cold Work till Thou inspire the whole;
What each, what all supply,
May court, may charm our Eye,
Thou, only Thou canst raise the meeting Soul!

Of These let others ask,
To aid some mighty Task,
I only seek to find thy temp'rate Vale:
Where oft my Reed might sound
To Maids and Shepherds round,
And all thy Sons, O *Nature*, learn my Tale.

This arrangement makes clearer what is less obvious in the
poem in its familiar form: that what Collins means by Simplicity
is Aristotelian unity. At the beginning Simplicity is taught to
breathe, in poetry, the 'geneuine Thought' of nature, disdaining
such extraneous ornamentation as 'Gauds, and pageant Weeds,
and trailing Pall'. That is another way of saying that poetry should
imitate nature in the Aristotelian sense: a poem should be, in
Butcher's words, 'a unity which is unfolded and expanded according to the law of its own nature, an organism which develops from
within'.(15) That is the law, personified as Simplicity, by which
poetry was governed through the ages, until the passions proved
too strong for it. In the last stanza, which has a more personal note,
Collins himself aspires to be a poet, though a poet of humble degree, singing in a 'temp'rate Vale' among maids and shepherds.
If his rustic listeners are willing to learn his tale, as he expects, that
must be because it expresses the 'genuine Thought' of nature, har-
monizing with their instinctive thoughts and feelings.

When all that is said, however, it can hardly be denied that
there is some confusion of thought in the lines

Who first on Mountains wild,
In *Fancy* loveliest Child
Thy Babe, or *Pleasure's*, nurs'd the Pow'rs of Song!

105

We do not naturally think of Fancy as the child of Simplicity, and by adding 'or *Pleasure's*' Collins admits to an uncertainty hardly compatible with genuine inspiration. I believe that several years later he re-wrote the ode with a clearer vision, but at this point that is all that can be said.

It is customary among literary historians to speak of Collins as a precursor of the Romantic Movement. The same claim is made for Thomson, Akenside, Young and a number of others up to and including Cowper. So far as it concerns Collins it cannot be admitted on the ground usually alleged: that, like an earlier Blake, he acknowledged no law except the law of his imagination, which was a law unto itself.

It is true that Collins's imagination was peculiarly vivid, and we remember the picturesque language in which Dr. Johnson speaks of the lengths to which it could lead him. 'He . . . was eminently delighted with those flights of imagination which pass the bounds of nature and to which the mind is reconciled only by a passive acquiescence in popular traditions. He loved fairies, genii, giants, and monsters; he delighted to rove through the meanders of enchantment, to gaze on the magnificence of golden palaces, to repose by the waterfalls of Elysian gardens . . .' In his poems this predilection for the remote and unreal is apparent even when it is under control, and shows to the best advantage in 'How sleep the Brave'.

The immediate question, however, is whether his flights of imagination may be seen as marking out the path to be followed at the end of the century by Wordsworth, the dominating figure of the Romantic Movement. There is no need to labour the point that Wordsworth was never lured away from reality by fairies, genii, giants and monsters. In the earlier of the two periods of which he speaks in *Tintern Abbey* he revelled in the sights and sounds of nature for their own sake, with

> a feeling and a love
> That had no need of a remoter charm
> By thought supplied, or any interest
> Unborrowed from the eye.

In the Pantheistic phase which followed he still loved the cataract, the rock, the mountain and the wood as things of beauty in themselves, but he saw them also as witnesses to a pervading divinity with which, in elevated moments, his own mind was able to communicate:

> And I have felt . . .
> A motion and a spirit, that impels
> All thinking things, all objects of all thought,
> And rolls through all things.

His devotion throughout was to nature; flights of imagination which pass the bounds of nature would have had for him no interest and no meaning.

Coleridge, as is well known, attempted unsuccessfully to distinguish the imagination from the fancy, and his argument must have led him to attribute Collins's fairies, genii, giants and monsters to the lower faculty, the fancy. Imagination he believed to be the highest power of the human mind, for it was that by which 'the poet, described in *ideal* perfection, brings the whole soul of man into activity, with the subordination of its faculties to each other, according to their relative worth and dignity'. There is reason to believe, however, that at a later state Coleridge abandoned this theory,(16) though he never openly repudiated it, and came to see that 'that synthetic and magical power, to which we have exclusively appropriated the name of imagination' was, in fact, the intuitive reason, the power which unites men with the angels,(17) so that Plato and Aristotle were right after all. It is not because of his love of the unreal creations of the fancy, but because he displays in a lesser degree the power of intuition which we recognize in *Tintern Abbey*, that Collins may be considered as a forerunner of Wordsworth. If critics choose to call this power by the name of imagination, as they usually do, it is probably too late to protest against a well established habit; but we should not confuse the imagination of Wordsworth, if it must be so called, with the inventive power which gives rise to 'those flights of imagination which pass the bounds of nature'.

Southey, the third of the 'Lake poets', has declined steadily in reputation since the time when the *Edinburgh Review* spoke of him as the leading member of the group. It could be argued that as a critic and essayist he has received less than justice, whatever may be said of him as a poet. He, like Wordsworth and Coleridge, admired the ode *To Evening,* and wrote of it in a critical essay which seems to have escaped the attention of literary historians because it is, nominally, a review of 'The Collective Works of the late Dr. Sayers'. He points the contrast with Gray on lines which, however familiar today, might have passed in his time as original cricitism: 'Lyric poems, of the most opposite kind, but which have become equally popular, were produced by Gray and Collins: those of the former were the highly finished compositions of a patient and fastidious artist; those of the latter, the effusions of an ardent, poetical spirit.'

Southey also anticipated an observation which has been made independently by later critics : that the metre of the ode *To Evening* is the unrhymed stanza which Milton had employed for his translation of Horace's 'Pyrrha' ode (I, 5). Mr. Garrod has pointed out that Collins may have owed the suggestion to Thomas Warton, who had used the same metre for his translation of Horace's 'fons Bandusiae' ode (III, 13), and that Warton, in his turn, may have been indebted to his father, who had used Milton's adaptation of Horace's metre for his *Ode to Taste,(18)* a poem in other respects neither Horatian nor Miltonic.

NOTES TO CHAPTER VII

1. *Autobiography*, p. 216.
2. *Autobiography*, Chapter VIII.
3. *Autobiography*, p. 206.
4. *James Thomson*, p. 247.
5. Ibid., pp. 110-1.
6. *The Sister Arts*, p. 279.
7. *James Thomson*, p. 157.
8. *Spring*, 11. 467-475.
9. Here, and elsewhere in this chapter, I have made some slight use of an article of my own on 'Coleridge and the Theory of Imagination'. (*University of Toronto Quarterly* Vol. IX, No. 4, July, 1940.)

10. It is generally supposed that Johnson alludes to Collins's work in the Preface to the *Preceptor*, where, speaking of 'the the art of poetry' as an educational subject, he says that 'a more accurate and philosophical account is expected from a commentary upon Aristotle's Art of Poetry, with which the literature of this nation will be in a short time augmented'. (Johnson's *Works*, ed. Lynam, 1825, Vol. V, p. 220.)
11. *Collins*, p. 52.
12. Garrod, *Collins*, p. 56.
13. *Studies in English by Members of University College, Toronto* ('Collins and the Creative Imagination', by A. S. P. Woodhouse), p. 110.
14. *The Sister Arts*, pp. 271-2.
15. *Aristotle's Theory of Poetry and Fine Art*, pp. 186-7.
16. See note 9, above.
17. Milton, *Paradise Lost*, Book V, 486-90; one of Coleridge's favourite quotations.
18. *Collins*, p. 25.

VIII

The Odes Completed

WE have no exact knowledge of the order in which the odes were composed. There was probably a certain amount of overlapping, and one, at least, the ode *To Liberty*, seems from internal evidence to have been begun at one period and finished at another after a considerable interval. In the ode *To a Lady* we detect echoes of the militant exultation which immediately followed the news of Culloden, and there are others which seem, though with less certainty, to relate themselves to the events of the day and to the prevailing mood of the country.

The ode *To Evening* is followed in the published volume by the ode *To Peace*, which is in the same metre as the rhymed *Ode to Evening* and the odes *To Pity* and *To a Lady*. That, it is true, is by no means a certain indication that it was the next in order of composition, but the subject is one which would be likely to suggest itself as soon as the excitement over a complete and decisive victory had subsided. 'I doubt not,' says a contemporary writer, speaking of the Duke of Cumberland, 'but he will endeavour to increase his honours with the increase of years; and after we have, by a successful war, procured tranquillity to the public, . . . I hope and believe that he will render himself conspicuous in promoting the fairer and more lovely triumphs of *Peace*, "Dear nurse of arts, plenties, and joyful births".'(*1*)

The first stanza of the ode obviously refers to the Jacobite rebellion:

110

O Thou, who bad'st thy Turtles bear
Swift from his Grasp thy golden Hair,
  And sought'st thy native Skies:
When *War*, by Vultures drawn from far,
To *Britain* bent his Iron Car,
  And bad his Storms arise!

These lines though not comparable on any other ground with the work of Collins's inspired moments, have one peculiarity in common with the ode *To Evening:* the faults of syntax, diction and imagery, the presence of which is indisputable, are in some mysterious way brought into service so as to contribute to the imaginative effect of the whole. It will be helpful to illustrate that by quoting at length two comments, one analytical and the other, if the word may be used in its literal sense, sympathetic. Mr. Garrod extends his view to the poem as a whole, but writes with particular reference to the first stanza, which he quotes in full. ' "Clarity of style"!' he exclaims, recalling some words of Swinburne which he had quoted on an earlier page. He continues:

But it takes some pains to discover that 'his', in line 2, refers to *War*, who, despite the colon at the end of line 3, is not mentioned until the fourth line ... In the fourth line, I have to think twice before I am sure that it is, not the Vultures, but *War* that is 'drawn from far'. Of the incongruous picture furnished by this first stanza – in which Peace bids her Turtles to loose her golden hair from the grasp of the Vulture-charioted *War* – I prefer to say nothing. 'The British Lion, Goddess sweet,' who, in the third stanza, kisses the feet of Peace, is almost equally disconcerting – till you make the discovery that the Goddess is, not the Lion, but Peace herself. If the truth must be told, no single stanza of this Ode has any redeeming felicity of sentiment, thought or phrase.(2)

In contrast with this we have the imaginative view of Mr. Woodhouse. Speaking of the odes generally, he says that

the suggestive and eminently visual character of the phrasing

111

compensates for its brevity. The result is a word-picture whose effect approximates to that of an allegorical painting or, more exactly, the sketch for an allegorical picture.

He then quotes the first stanza of the ode *To Peace* as an example, and continues,

One cannot doubt that the effect sought is almost wholly pictorial. The stanza is like a sketch of some allegorical painting by Rubens. Its features could be catalogued precisely as could be those of a painting: On the right is the male figure of War, borne through the air in an iron chariot, which is drawn by vultures and supported on dark storm-clouds; before him rises the female figure Peace, ascending to the heavens, with her doves circling around her; War is reaching forward to grasp her tresses, which are brushed from his hand by the doves; in the distance, beneath the storm-clouds, appear the isle of Britain, towards which War's flight is directed. Some of the details are, of course, but slightly suggested, and nothing is described minutely; but no one, I fancy, can fail to see that it is the effect of the allegorical painter that Collins is trying to rival.(3)

The reader who compares these impressions will be tempted to exclaim, as Mr. Garrod himself says of Johnson's opinion of Collins's style in contrast with Swinburne's, 'They cannot both be right'. Generally speaking – for we may not agree that there is any difficulty in deciding that it is War, and not the vultures, that is 'drawn from far' – the faults of expression discovered by Mr. Garrod's analysis are real, but so also is the pictorial effect of the whole, reminiscent of Rubens, which Mr. Woodhouse has observed. It is a matter within Mr. Hagstrum's domain, and we may regret that in his chapter on Collins in *The Sister Arts* he has not mentioned the ode *To Peace*. He does remark that 'nearly every one of the odes gives the impression that it was written with real or imaginary allegorical pictures in the back of the poet's mind', but in a qualifying note he adds:

112

I do not wish to suggest that Collins' form derives from a steady contemplation of real or imaginary graphic art ... It is not totally pictorial in that manner. Collins, gives, rather, the impression of glancing up at a picture that is not steadily contemplated but always ready to furnish pictorial and iconic details when called upon.(4)

If we accept that as generally true we may feel at the same time that Collins is occasionally led to make an exception, and that at the beginning of the ode *To Peace* he does, in fact, steadily contemplate the picture present to his mind. Thus, for a time, the art of the poet is subservient to that of the painter. The worst advice that could be given to a young poet would be to imitate Collins; yet if he had, against all advice, defied the rules and triumphed over them, as Collins occasionally does, that would be a hopeful sign of genius.

The subject of peace is one in which a poet ought to find inspiration; yet Collins seems to have found it necessary to search about for a model, and to have found it in an unexpected place. His figure of Peace has an obvious resemblance to the Venus of Thomson's *Nuptial Song*, who, after being implored to return to a land ready to receive her, is reminded that

> For long the furious god of war
> Has crushed us with his iron car,
> Has raged along our ruined plains,
> Has cursed them with his cruel stains,
> Has sunk our youth in endless sleep,
> And made the widowed virgin weep.

These lines were written in 1729 or 1730, but Collins might well have read them in 1746 as a prophecy, now fulfilled, of the Jacobite rebellion. Thus he would be able to complete the picture by recalling that the furious god of war had 'to *Britain* bent his Iron Car', and, his imagination being thus excited, the details of the imagery would supply themselves.

In the continuation it is said of War that

113

> Tir'd of his rude tyrannic Sway,
> Our Youth shall fix some festive Day,
> His sullen Shrines to burn.

That, again, is better understood if read against the background
of the *Nuptial Song*. It is universally agreed that war is an evil
and the restoration of peace a blessing, but, when all that has
been said, it remains true that war of the only kind known in the
eighteenth century had some compensations; it did provide scope,
and, for many young men, the only possible scope, for courage,
patriotic zeal and the spirit of adventure. Such Galahadian qualities as these are distinctive of youth at its best, and we may be surprised, therefore, that 'our Youth' should be foremost in the desire
to burn the 'sullen shrines'. That is explained when we realize that
Thomson's poem is addressed not to Peace but to Venus : it is she
who, now that the 'furious god of War' has been expelled, is
asked to restore happiness to 'a warring world, a bleeding age'.
We notice here, as when we compare the ode *To Evening* with
the rhymed ode, that Collins's borrowings are not always perfectly
assimilated.

It is natural that Collins's mood should have changed since he
composed the ode *To a Lady*. He does not forget that the war
across the Channel still continues, but he no longer exults in the
thought of heroes who 'wish th'avenging Fight', or in the prospect of seeing Cumberland's sword 'sated' with the blood of
enemies. No doubt he responded to the events of the time in much
the same way as the rest of the nation, and we know that the Duke
of Cumberland did not long retain the popularity which he had
won by his victory at Culloden. The Jacobites, it was felt, were
an honourable enemy fighting for a cause which in their eyes was
sacred, and Cumberland was devoid of the heroic virtue of
magnanimity. Alexander Carlyle speaks of Smollett's *Tears of
Scotland*, 'which . . . had such a run of approbation', and adds:
'Smollett, though a Tory, was not a Jacobite, but he had the feelings of a Scotch gentleman on the reported cruelties that were
said to be exercised after the battle of Culloden.'(5) Those feelings were shared by many people who were neither Scotch nor
Tories.

Thus it is reasonable to suppose that the ode *To Mercy* followed the ode *To Peace* at no long interval. Here again it is neither the rebel host nor the power of France, but war itself, that is the enemy. The poem is, as is generally agreed, superior to the ode *To Peace*, being simpler and more easily intelligible, though the picture in the first stanza of Valour submitting to the restraint of Mercy is not true to the facts if by Valour we are to understand the Duke of Cumberland. Collins's imagination is just as vigorous, but is better sustained throughout and better harmonized with the power of verbal description. Mr. Garrod, while denying to the poem any considerable merit, admits that the first section of the strophe (lines 1 to 6) 'has melody'.(6) Mr. Hagstrum says of these same lines that they 'are indeed pictorial, reminiscent of high Renaissance paintings of Mars disarmed by Venus'.(7) We cannot disagree with either. The melody is there, and so is the pictorial effect, but they support each other instead of struggling together for mastery. That is more than can be said of the first stanza of the ode *To Peace*.

The ode *To Liberty* is generally considered in relation to 'How sleep the Brave' and the odes *To a Lady*, *To Peace* and *To Mercy*, but, unlike the others, it has no obvious connection with any single event that is known to history. It has the appearance of having been written at different times over a period of several months, and would probably be more highly regarded if the first half had survived as a fragment.

The beginning of the poem reads as if the words had been written in letters of fire. We have here the expression of the martial spirit which must have been aroused in Collins in the autumn of 1745, when there was a possibility that the Jacobite adventure might succeed, and when, as his visit to Colonel Martin seems to indicate, he had serious thoughts of exchanging the pen for the sword. He was at this time, like his father, a Whig and a Protestant – by which is meant that he was a Whig in religion and a Protestant in politics – and it would be natural to him to think of the House of Hanover, now threatened with extinction, as the citadel of liberty.

Most critics have noticed that the plan of the poem has a general resemblance to that of Thomson's *Liberty*. In both, the

115

spirit of liberty is shown as settling for a time in one country after another as it wanders through the ages, until it finds an abiding habitation in contemporary Britain. In one respect, however, the two poems are at opposite extremes. Thomson moves from age to age and from country to country with a certain majestic deliberation, appropriate, as he must have thought, to his greatest work and to the grandeur of the theme. Collins plunges at once *in medias res,* and arrives at his goal by a far shorter route.

Thomson devotes the whole of his second Book to a description of the rise and fall of free institutions in Sparta and in Athens. Everything is generalized, and the poet seems to be striving, not always successfully, to harness his muse to the purposes of philosophic history. Collins dismisses in twelve lines what had occupied Thomson for five hundred. We hear nothing of 'Laconic force' or 'Spartan valour', of 'Athenian arts', or 'free social life, and polished manners fair', but we are allowed a momentary glance at some individual Spartans and Athenians whose achievements are left to the imagination. The amazing vigour of these opening lines almost defeats its own object, for the reader finds it easier to admire them than to discover what they mean. What is 'the Spartan Fife', and who are the youths whose locks 'applauding Freedom lov'd of old to view'? It needs some rapid mental adjustment to think of Sparta as the home of liberty, but perhaps we are to detect an allusion to its successful defence against the designs of Pyrrhus, King of Epirus, who was certainly, on this occasion, a tyrant and an aggressor.

The Athenians who follow in the next six lines could not have been identified with any approach to certainty if Collins had not quoted in a footnote 'that beautiful Fragment of *Alcaeus*', recalling how Harmodius and Aristogeton slew the tyrant Hipparchus at the Festival of Athene. Mr. Garrod has pointed out that Collins is wrong in attributing the lines in question to Alcaeus, who flourished a century or more earlier than the heroes whose fame he is supposed to have celebrated.(8) That is unanswerable, but it must be added that Mr. Garrod himself falls short of the strict accuracy to be expected of a critic who denounces the lapses of 'a bad scholar'. Collins is not responsible for the words 'sang the sword', which Mr. Garrod attributes to him in inverted commas.

He pleads for a 'New *Alcaeus*', who '*shall* sing the Sword', at some time in the future. We do not read Wordsworth's sonnet beginning 'Milton! thou shouldst be living at this hour' as betraying ignorance of the time when Milton actually did live.

It is essential to the understanding of the poem that the true authorship of these lines should be known. A little research will discover that they form part of one of the *scolia* preserved by Athenaeus, who flourished about 200 A.D., and who made a collection of such trifles in fifteen volumes. At this point we are able to add some important information furnished by Mr. J. M. G. Blakiston, the present Librarian of Winchester, which all but the most sceptical will accept as a convincing explanation of Collins's error. Mr. Blakiston found the lines in question in Casaubon's edition of Athenaeus, published at Lyons in 1657.(9) They are attributed to Carcinus ('Apud Carcinum hoc scolion extat'), but the *previous* extract is headed: 'Ex Alceo et Anacreonte scolion quoddam sumptum mihi cane.' The probability is, therefore, that Collins copied the extract without noting the name of the author, and that when he came to supply the omission at a later stage he was misled by the recollection of seeing in the adjacent column a note beginning, 'Ex Alceo——'

Alcaeus, though his metre found favour with Horace, is not, after all, a poet of the first magnitude, and Collins's error is hardly serious enough to justify a general charge of bad scholarship. Perhaps a better ground for such an accusation would be found in his selection of Harmodius and Aristogeton as typical champions of Athenian liberty. Our only information about them is derived from Thucydides,(10) and from him we learn that they killed Hipparchus from no other motive than to avenge a private injury, and were themselves killed by the guards. It was, to them, merely an accidental circumstance that Hipparchus and his brother Hippias happened to be tyrants, though they were, in fact, tyrants in the English sense of the word as well as in the Greek; but after Hippias had been deposed and driven into exile his name and that of his brother were held in execration, and Harmodius and Aristogeton, because they had slain Harmodius at the cost of their own lives, came to be revered as martyrs to liberty. A grain of historical fact grew into a legend, and it is from the

117

legend that Collins had taken the 'Deed renown'd' and the sword that 'leap'd in Gory forth'.

In passing from Greece in the age of the Pisistratids to Rome in the age of its decline Collins manages to maintain the strength and vigour of the opening lines, though it could be argued that this part of the poem is hardly relevant to the subject of liberty. From here it is easy to survey the course of time through and beyond the Middle Ages, and to speak first of Florence, San Marino and Venice, and then of Switzerland and Holland, as small communities which have remained strongholds of liberty. Moving rapidly over the ground traversed in more leisurely fashion by Thomson, he arrives at the ultimate home of liberty, which is his own country in his own time:

> The Magic works, Thou feel'st the Strains,
> One holier Name alone remains;
> The perfect Spell shall then avail,
> Hail Nymph, ador'd by *Britain,* Hail!

There the poem might have ended, for a poet who had an equal devotion to his country and to the House of Hanover could hardly wish to say more. Collins, however, does say more; he sets out along a different path which will bring him back, after some wandering, to the same conclusion. He recalls an old belief that England in some prehistoric time was physically joined to the Continent, and explains in a footnote: 'This Tradition is mention'd by several of our old Historians. Some Naturalists too have endeavour'd to support the Probability of the Fact, by Arguments drawn from the correspondent Disposition of the two opposite Coasts. I don't remember that any Poetical Use has been hitherto made of it.'

Actually Thomson mentions the tradition in the Fourth Book of his *Liberty,* the only difference being that what Collins reports as 'held of antique Story' Thomson records as the simple truth:

> For of old time, since first the rushing flood,
> Urged by almighty power, this favoured isle
> Turned flashing from the continent aside,

> Indented shore to shore responsive still,
> Its guardian she – the Goddess, whose staid eye
> Beams the dark azure of the doubtful dawn.

Mr. Garrod suspects that Collins had a bad memory, for he might be expected to have looked into Drayton's *Polyolbion*.(*11*) Mr. Woodhouse thinks that we must accept Collins's statement 'as made in good faith', and that 'the work on which Collins appears to have drawn most largely is Camden's *Britannia*'. But he also detects the influence of Waldron's *History and Description of the Isle of Man* and, as in the ode *To Fear*, that of Nashe's *Pierce Penniless*.(*12*)

Mr. Woodhouse does not rest his case on exact verbal parallels; he admits that 'one would not for a moment suggest that the reminiscences are all conscious', and does not claim more than 'a general and approximate accuracy for the whole'.(*13*) On that understanding may we not include the legend of the island of Atlantis, in the *Timaeus* of Plato, among the possible 'sources of Collin's imagery'? The fact that the Athenians are said to have fought successfully against a race of powerful enemies who were trying to enslave them would be enough in itself to commend the story to the author of a poem on Liberty.

According to Plato the defeat of the invaders was followed by terrific earthquakes and floods; the island of Atlantis sank into the sea, and with it both its inhabitants and the Athenian warriors disappeared. According to Collins,

> This pillar'd Earth so firm and wide,
> By Winds and inward Labors torn,
> In Thunders dread was push'd aside,
> And down the should'ring Billows born.

It was then that England, with its attendant islands, was torn away from the rest of the Continent, and enabled to become, in the course of ages, the last refuge of liberty.

> To Thee this blest Divorce she ow'd,
> For thou hast made her Vales thy lov'd, thy last Abode!

When we come to the concluding section, or Second Epode, we can hardly fail to notice a change of tone, suggesting that these lines were added after an interval. We have a highly imaginative description of a Temple of Liberty, said to have had a material existence in the centre of England in prehistoric ages. Somewhere beyond the clouds 'the beauteous *Model* still remains': a line happily interpreted by Mr. Garrod as meaning 'a Platonic Idea laid up in the heavens'.*(14)* There the British warriors of ancient times are even happier than the Athenian heroes in the Islands of the Blest, but what makes them so is not the consciousness of martial glory but the presence of Concord:

> Concord, whose Myrtle Wand can steep
> Ev'n *Anger's* blood-shot Eyes in Sleep:
> Before whose breathing Bosom's Balm,
> *Rage* drops his Steel, and Storms grow calm.

The sentiment anticipates some lines of *Locksley Hall*, and will seem even more admirable today than in times when wars were fought according to rules by small professional armies, but it would be an understatement to say that it differs from that expressed at the beginning. The most likely explanation is that the poem was begun during Collins's warlike mood, a little before or immediately after the Battle of Culloden, and finished at a time when the country was sated with the fruits of victory at home and wearied by the prolongation of the war with France. Thus the beginning would belong to the same period as the ode *To a Lady* and the conclusion to the same period as the odes *To Mercy* and *To Peace*.

That, by all the rules of proportion, is as much as should be said of the ode *On Liberty*, but in an interesting article entitled 'In Yonder Grave a Druid Lies',*(15)* published in 1946, Miss J. M. S. Tompkins has presented a new problem which cannot be passed over in silence. 'The word "Druid",' she writes, 'has given the critics some trouble,' and after quoting Mrs. Barbauld's opinion, approved by Mr. Garrod, that 'there is no propriety in calling Thomson a Druid or a pilgrim', she continues: 'Yet the word, while it is meant to stimulate reflection and to diffuse a colouring of awe over the line, cannot be meant to baffle us. It is essential that it should be understood, for it tells us at once under what aspect the dead poet is to be lamented.'

Miss Tompkins is mainly concerned with the ode *On the Death of Mr. Thomson*, as her title indicates, but, as is to be expected, the mention of the Druids in the ode *On Liberty* is also taken into account. 'In Collins's ode,' we are reminded, 'the Druids are found singing before the British chiefs in the celestial temple of Liberty.' The writer continues:

> I do not know where Collins got the notion of this temple, which stood, he says, 'an hoary Pile' in some forgotten 'religious Wood . . . midst the green Navel of the Isle'. Its overthrow, whether at the hands of Roman or Dane, is unrecorded, but its 'beauteous Model', its Platonic idea, still lies beyond the 'braided Clouds . . . amidst the bright pavilion'd Plains' of Heaven. The whole notion may be an unsupported sally of his imagination, stimulated, perhaps, by a hint in Thomson's poem; at all events it proves that Collins thought the Druids suitable inhabitants of such a temple.

It may be suggested that the origin of the idea is to be found in those lines which Collins has quoted in his footnote, and which he attributes to Alcaeus. There it is said that Harmodius is not dead, but still lives in the Islands of the Blest (οὔπω τέθνηκας, Νήσοις, δ᾽ἐνΜακάρων σέ φασιν εἶναι). These legendary islands are mentioned by Pindar (*16*) and elaborately described by Horace (*17*) as places where the souls of departed heroes find eternal happiness, and Collins would be aware, if only from his reading of *De Bello Gallico*, that the Druids also were reported to believe in some kind of immortality. As, however, according to Caesar, Britain was the headquarters of the Druids, and the place to which people of other nations resorted in order to settle doubt about their doctrines, the poet could hardly transport them to another island which, however fertile and beautiful, must be infinitely remote from the only place which they could feel to be their home. He overcomes the difficulty by keeping them in Britain but placing them above the sky, where they can enjoy a happiness

121

even greater than that of Harmodius in his divinely favoured but terrestrial islands:

> There happier than in Islands blest,
> Or Bow'rs by Spring or *Hebe* drest,
> The Chiefs who fill our *Albion's* Story,
> In warlike Weeds, retir'd in Glory,
> Hear their consorted *Druids* sing
> Their Triumphs to th'imortal String.

In the course of her article Miss Tompkins has related how interest in the Druids was revived in the seventeenth and eighteenth centuries, principally by the work of Toland and Stukeley. The latter, 'a more single-minded enthusiast than Toland', may be said to have brought the Druids into fashion. With hardly any support from authentic history for his facts, and none at all for his theories, Stukeley entertained the reading public with a portrayal of the Druids as masters of all knowledge and all wisdom, deriving the secrets of their religion from the son-in-law of Abraham, and even attaining 'a knowledge of the plurality of persons in the Deity'. All this would have appealed to Collins's imagination, but it must be added, regretfully, that we find no reason to believe that he was acquainted with it. He may have explored this fairyland of research in the last few years of his life, as his love of antiquarian studies seems to have grown as his power to write poetry declined, but of that we have no certain knowledge.

It will be noticed that in the passage last quoted from the ode *On Liberty* Collins thinks of the Druids not as philosophers or astronomers or prophets, and certainly not as theologians, but simply as singers, and in that he is following a literary tradition established by Beaumont and Fletcher's *Bonduca*, and continued by Milton. Sir Thomas Kendrick, in *The Druids,* a work to which Miss Tompkins acknowledges some indebtedness, observes that the third Act of *Bonduca* 'begins with a solemn entry of the druids singing; and it will be noticed that song seems to be their principal function'. He adds that 'this notion of the druids as being primarily bards gained further currency in Milton's *Lycidas*', and quotes the four lines ending, 'Where your old Bards, the famous druids,

lie'.(*18*) Miss Tompkins herself quotes this line with the comment:
'To Milton bards and Druids are synonymous, ... and in the
eighteenth century every bard can be referred to, if the verse re-
quires it, as a Druid.'

For his vision of a chorus of Druids celebrating the triumphs
of heroes Collins was certainly indebted to Milton, and, in particular, we may add with some confidence, to a passage in the
epistle *Ad Mansum*. There it is said that the Druids were accustomed, in the course of their religious rites, to sing the praises of
heroes and their illustrious deeds (*Gens Druides antiqua sacris
operata deorum Heroum laudes imitandaque gesta canebant*).
We hardly need evidence that Collins was familiar with this poem,
but in the fragment numbered 10 in Mr. Cunningham's collection – possibly, if the suggestion may be offered, a continuation of
the one printed separately as Fragment 9 – we find reason to suspect that Collins had not only read *Ad Mansum* but read it with
more than ordinary attention, and used it as a model for a poem
of his own. The concluding lines of Fragment 10 read:

> Nor, for they boast no pure Augustan vein
> Reject her poets with a cold disdain
> O Think in what sweet lays how sweetly strong
> Our Fairfax warbles Tasso's forcefull Song
> How Spenser too, whose lays you oft resume
> Wove their Gay [—] in his fantastic loom
> That Cynthio prompted oft ev'n Shakespear's flame
> And Milton valued ev'n Marino's name!

That is clearly a free adaptation of Milton's plea:

> Sed neque nos genus incultum, nec inutile Phoebo,
> Qua plaga septeno mundi sulcata Trione
> Brumalem patitur longa sub nocte Boöten.
> Nos etiam colimus Phoebum,—

Milton then speaks of the ceremonial dances of the Druids and of
their incantations, in the lines already quoted, and continues:

123

Fortunate senex, ergo, quacunque per orbem
Torquati decus, et nomen celebrabitur ingens
Claraque perpetui succrescet fama Marini,
Tu quoque in ora frequens venies plausumque virorum,
Et parili carpes iter immortale volatu.

Mr. Cunningham has a note on the line 'And Milton valued
ev'n Marino's name!' which reads: 'Milton names Marino in his
"Mansus".' That is true, but it will be seen from the passage
quoted that Milton's mention of Marino arises out of his tribute
to the glory of Tasso (Torquati decus), so that the parallel with
Collins's lines is much closer than Mr. Cunningham's remark
would indicate. Finding, then, from evidence not available to Miss
Tompkins in 1946, that Collins knew *Ad Mansum* well enough to
recall certain lines of it in a poem of his own – lines which immediately follow the passage about the Druids – we must suppose
that the singing Druids of the ode *On Liberty* owe their origin to
Milton's singing Druids, although, as has been said, the invention
for them of a celestial home, a place of even greater happiness than
the Islands of the Blest, may have been inspired by the lines quoted
from the pseudo-Alcaeus. That conclusion is not inconsistent with
the belief that the 'hoary Druids' of Fragment 3 are the Druids of
familiar talk and popular fancy.

The next poem to be considered, the ode *On the Poetical
Character*, must be approached with some trepidation, for it is
hardly possible to say anything about it that could pass as uncon-
troversial. Even to describe it as difficult or obscure might be open
to challenge, for there have been critics who have seemed to find
it as easily intelligible as 'How sleep the Brave'. Apart from the
fact that it was included in the volume published at the end of
1746, where it followed the ode *To Simplicity*, we have nothing
to indicate the date of composition, but that is a comparatively
small matter. More than one interpretation of the allegory has been
suggested, and no attempt will be made here to add another.
What is now to be said concerns the background of the poem
rather than the poem itself.

Bronson observed that the lines describing the Creator's infatua-
tion with Fancy are reminiscent of 'Jupiter Amans'. Most critics

124

are content to ignore the charge of blasphemy or to treat it lightly, perhaps because they feel that enough eloquence has been expended by Mrs. Barbauld in labouring the obvious. 'Some of the right things about Mrs. Barbauld,' says Mr. Garrod, 'have been said already by Wordsworth; and I pass her by.' He does not, however, as is usual, pass by the accusation itself. 'I am not sure,' he continues, 'whether either Shelley or Keats, certainly not Milton or Wordsworth, would have ventured to conceive God himself as wooed "by the lov'd Enthusiast", Fancy; to speak of God as "Himself in some Diviner Mood" retiring and sitting alone with Fancy; of Fancy seated on the Sapphire Throne – to Collins, the Throne of God; in Milton, the Sapphire Throne is the throne of Christ.'(19)

Mr. Garrod writes with restraint, but he accepts as unquestionable the assumption that the Creator described in the poem is the true Creator according to Christian doctrine. If we are obliged to admit that interpretation there is no escape from the charge of blasphemy; but we must allow Collins the benefit of the doubt if there is any room for doubt, and it is a fact that there is not the slightest taint of blasphemy in anything else that he ever wrote or spoke, so far as we know. We shall not willingly believe, therefore, that on this one occasion he was blasphemous to a degree beyond anything to be imagined of Shelley, to say nothing of Keats.

We must remember that Collins had a natural love of mythology and legend, and we must remember also, in connection with that, that there are other accounts of the Creation besides the one in the Old Testament. In a letter to John Gilbert Cooper, to be quoted in full in its place, he borrows a phrase from the First Book of Ovid's *Metamorphoses*, and that would be sufficient evidence, if evidence were needed, that he was familiar with the story of the Creation according to Ovid. It is possible, therefore, that the lines,

> When He, who call'd with Thought to Birth
> Yon tented Sky, this laughing Earth,
> And drest with Springs, and Forests tall,
> And pour'd the Main engirting all,

refer to 'whichever of the gods it was' (*quisquis fuit ille deorum*) who fashioned the world in the manner described in the *Meta-morphoses*. It would, of course, be hopeless to search for exact verbal parallels, for Collins was a poet and not a copyist; but it could be argued that the lines just quoted have a closer resem-blance to those of Ovid than to anything in the Old Testament. Collins's sky is 'tented', a good poetical equivalent of Ovid's *con-vexum*. 'This laughing Earth' accords well with the tone of Ovid's narrative, which, in contrast to that of the First Chapter of Genesis, is joyful rather than sublime. 'And dressed with Springs, and Forests tall' could have been suggested by Ovid's mention of *fontes* as among the earliest works of the creation and by the statement, a few lines later, that the forests were ordered to be covered, or dressed, with foliage (*fronde tegi silvas*). 'And pour'd the Main engirting all,' implying that the sea was called into be-ing after the creation of the earth, does not agree with either the Old Testament or the *Metamorphoses,* in both of which the dry land was made to appear by the parting of the waters; but, in a choice between the two, we must consider as the more likely source, on grounds of verbal resemblance, the words of the *Metamor-phoses*: 'The water, streaming round, filled the farthest places, and girt about the solid globe' (*circumfluens umor Ultima possedit solidumque coercuit orbem*). If, then, we admit even the possibility that the Deity of the poem is the Creator according to Ovid and not according to the Book of Genesis, the charge of blasphemy must be dismissed, for there is no blasphemy in attributing to this imagined predecessor of Jupiter conduct like that of Jupiter him-self.

What is remarkable about Ovid's story is that the creation of the world – or, strictly speaking, its fashioning out of a pre-existing Chaos – is said to be the work of one of the gods, who, by his own power, if we may describe his action in Collins's words,

> call'd with Thought to Birth
> Yon tented Sky, this laughing Earth.

Generally speaking, the ancient poets think of the gods as inhabit-ants of the world like man himself, though on a higher plane of existence. Zeus, as the supreme deity, may, within certain limits,

order the course of events on earth when they happen to interest
him and when he is not otherwise occupied, but he is not imagined
as the creator of the world which he controls. This is a point which
Mr. A. H. Armstrong insists upon at the beginning of a recent
book, and I mention it because in the continuation Mr. Armstrong
speaks of Pherecydes of Syros, a Greek who flourished some five
or six centuries before the time of Ovid, as a single exception.
Mr. Armstrong, of course, is not concerned with Collins's poem,
but I think that his remarks upon Pherecydes, whether taken alone
or in conjunction with the *Metamorphoses*, may be helpful to the
interpretation of the allegory. After reminding us that 'the gods
are part of the family, *in* the world, not its outside causes or
makers', he continues:

> The teller of stories about the origin of the gods called Phere-
> cydes of Syros ... does seem to speak, in an odd and allegorical
> way, of Zeus making at least the world we know; for he de-
> scribes him making a great tapestry or embroidered cloth with
> Earth and Ocean on it as a wedding-present for his bride
> Chthonie – perhaps the Earth-principle, or basic earth, the
> substructure as distinguished from the variegated surface.(20)

The writings of Pherecydes are known only by a few fragments,
and I confess that my own knowledge of them is very slight and
very recently acquired. What I understand by the passage summarized is that the Deity fell in love with the earth as it then was –
the 'basic earth', as Mr. Armstrong says – and was moved to
present her with a wedding-garment. The wedding-garment
must be symbolic of the grass, the trees, the flowers and the whole
of that outer covering of vegetation, as well as the hills and rivers,
without which the earth would not be a thing of beauty. May we
suppose, then, that Collins was thinking of Pherecydes as the
author of those 'Fairy Legends' from which, at the beginning of
the poem, he professes to have derived his story? It is an attractive
possibility, enabling us to conclude that the Deity by whom the
world was 'call'd with Thought to Birth' is the creator Zeus as
Pherecydes imagines him; 'young Fancy', the 'lov'd Enthusiast'
by whom he was wooed and whom he placed on his 'Saphire

Throne', must be his bride Chthonie; and the 'Cest of amplest
Pow'r', the 'Band' which,

> as Fairy Legends say,
> Was wove on that creating Day,

must be the wedding-garment. This, I think, is not incompatible
with the idea, already suggested, that Collins may have been
guided partly by certain lines in the *Metamorphoses*.

There remains, however, one difficulty not to be resolved even
with the combined help of Pherecydes and Ovid. Why is the account of the creation interrupted by the sudden introduction of
Apollo? For it must be Apollo, always depicted as young and as
having a luxuriant head of hair, of whom the poet speaks in the
lines,

> And Thou, Thou rich-hair'd Youth of Morn,
> And all thy subject Life was born!

It is possible to consider Apollo as the sun-god, and his 'subject
Life' as, in the words of Mr. Woodhouse, 'the vegetable and ani-
mal life on earth, which is dependent on (subject to) the sun':(21)
everything, in fact, that is symbolized in the narrative of Pherecydes by the wedding-garment. But Collins must have remembered
that, besides being the sun-god, Apollo is also the god of poetry,
to whom alone is reserved the power to distinguish poets of the
highest order by the gift of a laurel crown. Yet at the beginning
the girdle, or 'Cest of amplest Pow'r', the symbol of poetic inspiration, has been assigned not to Apollo but to Fancy, the 'lov'd Enthusiast', to be bestowed by her upon a certain 'few' of her own
choice, and it thus appears that the goddess has been allowed to
encroach upon the prerogative of Apollo. That there is confusion
between Apollo the sun-god and Apollo the patron of poets is a
conclusion which may be open to challenge but cannot be dismissed as impossible, or even as very unlikely, for we know of other
poems in which Collins has made use of borrowed ideas without
giving perfect cohesion to his borrowings. The ode *To Peace* and
the earlier version of the ode *To Evening* are two examples.

I have said that Collins must have remembered that Apollo is
the god of poetry as well as the sun-god. He must have been very
familiar with the well-known ode (III, 30) in which Horace boldly
prophesies his own fame in future ages, and, in the closing lines,
claims the Delphic laurel, or crown of Apollo, as his by right:

> Sume superbiam
> Quaesitam meritis, et mihi Delphica
> Lauro cinge volens, Melpomene, comam.

I suggest that it is this crowning honour – for the girdle is in the
poem, the equivalent of the Delphic laurel as being the mark of
Apollo's favour – which Collins has in mind when he asks the
tremendous questions,

> Where is the Bard, whose Soul can now
> Its high presuming Hopes avow,
> Where He who thinks, with Rapture blind,
> This hallow'd Work for Him design'd?

Where, that is, is the Horace of the modern age, who will dare
to apply to himself the language of this sublime assurance? He
is preparing to answer that there is one such poet, and only one,
and that that one is Milton.

This interpretation would gain some support if we could detect
other signs of the influence of Horace, and one such sign is to be
found in the line, referring to the Creator, 'Himself in some
Diviner Mood'. It will be remembered that on the occasion when
Hampton kicked over his tea-table Collins quoted spontaneously
line 62 of Horace's Fourth Satire, Book I: 'Invenias etiam disiecti
membra poetae.'(22) A little earlier in the same satire (lines 41-4)
he would at some time have read:

> neque, si quis scribat, uti nos,
> Sermoni propiora, putes hunc esse poetam.
> Ingenium cui sit, cui *mens divinior*, atque os
> Magna sonaturum, des nominis huius honorem.

129

'Diviner Mood' does not make good sense in English, because the adjective *divine* does not admit of degrees of comparison, and cannot be used correctly to qualify a mood. It may be explained as a rough rendering of the words which I have italicized in the quotation from Horace. A better equivalent would be *afflatus,* or *inspiration,* or, in the eighteenth century sense of the word, *enthusiasm.* Whether the Horatian influence extends any farther than this is uncertain. The line, 'Breath'd her magic Notes aloud', referring to the personified Fancy, may have been suggested by Horace's inclusion of the power of expression (*os magna sonaturum*) among the attributes of the true poet; but the prevailing tone is Miltonic, and we easily detect some Miltonic echoes. The 'Saphire Throne' and 'Seraphic Wires' recall the 'sapphire-coloured throne' and 'harps of golden wires' of *At a Solemn Music.* '*Truth,* in sunny Vest array'd', resembles the 'white-robed Truth' of *On the Death of a Fair Infant,* and the 'ambrosial Flow'rs' could have been gathered from *Paradise Lost* (II, 245).

The reader may sometimes be tempted to wonder whether Collins himself could have fitted every detail of the poem into an intelligible pattern. The main contention, however, seems to be, as is generally agreed, that the faculty which Collins personifies as Fancy, and which Coleridge was to call the 'shaping spirit of imagination', is that which distinguishes the poetical character at its highest. 'A powerfully imaginative mind,' says Ruskin, 'seizes and combines at the same instant, not only two, but all the important ideas of its poem or picture; and while it works with any of them, is at the same instant working with and modifying all in their relations to it, never losing sight of their bearings on each other.'(*23*) A little later he adds: 'It may seem to the reader that I am incorrect in calling this penetrating possession-taking faculty Imagination. Be it so; the name is of little consequence; the faculty itself, called by what name we will, I insist upon as the highest intellectual power of man.'(*24*) On that understanding we may conclude in the words of Mr. Woodhouse: 'The poem . . . appears to be an allegory in a somewhat stricter sense than Collins's remaining odes, an allegory whose subject is the *creative imagination* and the poet's passionate desire for its power.'(*25*)

It remains to add *The Passions* to the poems already mentioned as being included in the volume of 1746. It will be remembered that when Collins and Warton met at Guildford Races and read each other's odes they agreed, as Warton says, 'to join our forces, and to publish them immediately.'(26) The two authors, it is generally assumed, carried out the project so far as lay in their power, but were thwarted by a publisher who knew his business only too well. Collins's odes pleased the gods but Warton's pleased Dodsley, and so the plan of joint publication collapsed. From the facts that we know it is virtually certain that Collins, through his friendship with Thomson, had already met Thomson's publisher, Andrew Millar, who was then living at Richmond, and the probability is that Millar, being approached, undertook the publication but either suggested, or agreed to the suggestion, that another and a longer poem should be added, to serve as the keystone of the arch. Collins then, with careful deliberation, chose a broader and more ambitious subject, and wrote *The Passions*. This, it must be admitted, is partly conjecture. For those who will have the facts and nothing but the facts, all that can be said is that Collins's odes and Warton's were published separately at the end of the year, the former by Millar and the latter by Dodsley, and that *The Passions* appears as the last of Collins's collection.

There have been critics who considered *The Passions* as the best of Collins's poems, not excluding even the ode *To Evening*. Whether we accept that judgment will depend on whether we think of Collins as primarily an artist striving to express in words the effects which a painter produces by line and colour. The poem is, in fact, a series of verbal pictures. Each of the pictures, considered in itself, is of high merit; if the series, considered as a unity, had been of equal merit, Collins would have achieved the impossible, for it is impossible that an art whose medium is time should invade successfully the domain of another whose medium is space. We cannot say of *The Passions*, as could be said of *Fear*, that the pictures, vivid as they are in themselves, are still subordinate to the theme. Mr. Hagstrum, as we should expect, quotes at considerable length, from 'Melancholy' to 'Mirth', and comments enthusiastically:

This is a pattern of rich and subtle sound, but it is the pictorial

131

K

effects that are the loveliest: Cheerfulness is a Diana-like figure ('Her buskins gem'd with Morning Dew'); the satyrs and other sylvan creatures are seen emerging from the woods ('Peeping from forth their Alleys green'); the 'gay fantastic Round' in which Mirth dances with streaming hair and flowing robe is a pictorial bacchanal.(27)

That is true; but a little earlier, in approaching the poem, Mr. Hagstrum had remarked that 'it lacks the metrical suppleness and the dramatic human scenes of Dryden's "Alexander's Feast"', and that, 'as a whole . . . it lacks inspiration.' That also is true. We are all familiar with the distinction between imagination as the image-making and image-blending faculty, submitting to no control, and imagination as the 'shaping spirit', the real subject of the ode *On the Poetical Character*. It is imagination in the former sense which displays itself in *The Passions*. The reader feels that he is strolling through an art gallery. If he is inclined to think that the collection of pictures makes a perfect whole, let him ask himself whether he has the same impression in reading *Alexander's Feast*.

The allusion to '*Caecilia's* mingled World of Sound' at the end of the poem justifies the belief that Collins was willing to challenge comparison with Dryden. If that is so we must conclude that his reach on this occasion exceeded his grasp. *Alexander's Feast* may not be verse of the highest order, but in its own kind it is unsurpassable. It is the product of a kind of Indian summer of inspiration, displaying to perfection, in one brief achievement, the whole power which had been struggling for expression in the author's earlier life. There is continuous movement, graceful but rapid, and directed to an end, and it is in reaching the end that the poet's sense of mastery is most apparent. That would not be true of *The Passions*. Except for the unfavourable comparison of modern music with ancient, which does not perfectly harmonize with what has preceded, the poem ends where it began. Collins may have been a greater poet than Dryden, but he was not a greater Dryden. If he had lived to be as old as Dryden the perfect work of his maturity would not have resembled *Alexander's Feast*; for that matter, it would not have resembled *The Passions*, for we cannot think of *The Passions* as revealing a natural development of the powers which had produced the ode *To Evening*.

From the next of Collins's actions of which we have any record we must suppose that soon after completing his collection of odes he decided to take a holiday. On 1st August, 1746, Mulso writes to Gilbert White:

> I have just receiv'd a Letter from Collin's, dated Antwerp. He gives me a very descriptive Journal of his Travells thro' Holland to that Place, which He is in Raptures about, & promises a more particular Account of: He is in high spirits, tho' near ye French. He was just setting out for ye Army, which He says are in a poor way, & He met many wounded & Sick Countrymen as he travell'd from Helvoet-Sluys.(*28*)

Collins's journey has been confused with his earlier visit to Flanders in the summer of 1745, and both have been confused with his application for a Curacy in 1744. It has been assumed that he was in desperate need of money, and that he went to Holland to appeal to his military uncle for some kind of assistance. If that had been the case he would hardly have been in high spirits when he wrote to Mulso, and he would hardly have spent time in rambling about Antwerp before he had ascertained where Colonel Martin was to be found. The truth is that the Colonel was still in Scotland, although, as it happened, preparing to leave for Holland. After Culloden, according to the official History, 'the King's Regiment was encamped for a short time near Perth; it subsequently marched southward in charge of prisoners; and during the summer it was ordered to the Netherlands, where the war between France and the Allies was continued.'(*29*)

That, in the matter of dates, is somewhat vague, but more precise information is conveyed by a single sentence of a letter written by Lord Albemarle to the Duke of Richmond from Fort Augustus on 13th July, 1746: 'Martin marched two days ago to Perth, and from thence to Holland.'(*30*) Finally, we have a letter to the Duke of Richmond from a certain Captain Richard Meggott, from which we learn that the Regiment took six days to reach Perth and remained there for a further eight days, and that on 1st

August, the date of his letter, it was still waiting 'for Water enough to carry Us out of the Harbour'.(*31*) 1st August happens to be also the date of Mulso's letter to Gilbert White, from which we gather that Collins had then been in Holland for at least a few days. We must conclude, then, that his object in going abroad, whatever it may have been, was not to interview Colonel Martin about urgent financial problems.

For some months after this we lose sight of him. The next event in his career is, as the literary historian sees it, the most important of all. The *Gentleman's Magazine* for December, 1746, included among 'Books and Pamphlets published this Month':

5. Odes on several descriptive and allegoric subjects. By *W. Collins*. pr. 1*s*. *Millar*.

6. Odes on several subjects. By *Thos. Warton*, B.A. pr. 1*s*. 6*d*. *Dodsley*.

The cautious Dodsley proved to be wise in his generation. While Warton's poems had a fair measure of success, and went into a second edition the following year, there was hardly any demand for those of Collins. Collins was certainly disappointed, but probably less acutely than has been believed. From the number of obvious printer's errors in the book we should suppose that the proof-reading had been left to Millar, or not done at all, and that indicates a certain indifference. On the other hand, it has been said that 'so deeply did the author feel the coldness with which they were received, that he shortly afterwards obtained the unsold copies and burnt them with his own hand'.(*32*) That story must be accepted with a certain reserve. Anyone who has ever attempted to burn even one book will have discovered that it is a work of time and patience, and Millar had printed no less than a thousand copies.

However that may be, we can trace the existence of two copies which escaped the holocaust, if holocaust there was, besides those now treasured by the British Museum and a few other libraries. One, together with Warton's volume, was acquired by Gray, who hastened to record his opinion:

Have you read the works of two young authors, a Mr. Warton and Mr. Collins, both writers of Odes? It is odd enough, but each is the half of a considerable man, and one the counterpart of the other. The first has but little invention, very poetical choice of expression, and a good ear. The second, a fine fancy, modelled upon the antique, a bad ear, great variety of words and images, with no choice at all. They both deserve to last some years, but will not.(*33*)

Gray's impartiality does him credit, as his personal sympathies must have been with Warton. Allowing for some exaggeration at either extreme for the sake of the contrast, we feel that he shows himself a good critic though a bad prophet.

Though we have no conclusive evidence, it is virtually certain that another copy found its way into the hands of Alexander Carlyle. It has already been remarked that Carlyle's *Fannie Weeping* was published for the first time in the *British Magazine* for July, 1747. In the same number there appeared anonymously Collins's ode *To a Lady*, under the title, 'An Ode to the Memory of Colonel Charles Ross of Balnagown, who was killed in the Action at Fontenoy'. The text could not have been taken from Dodsley's *Museum*, as it includes the two stanzas which are absent from the Dodsley version. Whoever sent it to the *British Magazine* must, therefore, have been one of the very few persons who had acquired a copy of Collins's volume of Odes, and must also have been, in 1747, in contact with literary circles in Edinburgh. It is difficult to imagine anyone other than Alexander Carlyle as answering to that description.

NOTES TO CHAPTER VIII

1. *The Craftsman*, No. 1035, reprinted in the *Gentleman's Magazine*, Vol. XVI, p. 244.
2. *Collins*, p. 83.
3. Op. cit., pp. 96-7.
4. *The Sister Arts*, p. 282, note 27.
5. *Autobiography*, ed. Burton, pp. 199-200.
6. *Collins*, p. 84.
7. *The Sister Arts*, p. 272.

8. *Collins*, p. 36, note 1.
9. Unfortunately Mr. Blakiston cannot say with certainty whether the actual copy of this book now in the Library was there in Collins's time, but he feels obliged to add that he thinks it improbable.
10. Book VI, 54-7.
11. *Collins*, p. 89.
12. Op. cit. pp. 105-6 (note 31); pp. 113-4 and note 41.
13. Op. cit., p. 118.
14. *Collins*, p. 90.
15. *Review of English Studies*, Vol. XXII, pp. 1-16.
16. *Ol.* ii, 68 et seq.
17. Epod. 16, 41-66.
18. *The Druids*, p. 23.
19. *Collins*, p. 69.
20. A. H. Armstrong and R. A. Markus, *Christian Faith and Greek Philosophy*, p. 1. It is explained in the Preface that the first half is the work of Mr. Armstrong and the second of Mr. Markus, which is my reason for attributing the words quoted in the text to Mr. Armstrong alone.
21. Op. cit., note 10.
22. See p. 23, above.
23. *Ruskin as Literary Critic*, ed. A. H. R. Ball, p. 110.
24. Ibid., p. 117. Ruskin is clearly wrong according to the literal meaning of *imagination*, but the use of the word to denote what Platonists and the mediaeval philosophers would have called *intuition*, or *intuitive reason*, has a long history. According to Dean Inge, 'It was Philostratus who first raised φαντασία from the humble position which Plato gives it, and declared that imagination, not imitation, is the creative spirit in all great works of art'. ('Plato and Ruskin', in *Essays by Divers Hands*, 1935, p. 51.) For a full discussion of the rise and development in English literature of the theory of the creative imagination from the time of the Reformation (with which, it may be remarked in passing, it is closely connected) see A. S. P. Woodhouse, *Collins and the Creative Imagination*, cited in the text.
25. Op. cit., p. 60.
26. See pp. 72-3, above.
27. *The Sister Arts*, p. 277.
28. *Letters to Gilbert White*, p. 15.
29. *Historical Record of the King's Regiment of Foot*, p. 53.
30. Lord March, *A Duke and his Friends*, p. 523.
31. Ibid., pp. 156-7.
32. *Poetical Works of Gray, Beattie and Collins*, p. 392. ('Memoir of William Collins', by Thomas Miller.)
33. *Correspondence of Thomas Gray* (1935), No. 129.

IX

Farewell to Richmond

COLLINS must have been in Chichester on 1st May, 1747, when, jointly with his sisters, he sold his father's old premises in East Street.(*1*) This was in accordance with the terms of his mother's will.

If internal evidence could decide the question we should suppose that soon after this he was writing for Dodsley, who must, in that case, have liked his prose better than his poetry. Mr. Frederick Page, in a letter to the *Times* Literary Supplement,(*2*) proposed to attribute to him a long essay in Dodsley's *Museum* for 4th July, 1747, entitled 'Of the Essential Excellencies in Poetry'. The sentiments are certainly those of Collins, though not peculiar to him. The passage about 'this great, this divine Power that distinguishes true Poets from mere Versifiers' may well have sprung from the same Horatian source as certain lines of Collins's ode *On the Poetical Character*,(*3*) and if their influence can be traced also in the essay in question that will strengthen Mr. Page's argument. From what follows it will appear that Collins was at this time turning his thoughts to literary criticism.

To Collins, as to most people, the writing of a chatty letter to a friend would be a mere incident in the day's routine, but his letters have a special importance because only two of them are known to have survived. The earlier in date was not discovered until 1924, when Mr. E. H. W. Meyerstein made it the subject of an article in the December number of the *London Mercury*. It is addressed to John Gilbert Cooper, afterwards known as the author of *Letters on Taste,* highly praised by Dr. Johnson. Cooper had in 1746 contributed to Dodsley's *Museum,* and it may have been on that common ground that he and Collins had first met. The letter was published again, fully annotated, by Mr. H. O. White in the *Review of English Studies* for January, 1927, and the original is now in the British Museum. In the copy now to be given everything in square brackets is due to Mr. White.

London Tuesday Nov 10th 1747.

Dear Cooper,

Your obliging Paquet reach'd me last night, in an hour which I had assign'd for the carrying on my design. I will not lose a line in telling you how sensible I was of your kind promise. I hope our Hearts are form'd so much alike, that Yours will imagine the force with which such generosity must affect mine without my [having] recourse to those symptoms of vulgar Friendship verbal acknowledgments – I had wrote to you by Saturday's post, to tell you my thoughts of changing the title which I still think should be – The Friendly Examiner, or Letters of Polemon and Philethus; or, the Plain Dealer, with the same Appendix. In regard to the Clar[endon Review] I think it *nimis fatuosum* (to talk like Le Sage's Salzedo) and apprehend it may be dislik'd by a *particular Body of Jealous Literati,* at the same time that I conceive the above to be more modest and equally comprehensive. You found by my last that I propos'd the more literary papers should fall under the name of Polemon, and the more lusory or Comic under that of Philethus.(4) In order to Hint this at the head of the Paper, I shall have a Medallion engrav'd of two Elegant Heads à l'antique thus [here is a small sketch of two heads] (Don't you think 'em à l'antique?) over the lower part of the necks of which a little *Art* shall appear writing on a Roman scroll, and a *Satyr* either in contrast holding up another, or writing on part of the same [I] suppose the Veil be upheld by *Friendship,* who may at the same time point to the Relievo of the Medallion while she discovers the Ornaments of the base by supporting the Veil. The Motto to the first Paper shall be with your approbation,

Duo turba sumus. That to the second part, or the Paper of
Philethus, Idonea dicere vitae or Illustrans commoda vitae, and
that which shall appear at the head of the next of Polemon
Usus vetusto genere, sed rebus novis. Phaedr: or Plus operis
quanto veniae minus, or etc. etc. etc. etc. In the course of the
Paper may be introduc'd New Characters, if it be not too ancient, Athenaeus, from whom whom [repeated] any Poetical
fragments of our best writers, such as some MSS of Fairfax
which I can procure, or any anecdotes of their lives etc. might
with the greatest propriety come.

Thus far a desire of consulting you has carried me into a
forgetfullness of the Essay, with which I have been so much
charm'd till this half hour, when I began talking to you.

It is my sincere opinion that the subject could not have been
treated in a more Picturesque or forcible Allegory, and I am
confident I am at least qualified to give the Public one Beauti-
full Paper. Allow me, dear Cooper, to thank you from the
sincerest Gratitude yet, before I leave you, tho' I think it un-
necessary, yet I think it too natural for to be resisted. Yours most
affly. and sincly

Wm. Collins.

The Town has enough of Foote. He played Saturday at C.
Garden for the 3rd time to almost an Empty House. There is a
Song of Colley Cibber's performed to-night at Drury Lane,
call'd Tit for Tat, or the Sailors Rendezvous at Portsmouth.
Rich is to entertain the Town with a New Actor in the Pierre
[word scratched out] Name is Sowden, a Man of great Pretence
and fortune. The Opera was crowded, but went off, as the
Musicians term it, ill.

Frasi is engaged for Ranelagh next Season with Beard.

It is worth remarking that Collins's choice of the name
Athenaeus, 'if it be not too ancient', as suitable for an imaginary
contribution of 'Poetical fragments of our best writers', is a further
indication of his knowledge of the real Athenaeus and his collection of *scolia*. It was from that collection, as we have found reason
to believe, that he copied the lines on Harmodius and Aristogeton

139

which he wrongly attributed to Alcaeus in his footnote to
Liberty.(5)

The letter has other points of interest. Mr. Hagstrum describes
as 'revealing' the passage about Polemon and Philethus, and the
'two Elegant Heads'. He remarks that 'Collins is obviously excited by his ability to achieve a quality of antique elegance. Moreover, the design he has drawn seems to suggest the kind of effect
he achieves in his poetical allegories.' This leads the writer to en-
quire 'if there is the sculpturesque as well as the picturesque in
his poetry, and, if so, how it can be discriminated'. He thinks that
'in Collins the statuesque is less obvious' than in Pope and Thomson, and 'cannot be easily separated from the picturesque and isol-
ated as a thing apart'. He continues:

And yet it is pervasively present in the odes. There are subtle
similarities between Collins' figures and the classical figures en-
graved on the pages of *Polymetis* ... Joseph Spence's hand-
some folio appeared in 1747, too late to have influenced the
odes that had appeared some months earlier. But, as we have
seen, neoclassical authors admired ancient marbles, coins, and
medallions; borrowed images from the sculptures of antiquity;
and associated ideal forms with classical marbles. Of these neoclassical habits of mind both the *Odes* of 1746 and *Polymetis*
of 1747 are separate embodiments. In the economy and con-
centration of Collins' allegories, which are stripped of unessen-
tial ornament and are free from the floridity and excessive
detail of an allegorist like Rubens, one can perhaps see the
statuesque. And is not the grace of Collins' figures partly that
of sculptured stone? One important equivalent of the poet's
personified abstractions, which so often take the form of a
nymph, an anchorite, and even the Virgin without being directly
Christian or even religious, may be the 'moral Venus' of
the eighteenth century – the Venus of the Medici transformed
into a figure with modesty, elegance, and virginal reserve.(6)

I have quoted this passage at length partly because it does not,
so far as I understand it, lend itself to summary, and partly because I have not succeeded in following the meaning of the

last sentence. Collins's personified abstractions often, it is true, take the form of a nymph, and an anchorite is not unknown, but 'the Virgin without being directly Christian or even religious' is a figure whom I have failed to identify, and the attempt has not been made easier by the conjecture that she may be one equivalent, among others, of 'the "moral Venus" of the eighteenth century'. Perhaps others of Mr. Hagstrum's readers may be more successful.

Concerning the principal subject of the letter, the projected 'Clarendon Review', some further information is furnished by a letter addressed by Thomas Warton to Hymers, probably about the time when Ragsdale was writing to the same correspondent. It was published some sixty years later in *The Gleaner*,(7) reprinted from a still more obscure periodical, *The Reaper*.(8) The younger Warton, like Ragsdale, was apparently replying to a request to set down any recollections of Collins which might be of use to a biographer. At the beginning he says that he often saw Collins in London in 1750. He continues: 'He then told me of his intended History of the Revival of Learning, and proposed a scheme of a review, to be called The Clarendon Review, and to be printed at the university press, under the conduct and authority of the university.' We have already noticed evidence that the 'Review of the Advancement of Learning' was understood to be within sight of completion in December, 1744,(9) but it is possible that Collins had first abandoned the scheme and then returned to it after an interval of several years. The *Clarendon Review*, which never, so far as is known, reached the stage of print, must also have been on the way for more than two years, as we know from his letter to Cooper that Collins was absorbed in the project in November, 1747.

It was Bronson's belief that the real reason for Collins's failure to launch the *Clarendon Review* was that he made the attempt fifty years too early. 'When it is remembered,' he says, 'that the reviews of the eighteenth century were booksellers' organs, written by literary hacks, Collins's idea is seen to be original and bold. It has since been realized, in substance, by the great independent reviews established in the first quarter of the present [nineteenth] century; in 1750 the project probably was not practicable.'(10)

141

It may be doubted whether the case is quite so simple as that. The *Edinburgh Review* as conducted by Jeffrey and Sidney Smith was the organ of a political party, and it was because that fact was generally recognized that the *Quarterly* was founded in the interest of the opposing party. Neither depended for its circulation mainly on its literary articles; both, in fact, were accused of subordinating their judgement in matters of taste to political loyalties. A strictly literary periodical would have found far greater scope in the tranquil years of the eighteenth century than in the turmoil of the Napoleonic Wars and the Industrial Revolution. In the hands of Cave or Dodsley it would have had a good chance of success; but Cave and Dodsley, unlike Collins, were primarily men of business.

The social and intellectual life of Richmond must have been very delightful at the time when Thomson was finishing the *Castle of Indolence*, and perhaps it is partly for that reason that Collins was inactive, so far as we know, for the greater part of a year after the date of his letter to Cooper. M. Morel, the French biographer of Thomson, thought that he recognized Collins in the description in the *Castle of Indolence* of the 'man of special grave remark' who buried his talents and spent his days lying on the ground and communing with nature:

> Yet not in thoughtless slumber were they past:
> For oft the heavenly fire, that lay concealed
> Emongst the sleeping embers, mounted fast,
> And all its native light anew revealed.
> Oft as he traversed the cerulean field,
> And marked the clouds that drove before the wind,
> Ten thousand glorious systems would he build,
> Ten thousand great ideas filled his mind;
> But with the clouds they fled, and left no trace behind.(*11*)

That these lines refer to Collins has been disputed. Mr. Douglas Grant remarks that they 'are generally accepted as a portrait of William Paterson', and that 'the poet told Paterson in his letter to him of April 1748 that he had an "apartment" in *The Castle of Indolence,* "as a night pensioner".' But, in spite of this strong evidence, 'there has always been a suspicion', Mr. Grant continues,

> that the verses are in fact a portrait of William Collins, to whose
> appearance and character they are so exactly fitted. Collins's
> countenance was 'o'erspread' with a 'tender gloom' of thought;
> he particularly loved the sun's 'latest ray', and his *Ode to Even-
> ing* is the matchless evocation of that hour; and he too built
> 'ten thousand glorious systems' which 'left no trace behind'. His
> friend, Dr. Johnson, reflected upon this last fault : 'He designed
> many works, but his great fault was irresolution . . . He planned
> several tragedies, but he only planned them.' We know nothing
> about Paterson to suggest that he was possessed of a genius
> comparable to that described in these verses, and if they were
> intended for him, the poet must have exaggerated his
> quality.(*12*)

It could be argued, on the other side of the case, that if the
verses were intended for Collins the poet must have exaggerated
his indolence. From our knowledge of his restlessness at Oxford,
his varied activities in London and his life at Richmond according
to Ragsdale, supplemented by his self-portrait in *The Manners*
and the liveliness revealed by his letter to Cooper, we gather that
he could enter with energy and zeal into creative work of his own
choosing, and that it was only when confronted with a disagreeable task imposed upon him by necessity that he was liable to an
acute form of ergophobia. I say this as an *advocatus diaboli*, still
hoping that Mr. Grant may be able to strengthen his case and be
proved to be right.

On 27th August, 1748, Thomson died suddenly from the effects
of a chill. His biographer, Murdoch, felt some resentment that the
other poets of the day did not exert themselves on this occasion
as they had done four years earlier to honour the memory of Pope,
'who had been the terror of poets all his lifetime'. There was, however, a notable exception. 'Only one gentleman, Mr. Collins, who
had lived some time at Richmond, but forsook it when Mr.
Thomson died, wrote an Ode to his memory.'

Actually Murdoch was mistaken. Mr. Grant reminds us that
William Shiels, a fervent admirer of the poet and his first bio-

grapher, published a competent, if uninspired, elegy entitled *Musidorus:A Poem sacred to the Memory of Mr. James Thomson'*, and he adds that 'two poems on his death were also printed in the *Scots Magazine* for September and October 1748'.*(13)* We can be sure that Thomson himself would have been content if he could have foreseen that he was to receive two or three sincere tributes, and would not have desired more. The kind of magnetism by which Pope had drawn friends and enemies in crowds to Twickenham was foreign to his nature. He was the object of a devotion which Pope never knew, but was little known outside the circle of his chosen friends except as the author of *The Seasons*.

Mr. Garrod thinks the ode on Thomson cold and artificial, and perhaps he is right. 'Neither the thought nor the phrases of his poem,' he says, 'are those which one would expect for the expression of a personal and near grief,' and he proceeds to demonstrate the point by a searching analysis of lines and words. He is surprised and shocked by Collins's habit of speaking of his hero as 'the friend', instead of '*my* friend'. ' "The friend"!' he exclaims. 'Just as we might think that Collins was going to say something from the heart, say something of himself and Thomson, he drifts into that frigidity.'*(14)* The probability is that Collins was following a precedent set by Thomson himself in addressing Lyttelton:

> These are the sacred feelings of thy heart,
> Thy heart informed by reason's purest ray,
> O Lyttelton, the friend!*(15)*

It is a formula which might suggest itself to a poet who was prepared to surmount a barrier without pretending that the barrier did not exist. Between Thomson and Lyttelton it was a barrier of rank, which, to a Scotsman of the time, was even more closely hedged with divinity than to most Englishmen. Between Collins and Thomson it was a barrier of age. Thomson died within a month of his forty-eighth birthday, and Collins at that time was twenty-seven. So extensive a gap could be bridged by respect, by admiration, by affection, but hardly by friendship on an equal footing.

For this reason it is not to be expected that the ode on Thomson should have any resemblance to the lament of an earlier Tennyson for an earlier Arthur Hallam. Mr. Garrod complains that the poet 'is always just going to lapse, humanly and truly, into "my friend", and even "my boat"; when some demon of anti-sentimentality calls him too loudly and harshly back to the old conventions'.(16) That may be true, but perhaps there is something to be said for the demon's restraining action. If we had been with Collins in the autumn of 1748 we should not have expected to see him visibly weeping at the grave of Thomson; we should have thought it more natural if he had placed a wreath upon the grave and turned away. We should not have remarked that the wreath conformed to the old conventions; to say that would be to condemn it for being a wreath.

Collins's ode is not a spontaneous outpouring of emotion; it is a poem, and it would not be such a poem as Collins would have acknowledged if it did not conform to the conventions which he, in common with his age, respected. He composed it carefully as a labour of love, as if he had been making a wreath with his own hands; he offered his tribute and then turned away. Perhaps the perfect expression of his grief is the fact that having lived for some time at Richmond, he 'forsook it when Mr. Thomson died'.

It would not be right to speak of Mr. Garrod's criticism of certain features of the ode without adding that he has detected its elusive merits as well as its obvious faults. He concludes with an excellent appreciation which Hazlitt would not have disowned, and which is worth oceans of gushing hyperbole:

I say all this, or take what others have said, and yet, though there is nothing of it that I do not feel to be true, I am left with a perplexed sense that this is a better poem than I seem to have allowed – I had almost said, a better poem than it should be. It is easy to point out the faults of it; and hard to define its obscure excellence. Yet when you have said what is the matter with it – that it ails here, and here – you have to reckon with some fundamental *rightness* in it. Wordsworth knew what this was; and he was not easily deceived into thinking the bad good (in the poetry of others) or the false true. I must leave it at that

145

– this poem has some fundamental rightness of life which must
plead for it against all the critics.(17)

One wonders whether, after writing that, Mr. Garrod would still
concede that 'Mrs. Barbauld must have it, this time, all her own
way', and whether, after all, Langhorne may not have been right
when, speaking of the ode on Thomson, he said of Collins, 'From
his own great sensibility he felt what he wrote.'

Before leaving the ode on Thomson we must glance back at
Miss Tompkins's article, 'In Yonder Grave a Druid Lies', of which
something has been said already in connection with Mr. Cunningham's Fragment 3 and the ode *On Liberty*. After remarking that
the word 'Druid' is 'the single challenging word in a very plain
line of verse', and 'must have been Collins's approved choice',
Miss Tompkins continues: 'It is the loss of a poet-priest of nature
that we are invited to contemplate, and it is in this sense that those
readers, to whom the word "Druid" has not been a stumbling-
block, have taken it.' She quotes with approval J. L. Robertson's
words describing the youthful Thomson before he left Scotland:
'We see him, already a young Druid – the part for which, as
Collins happily noted, his genius was cast – in the alleys of Marle-
field woods.' She adds: 'Certainly this is the prime meaning of
the word in Collins's ode, and it is established by the other designations of Thomson, "woodland pilgrim", "sweet bard", "meek
Nature's child".'

That agrees with what I was trying to say when, in an earlier
chapter, I spoke of the 'popular' conception of the Druids.(18)
Had Miss Tompkins been writing a few years later she might have
quoted as a further illustration the words of Collins himself in the
fifth stanza of Fragment 3:

> But me by [——] Springlets laid
> That thro' the Woodland chide
> Let Elms and Oaks that lent their Shade
> To hoary Druids hide.

Miss Tompkins insists, however, that this is only the prime meaning of the word. In the eighteenth century, in certain poetical and

146

antiquarian circles, 'the Druids were believed to have been not only priests of nature but philosophers probing her secrets, metaphysicians, enlightened educators of youth, and ardent patriots, enflaming their people in the struggle for liberty and heartening them with songs to cast back the unconquered Roman over sea'. She then prepares the reader for a full discussion of the Druidic mystery by saying of Collins: 'Since, therefore, his characteristic diction is concentrated and densely associative, it is no very bold assumption that in his ear, at least, all these overtones vibrated together.'

Even with a strong emphasis upon the qualifying phrase, 'in his ear', that must be considered disputable; but Collins was writing for the reading public, and could hardly have expected that the single word 'Druid', with no elaboration, would evoke all those memories of history, tradition and legend which Miss Tompkins has called 'overtones'. We must agree, however, that it is proper to ask how the word 'Druid' is used by Thomson himself. 'Affection,' says Miss Tompkins, 'pays tribute most gladly in words that have a special significance for the hearer, and, if the ear of the friend is closed, the use of this language has a poignant satisfaction for the survivor.' That is well said, and, as the word 'Druid' is used by Thomson only twice, the test is not difficult to apply.

In Book IV of *Liberty*, speaking of the Britons, Thomson writes:

> For by the Druid taught, that death but shifts
> The vital scene, they that prime fear despised;
> And, prone to rush on steel, disdained to spare
> An ill-saved life that must again return.(*19*)

That is, obviously, a recollection of Caesar's statement that the Druids excite their warriors to valour and contempt for the fear of death by telling them that their souls do not die, but pass from one body into another. (*Imprimis hoc volunt persuadere, non interire animas, sed ab aliis post mortem transire ad alios, atque hoc maxime ad virtutem excitari putant metu mortis neglecto.(20)* Collins, no doubt, was familiar with this passage and with Thomson's adaptation of it, but we may say with some confidence that

147

L

it was not present to his mind when he spoke of Thomson himself as a Druid.

Thomson's second mention of a Druid occurs in the *Castle of Indolence*, and is not so easy to explain. Sir Industry is setting out to overthrow the demon Indolence, and sends a messenger to order the attendance of his bard. The poem continues:

> He came, the bard, a little Druid wight,
> Of withered aspect; but his eye was keen,
> With sweetness mixed. In russet brown bedight,
> As is his sister of the copses green,
> He crept along, unpromising of mien.
> Gross he who judges so. His soul was fair;
> Bright as the children of yon azure sheen.
> True comeliness, which nothing can impair,
> Dwells in his mind: all else is vanity and glare.(21)

Because of his musical gift, as well as a certain strange power which seems to be a mixture of magic and prophetic inspiration, the 'Druid wight' is treated with respect, but, in spite of that, we are left in no doubt that his status is that of a retainer. When he sings, as he does continuously through seventeen stanzas, he is obeying the order of a master. Thus he is totally different from the theocratic Druids of the same author's *Liberty,* and it is only in respect of his minstrelsy that he has any resemblance to the Druids of Milton's *Ad Mansum* and of Collins's *Liberty*. We cannot think that Collins intended to compare his friend either to this diminutive and servile Druid or to the brutal and despotic Druids encountered in the pages of Caesar, and must conclude that not only the prime meaning of the word but the whole meaning is sufficiently 'established', in Miss Tompkins's words, 'by the other designations of Thomson, "woodland pilgrim", "sweet bard", "meek Nature's child".'

NOTES TO CHAPTER IX

1. See pp. 46-7, above.
2. Volume for 1935, p. 488.
3. See p. 129, above.
4. Mr. White prints these names as Polémon and Philèthus, and that, no doubt, is according to the manuscript, which I have had the opportunity of seeing; but a name formed from a Greek word does not usually preserve the accents, and here both the accents are incorrect.
5. See p. 117, above.
6. *The Sister Arts*, pp. 284-5.
7. Published in four volumes by Nathan Drake, M.D., 1811. The letter in question is in No CLXXXVII. 'W.B.', writing from Haughton, 1st January, 1797, says that he met with it 'among the papers of a much respected and ingenious friend deceased, who had intended to give to the public a complete edition of the works of Collins, and an improved and more satisfactory account of his life and writings than has hitherto appeared'. A note appended by Drake says that the deceased friend was 'William Hymers, A.B., of Queen's College, Oxford'.
8. 'The Reaper', says Dyce, 'the greater part of which was written by the late Mr. Maude, of Wensleydale in Yorkshire, was originally published in the York Chronicle, from January 1796 to June 1797, and was reprinted in an octavo volume, though never published, in 1798. My only acquaintance with this scarce work is from the specimens of it in Dr. Drake's Gleaner.'
9. See pp. 99, 109, above.
10. *Poems of William Collins*, p. xxiii.
11. *Castle of Indolence*, Canto I, LIX.
12. *James Thomson*, p. 261.
13. Ibid., pp. 270-1.
14. *Collins*, pp. 109-10.
15. *Spring*, ll. 904-6.
16. *Collins*, p. 110.
17. Ibid., p. 111.
18. See p. 92, above.
19. Lines 630-3.
20. *De Bello Gallico*, VI, 14. Thomson seems to allude to the same passage in the *Castle of Indolence* (Canto I, stanza XVII), when he says of the Britons, 'Yet not the Roman steel their naked breast dismayed'.
21. Canto II, stanza XXXIII.

X

Back to Chichester

ANYONE who has looked for the last time upon scenes which hold memories of former happiness will understand what Collins's feelings must have been when he 'forsook' Richmond, as Murdoch says with imaginative sympathy, 'when Mr. Thomson died'. There is some slight evidence that he returned immediately to London, and stayed there long enough to see the *Ode Occasion'd by the Death of Mr. Thomson* through the press. The poem was published by Manby and Cox early in 1749, and, in contrast to the Odes, has no obvious printer's errors, so that Collins may have taken care to correct the proofs himself. Judging by what we know of his later years, however, we should suppose that he was already beginning to lose something of the energy and *joie de vivre* to be discerned in his letter to Cooper. When next we hear of him he is living quietly at Chichester, though still able to make new friends and to find pleasure in the labour of composition. Richmond had been to him a second home, but Chichester had its permanent place in his affections.

Colonel Edmund Martin, 'lying sick in the city of Chichester in the County of Sussex', made his will on 19th April, 1749, and died a week later.(1) He had been wounded at Val in 1747, and after that he had wished to retire, urging that he 'had been more than forty years an Officer, was upwards of sixty years of age, lyable to the Infirmitys of that Stage of Life'. This he explains in a letter to the Duke of Richmond dated from 'Ginnegen near

150

Breda', 21st January, 1748.(2) Either he changed his decision or he was not allowed to retire, as his subsequent letters to the Duke show that he was still on active service at various places in Flanders on 8th April, 25th July, 19th August and 21st September. The war was concluded by the Peace of Aix-la-Chapelle on 18th October, and there is no reason to doubt that Colonel Martin stayed to the end.

The effect of his death upon Collins's worldly fortunes was examined in an earlier chapter, and it has seemed unlikely that the event brought him any great acquisition of wealth; but nothing that has been said on that subject is meant to imply that Collins himself thought of it in terms of a possible legacy. Colonel Martin had all the military virtues superimposed upon the character of a sturdy peasant. After a lifetime of service to his country he had experienced his finest hour at Culloden, and we have the great authority of Wolfe for the statement that his prompt action saved the situation at a critical point of the battle.(3) It is one of the little ironies of history that his name has been saved from oblivion only by his indolent nephew's volume of poems: a volume which in all probability he never read and of which, if he did read it, he must have had a poor opinion.

Alexander Carlyle tells us that 'in winter 1749' his friend John Home, not yet famous as the author of *Douglas*, went to London from Scotland hoping to arrange for the production of his tragedy of *Agis*, a hope which was to be disappointed. Carlyle gave him an introduction to Smollett, 'with whom he contracted a sincere friendship, and he consoled himself for the neglect he met with by the warm approbation of the Doctor, and of John Blair and his friend Barrow, an English physician who had escaped with him from the Castle of Doune, and who made him acquainted with Collins the poet, with whom he grew very intimate'.(4)

We are not told that Home went from London to Chichester before returning to Scotland, but we shall find evidence that he did, in fact, make the journey, and that it was at Chichester that Collins presented him with the manuscript of the *Ode on the Popular Superstitions of the Highlands. In the meantime it is* desirable to collect whatever information can be gathered concerning his friend Barrow.

151

Thomas Barrow, if we may judge by his later career, belonged to a family of some importance in the south or south-west of England; it is very likely that he was related to the sturdy Whig Sir Charles Barrow, Member for Gloucester in the time of the Pelhams. At the outbreak of the rebellion he was a medical student at Edinburgh. He fought as a volunteer in the Battle of Falkirk, was taken prisoner, and, with John Home and some others, was committed to the castle of Doune. The whole party, under Home's leadership, succeeded in escaping, and became for a time minor heroes. Scott has described the affair in a note to *Waverley*, and speaks of Barrow as 'a brave young Englishman, a particular friend of Home's'.

To pass over for a moment his association with Collins in 1749, our next certain information about him concerns his marriage. On 2nd April, 1753, 'Thomas Barrow of the City of Chichester Batchelor and Mary Downer of the Parish of All Saints otherwise the Pallant Maiden were married with License by me Jno. Blair L.L.D.'(5) It is an interesting fact that Blair, one of those who had given Home his 'warm approbation', was the officiating clergyman at Barrow's wedding. He was a former Presbyterian who had known Carlyle as a student at Edinburgh, had met him again when Carlyle came to London in 1746, and remained on friendly terms with him after he had seceded to the Church of England.(6) The Barrows were still at Chichester in 1757, and a daughter, Mary Elizabeth, was baptized at All Saints on 6th June of that year.(7)

In the meantime, on 2nd April, 1757, Barrow had been appointed Deputy Paymaster of the Forces in North America.(8) We know from his letters that he was travelling about America in 1759.(9) He was back in England in 1769, when Carlyle and John Home 'dined with Mr. and Mrs. Barry, who had been old friends of John's, and Barry had ... escaped with him from Doune Castle'.(10) This was probably at Chiswick, where Barrow is known to have been living in 1770.(11) John Hill Burton, the editor of Carlyle's *Autobiography*, could not believe that 'Mr. Barry' is identical with Thomas Barrow (whom he calls erroneously 'John Barrow') because *'Barrow*, according to Carlyle's letter in the "Transactions", died paymaster of the forces in the

American war of 1756'.(*12*) Carlyle was certainly, in his later years, capable of misspelling a name, but he could not have meant to imply that Barrow died in 1756. Actually Barrow died in New York in 1780, and his will was proved on 13th November of that year.(*13*)

It is well known that Barrow is the 'cordial youth' mentioned in the fifth line of the *Ode on the Popular Superstitions,* and from this it follows that his 'destin'd bride' must be Mary Downer. Carlyle found her 'very amiable'(*14*) when he met her at dinner in 1769; beyond that, hardly anything about her is known. She lived to be eighty-seven, and at the time of her death in 1814 was living in Portman Square, London;(*15*) but she was buried in Chichester,(*16*) and that is an almost certain indication that Chichester was her native place. It is unfortunate that Hymers, when he was enquiring for reminiscences of Collins, did not think of applying to Mrs. Barrow. She would almost certainly have remembered Collins as at one time a friend of her husband, and, if she was a native of Chichester, would have known the Collins family from her earliest youth.

From here we should like to return to the year 1749, but as no one who was with Collins in that year has left us his recollections we are obliged to look back on it from a point very much later in time. Johnson's *Lives of the English Poets* was first published in 1781, and Carlyle, turning to the 'Life' of Collins, came upon this passage: 'He was visited at Chichester by his learned friends Dr. Warton and his brother, to whom he spoke with disapprobation of his *Oriental Eclogues* ... He shewed them at the same time an ode inscribed to Mr. John Home on the superstitions of the Highlands, which they thought superior to his other works, but which no search has yet found.'

Carlyle remembered that Home had shown him a poem with some such title in 1749, and found the manuscript, though in an imperfect state, among his papers.(*17*) One stanza and part of another were missing, and some lines were defective by the omission of a word or a phrase. Carlyle, with the help of his friend Henry Mackenzie, set to work to repair the broken lines by supplying words of his own, and appears to have done so with considerable skill. Thus restored the poem was read, on 19th April,

1784, to the Royal Society of Edinburgh, which had been founded in the previous year. It need hardly be said that Carlyle was entirely frank about his interpolations and the reason for them.

After that the poem seems to have lain dormant for four years. In 1788 the Society published the first volume of its 'Transactions', and in that volume Collins's ode was printed for the first time, with an introductory letter by Carlyle. One passage in that letter needs elucidation:

> Soon after I found the poem, I shewed it to Mr. Home, who told me that it had been addressed to him by Collins, on his leaving London in the year 1749: that it was hastily composed and incorrect; but that he would one day find leisure to look it over with care. Mr. Collins and Mr. Home had been made acquainted by Mr. John Barrow (the *cordial youth* mentioned in the first stanza), who had been, for some time, at the University of Edinburgh; had been a volunteer, along with Mr. Home, in the year 1746; had been taken prisoner with him at the battle of Falkirk, and had escaped, together with him and five or six other gentlemen, from the Castle of Down. Mr. Barrow resided in 1749 at Winchester, where Mr. Collins and Mr. Home were, for a week or two, together on a visit. Mr. Barrow was paymaster in America, in the war that commenced in 1756, and died in that country.

According to Carlyle, then, Home was leaving London when Collins presented him with the ode in 1749. This at first sight agrees with the opening lines of the ode itself:

> Home, thou return'st from Thames, whose Naiads long
> Have seen thee ling'ring, with a fond delay,—

But two lines later we read:

> Go, not unmindful of that cordial youth,
> Whom, long endear'd, thou leav'st by Lavant's side.

Collins, then, seems to say in one sentence that Home was returning from the Thames and in the next that he was bidding farewell to Barrow by the Lavant. If, however, Home spent a few days as Barrow's guest at Chichester before returning to Scotland, there is no real contradiction. His intention when he left Scotland had been to interview certain persons in London about the production of his play,(*18*) and his visit to Chichester would be a mere incident following the completion of his business. It would be true, therefore, to say when he started on his journey back to Scotland that he was returning from London, even though his actual point of departure was Chichester.

Inadvertently Carlyle has increased the confusion by saying that the 'cordial youth', Barrow, lived at Winchester, and that Collins and Home were also at Winchester at the critical time. Both Winchester and Chichester would be mere names to him, as he had never himself been within many miles of either, but Winchester, as a name, would be more familiar. The kind of muddle in which we are now involved may be illustrated by this passage in Leslie Stephen's account of Collins in the *Dictionary of National Biography:* 'In the autumn of 1749 he met John Home the author of "Douglas", at Winchester, where they were visiting a common friend, an officer named Barrow, who died in America in the following war. To Home Collins gave an imperfect copy of the "Ode on the Popular Superstitions of the Highlands". Home gave it to a friend, among whose papers it was found by Alexander Carlyle.'

Carlyle has given another account of the finding of the manuscript in a fragment of a letter in the Lee Collection, published in the *Times* Literary Supplement for 26th June, 1943, by Mr. W. Forbes Gray. It is almost certainly addressed to Henry Mackenzie, as Mr. Gray has surmized, and, among other points of interest, states clearly that Chichester, not London or Winchester, was the place where Collins met Home and presented him with the manuscript. Carlyle writes:

I recollected that [blank in MS.] had asked me to show you a Poem of Collins's that Johnson in his life of the poet has mentioned with regret as lost, & which I fortunately have. The History of it is this: It has been hastily wrote on John Home's [author of 'Douglas'] leaving Chichester . . . (where Collins was a native) in the year 1749. John had got it imperfect & unfinished . . . He had lent it to a friend who died 30 years ago . . . [The *Ode*] had been all this time in my beaureau (*sic*) as a forgotten fragment when the remembrance of it was revived by the mention made of it in Collins's life. I sought for it and read it with admiration but with regret that it was unfinished. I showed it to [blank in MS.] and on her approbation I admired it the more. I have copied it literally excepting only a few gaps of single words that I have supplied. If you will be so obliging as to fill up some lines that are wanting, I shall have it printed next Winter. There seems to me to run a fine wild genius thro' the whole of it, and it will serve to illustrate some points that might be disputed hereafter & preserve the memory of the ancient Scottish fairy Mythology.(*19*)

Thus we are able to reconstruct the course of events with very little help from conjecture. In the autumn of 1749 Collins was settled permanently at Chichester. It is virtually certain that he was well acquainted with Mary Downer and with her fiancé, Thomas Barrow. Toward the end of the year John Home arrived in Chichester, probably at the invitation of Barrow, his old friend and brother in arms against the rebels. Home, we remember, had set out for London with an introduction to Smollett from Alexander Carlyle. If Collins had known Carlyle, as has seemed probable, and had even collaborated with him in 1746, that fact in itself would afford common ground between them, but it was probably Barrow who brought Collins and Home together.

Home, according to Carlyle, 'had a recommendation to Mr. Lyttelton, afterwards Lord Lyttelton', and was 'enraged, but not discouraged' when Lyttelton declined even to read his tragedy.(*20*) Collins, having moved in theatrical circles, and having himself attempted to write a tragedy, would be likely to sympathize, and perhaps he echoes some comforting words of his own when he speaks of Home as lingering in London

Mid those soft friends, whose hearts, some future day,
Shall melt, perhaps, to hear thy tragic song.

156

Home would not take long to discover that Collins was more a poet than a dramatist, and, as a poet, not altogether a stranger to print. He had considerable force of character, and when he spoke of the Scottish Highlands and the life and customs of the inhabitants Collins would be an attentive listener. Collins had not been a great traveller, but under the spell of Home's wizardry he must have travelled vicariously. To record his observations in verse was a risky adventure, for it could have been argued that to enter into the life of the Highlands much more was needed than to be transported there in the spirit. How far Collins achieved this apparent impossibility may be judged by the fact that the poem has always been admired in Scotland. Burns has given it the stamp of his approval by quoting two lines from it in the *Cotter's Saturday Night*, and Burns was the last person to mistake romantic sentimentality for genuine understanding.

In the *Times* Literary Supplement for 20th December, 1928, Mr. A. S. P. Woodhouse has discussed Collins's indebtedness, already suspected, to Martin Martin's *Description of the Western Islands of Scotland*. It is a bulky volume, and so it needs to be, for the title-page promises an account of 'The Ancient and Modern Government, Religion and Customs of the Inhabitants, particularly of their Druids, Heathen Temples, Monasteries, Churches, Chappels, Antiquities, Monuments, Forts, Caves, and other Curiosities of Art and Nature. Of their Admirable and Expeditious way of Curing most Diseases by Simples of their own Product. A Particular Account of the Second Sight, or Faculty of foreseeing things to come, by way of Vision, so common among them'.

Mr. Woodhouse suggested as an additional source, particularly of Collins's tenth stanza, the same Martin Martin's 'A Late Voyage to St. Kilda', published in 1698. This, he thinks, would have been recognized earlier if Knight had not misread *tree* for *bee*, *Warton's* for *Martin's* and *St. Hilda* for *St. Kilda* in transcribing one of Wordsworth's letters to Dyce. What Wordsworth actually wrote is, except that the italics are not his: 'I am almost sure that the very agreeable line, "Nor ever vernal *bee* was heard to murmur there", is from *Martin's* account of *St. Kilda*.' Mr. Woodhouse observes that Martin attributes to the inhabitants of St. Kilda a certain 'primal innocence', and he contends that in the poem this peculiarity is somewhat exaggerated, so that the St. Kildans as Collins portrays them are nearer to the state of nature than the real St. Kildans, according to Martin, actually were. Thus it would appear that Collins was feeling his way towards Romanticism, 'the cult of the primitive' being one of its distinguishing signs. That suggestion opens up a prospect of research which, tempting as it is, must be considered to lie beyond the scope of this volume. A question which we should like to settle at the outset is whether Collins was personally acquainted with Martin's work or whether he derived his knowledge of it from conversations with Home, who may have known it well enough to quote certain passages from memory, and who was certainly capable of a little harmless exaggeration. A fact which favours the first possibility is that a copy of the 'Description' was found in Thomson's library at Richmond, and Collins may be assumed to have had access to it; on the other side of the case it could be argued that he shows no sign of having read it earlier than the time of his meeting Home.

The story of the finding of the manuscript would not be complete without some mention of the rival edition, though modern editors of Collins do not take it very seriously. A few weeks after the publication of the ode in the 'Transactions' an Edinburgh publisher named Bell produced what was alleged to be a perfect copy. The fact that it was perfect in the sense of being complete to the last word and the last comma was in itself a suspicious sign, and Bell's story of its provenance was still more suspicious. He said that the manuscript had been found in the 'concealed drawers' of an old bureau, by 'a gentleman, who, for the present, chooses not to publish his name'. The anonymous gentleman was no less chary of answering questions prompted by his discovery than of revealing his identity, and the only reasonable conclusion is that neither he nor the old bureau with its contents ever existed. Bell did not admit that he had seen Carlyle's version in the 'Transactions', but Bronson, who examined the evidence exhaustively, has demonstrated that he must have been well acquainted with the notes.(21)

The nearest approach to an argument in favour of Bell's claim is that his edition was dedicated to the brothers Warton, and that they did not repudiate it. It is true that the Wartons had seen the poem when they visited Collins at Chichester in 1754, and Thomas Warton quotes the first line in his letter to Hymers, but he describes the continuation as 'very long', and would not be likely to have memorized it; he would be easily satisfied that Bell's version had a general resemblance to the poem which he remembered. According to Francis Horner, Bell finally admitted that 'the additions were a forgery of his own, of which he boasted to Mackintosh'.(22) Horner was not the man to report such a statement lightly. He was one of the most cautious politicians of his day, respected on both sides of the House for his fairness and moderation, and it is, perhaps, for that reason that he has left but a slight impression on the page of history.

NOTES TO CHAPTER X

1. Dalton, George the First's Army, Vol. II, p. 165, note 1.
2. Lord March, *A Duke and His Friends*, p. 511.
3. Beckles Willson, *Life and Letters of James Wolfe*, p. 63.
4. *Autobiography*, ed. Burton, p. 241.
5. B.M. Add. MS. 39456, f. 222.
6. *Autobiography*, ed. Burton, pp. 63, 194, 195, *note*.
7. B.M. Add. MSS. 5699, f. 166; 39475A (7), f. 584.
8. P.R.O. T. 1/478/482. According to his own statement he was appointed 'by Lord Duplin and Mr. Potter'.
9. B.M. Add. MS. 21644, ff. 337, 385, 404, 432. He was at Fort Ligonier in August and at Pittsburg in September and October.
10. Carlyle's *Autobiography*, p. 547.
11. See note 8, above. He applied to the War Office for a refund of £5,800, expended by him 'in defraying the contingent Expenses of his Employment'.
12. Carlyle's *Autobiography*, Supplementary Chapter by J. H. Burton, p. 590, *note*.
13. P.C.C Collins, 505. The probate note describes him as 'late of Chiswick in the County of Middlesex', and adds that he died in New York. Carlyle is right, therefore, in saying that he died in America.
14. *Autobiography*, ed. Burton, p. 548. Carlyle mentions that Blair was also present on this occasion.
15. P.C.C. Bridport, 455. She left considerable property in Sussex and in Canada to her three children.
16. B.M. Add. MS. 39475A (7), f. 582.

17. Carlyle's *Autobiography*, Supplementary Chapter by J. H. Burton, pp. 590-2.
18. See p. 151, above.
19. The words inserted in square brackets are due to Mr. Forbes Gray. There is another copy of this letter, also incomplete, among the collection of Carlyle's papers in the possession of Mrs. Carlyle Bell.
20. See note 4, above.
21. See the Introduction to his *Poems of William Collins*.
22. *Memoirs of Francis Horner*, 1843, II, 276; quoted by Birkbeck Hill in his edition of Johnson's *Lives of the English Poets*, III, 340, note 3.

XI

'The Thick'ning Horror'

ABOUT the time when Collins was travelling in spirit through the Highlands he received a sign that he was not entirely forgotten in London, in spite of the failure of his Odes. In October, *1749*, the *Gentleman's Magazine* printed his *Song from Shakespear's* Cymbeline at the head of the 'Poetical Essays' for the month, but with alterations which should serve as a warning to modern editors of the poems. 'I remember,' says Nichols, speaking of Edward Cave,

> that, calling on him once, he gave me to read the beautiful poem of Collins, written for Shakespeare's Cymbeline, 'To fair Fidele's grassy tomb', which, though adapted to a particular circumstance in the play, Cave was for inserting in his Magazine, without any reference to the subject. I told him it would lose [much?] of its beauty if it were so published: this he could not see; nor could he be convinced of the propriety of the name *Fidele*: he thought Pastora a better and so printed it.(*1*)

That, happily, settles the question whether Collins was responsible for the change. Modern editors have rightly restored *Fidele*.

It is not certain whether we should think of the spring of 1746 or of a period of a few months from October, 1749, as the time when Collins's powers reached their height. The answer must depend partly on our opinion of the relative merits of the ode *To*

161

Evening and the ode on the 'Highland Superstitions'. In the former we have the essence of Collins as we know him; but we know him as a minor poet, though first, perhaps, among the minor poets who abounded between the age of Dryden and the age of Wordsworth. The ode *To Evening* is not, and is not designed to be, a *great* poem in the accepted sense of the word. The 'Highland Superstitions' is on a grander scale; it has not the perfection of the ode *To Evening,* but it points the way by which Collins might have achieved greatness if he had lived to be as old as Dryden. That is more than can be said of *The Passions,* in which he was attempting to go Dryden's way instead of his own.

If to the 'Highland Superstitions' we were able to add three other poems, two known only by their titles and the third by some slight fragments, we might have to decide that the period beginning in 1749 was the more brilliant. In 1928 Mr. A. D. McKillop discovered from an advertisement in two contemporary journals that Manby and Cox had ready for publication in February, 1750, 'An Epistle to the Editor of Fairfax his Translation of Tasso, by Wm. Collins'.(2) The occasion of the poem was probably, as Mr. McKillop suggested, the appearance in 1749 of a new edition of Fairfax's translation. In the ode on the 'Highland Superstitions', which must have been written about the same time, Collins describes how he had been captivated by those scenes in which 'th'heroic muse employ'd her Tasso's art', and with what delight he had heard 'his harp, by British Fairfax strung'. Again, in Fragment 10 of Mr. Cunningham's collection, of which something had been said already, we find the same sentiment expressed in very similar language:

> O Think in what sweet lays how sweetly strong
> Our Fairfax warbles Tasso's forcefull Song.

The second of the two lost poems is mentioned in a letter to Dr. William Hayes, Professor of Music at Oxford. This letter must be given in full, as it is the second of the only two which have survived from Collins's private correspondence. The text has been preserved by Seward in his *Anecdotes of Distinguished Persons.*(3)

Sir, – Mr. Blackstone, of Winchester, some time since informed me of the honour you had done me at Oxford last summer; for which I return you my sincere thanks. I have another more perfect copy of the Ode; which, had I known your obliging design, I would have communicated to you.

Inform me by a line, if you should think one of my better judgement acceptable. In such case I could send you one written on a nobler subject, and which, though I have been persuaded to bring it forth in London, I think more calculated for an audience in the University. The subject is the Music of the Grecian Theatre; in which I have, I hope naturally, introduced the various characters with which the chorus was concerned, as Oedipus, Medea, Electra, Orestes, &c., &c. The composition, too, is probably more correct, as I have chosen the ancient tragedies for my models, and only copied the most affecting passages in them.

In the meantime you will greatly oblige me by sending the score of the last. If you can get it written, I will readily answer the expense. If you send it with a copy or two of the Ode (as printed at Oxford) to Mr. Clarke, at Winchester, he will forward it to me here.

> I am, Sir, with great respect,
> Your obliged humble servant,
> William Collins.

Chichester, Sussex, November 8, 1750.

P.S. – Mr. Clarke passed some days here while Mr. Worgan was with me, from whose friendship, I hope, he will receive some advantage.

This letter has more than one point of interest, and we shall have occasion to refer to it again. Here we are concerned only with the ode 'written on a nobler subject', and must regret that Hayes did not, on hearing of its existence, call for his horses and chariots and make a dash to Chichester to secure the poem at once, finished or unfinished. Among Mr. Cunningham's 'Drafts and Fragments', however, is a Fragment of an Ode for Music', which 'may', as the editorial note suggests, 'be connected with it'.

M

Mr. Cunningham's extreme caution is partly explained by his next sentence: 'The fragment may, on the other hand, be connected with the "Ode on the Use and Abuse of Poetry", which Joseph Warton quotes from in his *Essay on the Writings and Genius of Pope* . . . and which has been thought to be the work of Collins.'

Of the two alternatives thus presented, the first seems by far the more probable. It is a matter on which opinions may differ, but one reader would think it not too bold a conjecture that in these eighteen lines we have the whole of the ode on the 'Music of the Grecian Theatre' that was ever written. Taken literally, it is true, Collins's words convey that the composition was already complete; but a poet of his temperament might have written in those terms if the project were shaping itself in his mind and if, after writing the introductory lines – often the most difficult – he was satisfied that he could see his way clearly through the continuation. The poem, so far as it goes, has a strong resemblance to *The Passions*, and is obviously intended to be set to music. It promises to be just such a poem as Hayes would be led to expect after reading Collins's letter.

The third lost poem, as well as some attempts at others, was remembered by Thomas Warton, as he explains in his letter to Hymers, as having been shown to him and his brother when they visited Collins at Chichester in 1754. After speaking of the ode on the 'Highland Superstitions', Warton continues:

He also showed us another ode, of two or three four-lined stanzas, called the Bell of Arragon; on a tradition that, anciently, just before a king of Spain died, the great bell of the cathedral of Sarragossa, in Arragon, toiled spontaneously. It began thus:

> The bell of Arragon, they say,
> Spontaneous speaks the fatal day.

Soon afterwards were these lines:

> Whatever dark aerial power,
> Commission'd, haunts the gloomy tower.

164

The last stanza consisted of a moral transition to his own death and knell, which he called 'some simpler bell'. I have seen all his odes already published in his own handwriting; they had the marks of repeated correction: he was perpetually changing his epithets. Dr. Warton, my brother, has a few fragments of some other odes, but too loose and imperfect for publication, yet containing traces of high imagery.

That is all that can be said of the three missing poems, and we may now return, for a moment, to the letter to Dr. Hayes. Mr. H. O. White makes an interesting comment on the last paragraph, the significance of which, he thinks, has not been sufficiently appreciated. He had discovered that an edition of *The Passions*, with a new ending by the Earl of Lichfield, was printed at Oxford in 1750, and that the work in this form, with music by Hayes, was performed at Oxford on 2nd July of the same year. Mr. White discovered further that an edition of *The Passions* already known to have been published at Winchester in 1750 is, in fact, a reprint of the Oxford edition. 'The inference,' he says,

is obvious. Collins wrote to Dr. Hayes for copies of the music and of the printed ode, because his friends were contemplating a public performance of the ode at Winchester. That such a performance took place we may safely infer from the fact that the ode with the new termination was specially printed at Winchester, evidently for distribution among the audience. When this took place I have so far been unable to determine; but one is tempted to hope that it was during the poet's lifetime, and that he, who enjoyed so few poetic triumphs, had the satisfaction of being present.(4)

It appears from the evidence to be virtually certain that a performance at Winchester was projected, but we know that such schemes sometimes fail because of some unforeseen hitch or through lack of interest. Mr. Blakiston, the present Librarian of Winchester, allows it to be stated that when he was preparing the Collins Exhibition which he organized in 1959 he searched for a record of the event both among the College archives and in other likely places, but was unrewarded. So far, therefore, the probability established by Mr. White must remain a probability, though we may still hope that the final proof may yet be found.

According to Thomas Warton Collins had a severe illness, and believed himself to be dying, about Easter, 1751, after he had finally retired to Chichester. Although he had recovered by the following June, as Warton judged from a letter received at that time, it is generally assumed that this was the first stage of the malady which finally overwhelmed him, and that for the rest of his life he must have been incapable of composition. That is not a necessary conclusion. I believe that three poems, one published six years after his death and the two others appearing for the first time in Mr. Cunningham's collection, may, with reasonable probability, be assigned to a period between 1751 and 1754.

In May, 1765, there was published in the *Gentleman's Magazine* a poem with the title, *Written on a Paper, Which Contained a Piece of Bride Cake Given to the Author by a Lady*, and said to be 'by the late Mr. Collins'. Bronson was unaware 'on what evidence this poem was ascribed to Collins', and that mystery remains; but Bronson decided to include it 'wholly on internal evidence'. Critics generally have agreed, as the poem breathes the spirit of Collins in every line.(5) What is more disputable is Bronson's opinion that it seems 'to belong to the poet's younger and mildly amorous muse'. Bronson's judgement is not to be lightly set aside, but it must be remembered that he accepted as genuine the lines 'To Miss Aurelia C——r' and 'Young Damon of the Vale is dead', and, apart from those trifles, it does not appear that Collins's muse was ever mildly amorous.

The whole poem has a tone of wistful melancholy, and in the last stanza the poet says clearly that he has no peace by day and only brief intervals of rest by night:

> Sweet *Peace*, who long hath shunn'd my plaintive day
> Consents at length to bring me short delight,
> Thy careless steps may scare her doves away,
> And grief with raven note usurp the night.

We can hardly imagine Collins writing in that strain in his younger

days, when he was moving in the gay society of London or when
he was living quietly but happily at Richmond, or, in fact, at any
time before his first attack of illness; but the tone is exactly what
we should expect of him at a time when he knew himself to be a
nervous invalid but was still able, with an effort, to express himself in verse.

Thus we are led to ask ourselves whether we know of any
marriage among Collins's friends which would be likely to inspire
him to make such an effort. The answer is that we know of one,
and only one. There may have been others, it is true, of which we
have no record, but it is evident from the opening lines of the
'Highland Superstitions' that Thomas Barrow, the 'cordial
youth', and Mary Downer, his 'destin'd bride', were very special
friends, and we have already found that their marriage took place
at Chichester on 2nd April, 1753.(6) Collins, we may be reasonably sure, was invited to the ceremony, and if he was unable to
attend that would be all the more reason why, on receiving a piece
of wedding cake, he should be moved to express his felicitations in
verse.

Another poem which we should suppose to belong to the same
period is the second of Mr. Cunningham's 'Drafts and Fragments'. The sixth stanza of that poem was quoted in full in an
earlier chapter, with the comment that Delia, to whom it refers,
seems to have lived by the Medway, and not at Harting, the alleged home of Elizabeth Goddard. The present difficulty is about
the probable date of composition. Collins adds a footnote reading,
'Dic quibus in terris &c', and in an editorial note Mr. Cunningham explains: 'Collins's footnote refers to Virgil, *Ecl.* iii. 106.'
Lines 106-7 of the Third Eclogue read,

> Dic quibus in terris inscripti nomina regum
> Nascantur flores: et Phyllida solus habeto,

and there would be nothing relevant to the theme of the poem in
asking what land brings forth flowers inscribed with the names of
kings. The allusion intended by Collins must be to lines 104-5:

> Dic quibus in terris, et eris mihi magnus Apollo,
> Tres pateat coeli spatium non amplius ulnas.

167

That is highly relevant. Collins compares himself to a man look-ing up from the bottom of a well, who can see only so much of the sky (about three ells) as the width of the well allows. At what period was he living in this unnatural seclusion, so that he could say, in the words of the poem,

> Confin'd within my Native dwells
> The world I little know?

Not in 1745 or 1746 – the time, we must suppose, of his acquain-tance with Elizabeth Goddard – when he was busy in London or living happily among his friends at Richmond. The most likely time is between Easter, 1751, when his first illness occurred, and the autumn of 1754, when, in all probability, the poem was shown to the Wartons as one of the 'fragments of some other odes'. That is another reason why we cannot, with any approach to certainty, identify the Delia of the poem with Elizabeth Goddard. It is pos-sible that Collins's devotion to Miss Goddard persisted through the years, but it is also possible that she was the Rosaline of his life, and that long before 1754 she had been superseded by Juliet. Only if we had evidence that she was living by the banks of the Medway between 1751 and 1754 should we be safe in concluding that she and Delia were the same person.

The last of the three poems to be assigned to the later period is the one which Mr. Cunningham has placed first in his *Drafts and Fragments*. Mr. Cunningham speaks of it in his note as 'an early draft of the "Ode to Simplicity"', and that is what, at first sight, we should suppose it to be; but on closer acquaintance we can hardly fail to agree that, besides being free of the obvious faults of the published ode, it is in every respect positively superior. There is no aimless wandering through the ages, no 'jump from Augustus to the troubadours', in Mr. Garrod's words, by 'a verit-able *salto mortale*'. The indebtedness of the modern world to Greece is acknowledged in a single stanza, but before that stanza is reached the poet has already struck the key-note in the lines:

> Return sweet Maid at length
> In all thy Ancient strength
> And bid our Britain hear thy Grecian song.

168

As an illustration of the superior merit of Fragment 1, it will
be instructive to quote at length Mr. Garrod's remarks on the
eighth stanza of the familiar version and then to observe how in the
equivalent stanza, the fifth, of Fragment 1, Collins has removed
every one of the imperfections noticed, as if he had foreseen the
criticism and profited by it. Mr. Garrod writes:

> In the eighth stanza, the 'meeting Soul' of the last line is suf-
> ficiently obscure; and I do not know that the obscurity of it is
> altogether excused by its derivation from Milton's *L'Allegro*. In
> the same stanza,
>
> > Tho' Taste, tho' Genius bless,
> > To some divine Excess
>
> can be imputed, I am tempted to say, neither to taste nor to
> genius in Collins. *Taste* recalls the elder Warton's ode to that
> deity. But the 'divine Excess' spoken of sorts with the function
> only of genius, not of Taste – who has no excesses. In the line
> that follows 'the *cold* Work' is such as might be expected, cer-
> tainly, from mere taste, but matches ill with the idea either of
> genius or of 'divine Excess'. We feel Collins to be losing his drift;
> and we are not in any degree reassured when we reach lines 4-5:
>
> > What each, what all supply,
> > May court, may charm our Eye.
>
> We were speaking of what Taste and Genius supply to *poetry*;
> and not the eye, but the ear, is in question.(7)

Turning to Fragment 1, we shall find it helpful to glance first
at the last three lines of stanza 4, so as to establish the context.
They are:

> For Wisdom learn'd to please
> By thy persuasive Ease,
> And Simplest Sweetness more ennobled Truth.

169

The poet then continues:

> Nor modest Picture less
> Declin'd the wild Excess
> Which frequent now distracts her wild design
> The Modest Graces laid
> Each soft unboastfull shade
> While Feeling Nature drew th'impassion'd line!

We notice at once the absence of the 'meeting Soul', condemned by Mr. Garrod as obscure. The 'divine Excess', which the critic would allow to genius but not to taste, is mentioned only to be excluded, with no exception even in favour of genius. No reader is likely to feel that Collins is 'losing his drift'. Finally, there is not here any ground for the statement that 'we were speaking of what Taste and Genius supply to *poetry*; and not the eye, but the ear, is in question'. Here we are speaking not of poetry but, more particularly, of pictorial art in its relation to art in general.

The poem has some slight defects which could easily have been removed in the course of a final revision, such as the repetition of *modest* and of *wild* in the lines just quoted. Making allowance for that, we shall find it difficult to believe that this is, in fact, an early draft, and that Collins remodelled it into the comparatively heavy and shapeless mass of stanzas which we know. It seems far more likely that at some later stage, when his volume of odes was already in print, he re-wrote it for his own private delectation, leaving it incomplete in some points of detail.

That would account for the cryptic phrase 'And 'midst my Cave', in the third line of stanza 6. That these words were chosen with deliberation is proved by the manuscript, in which they are substituted for 'ever near my view'. Collins could not have spoken of himself as inhabiting a cave when he was living an active life in London or when he was moving in the congenial society of Richmond, but, as we have noticed already, in Fragment 2 he uses words which convey the same idea of isolation:

> Confin'd within my Native dells
> The world I little know.

170

Thus Fragment 1 would appear to belong to the same period as
Fragment 2, not earlier than the spring of 1751.

The most satisfactory evidence, however, of a later date is that
in Fragment 1 Collins has removed the ambiguity apparent in
the lines of the familiar ode:

> In *Fancy* loveliest Child,
> Thy Babe, or *Pleasure's*, nurs'd the Pow'rs of Song!

These lines are fanciful in the common and colloquial sense of the
word, but they lend themselves even better than the examples cited
by Mr. Garrod to the criticism that 'we feel Collins to be losing
his drift'. That remark is suggested to Mr. Garrod by the third
line of the eighth stanza, but it is more obviously true if applied
to that stanza as a whole:

> Tho' Taste, tho' Genius bless,
> To some divine Excess,
> Faints the cold Work till Thou inspire the whole;
> What each, what all supply,
> May court, may charm our Eye,
> Thou, only Thou can'st raise the meeting Soul!

We must remember that Collins is still addressing Simplicity. Is
it Simplicity, then, that inspires the whole, that raises a soul in
what without it is lifeless? Is it not rather the power which in the
ode *On the Poetical Character* Collins had personified as Fancy,
and which today we should prefer to call Imagination? That question Collins must have reconsidered at some time after he had
written the ode *To Simplicity* as we know it. Fragment 1, though
entitled *To Simplicity*, begins with the line, 'O Fancy, Alter'd
Maid', and the whole poem is consistent with the supposition
that it is Fancy who is addressed throughout. Thus the new version of the poem is brought into harmony with the ode *On the
Poetical Character*. In the latter Fancy is considered as the *creative*
power; in Fragment 1 it is the *unifying* power. Except in thought
the two are inseparable, for the act of creation – or what, by
analogy, we call creation in the sphere of art – implies the act of
imparting unity.

171

In the absence of some new discovery which we have no reason
to expect, we must believe that Collins's life as a poet had come
to an end when he showed his fragments to the Wartons in 1754.
He had already had an illness of some severity, accompanied by
all the symptoms of a nervous breakdown, and it recurred at intervals. 'The approaches of this dreadful malady,' says Johnson,
'he began to feel soon after his uncle's death,' but we can say on
the authority of Thomas Warton, who was better informed, that
the interval was fully two years. Johnson was guided throughout
by his fixed belief that Colonel Martin's death brought his nephew
a considerable fortune, but too late to save him from the effects of
years of privation. The assumption that Collins went on with his
translation of Aristotle until Colonel Martin's bequest enabled
him to repay the money advanced by the publisher must be explained in the same way.

Colonel Martin, as we remember, died in April, 1749. Thomas
Warton, after saying that he often saw Collins in London in 1750,
adds, 'This was before his illness'. He then speaks of Collins's
literary projects, his 'History of the Revival of Learning' and the
'Clarendon Review', and continues:

About Easter, the next year, I was in London; when, being
given over and supposed to be dying, he desired to see me, that
he might take his last leave of me: but he grew better, and in the
summer he sent me a letter on some private business, which I
have now by me, dated Chichester June 9, 1751, written in a
fine hand, and without the least symptom of a disordered or
debilitated understanding.

After this, apparently, Warton lost sight of him for three years,
as the next sentence refers to the year 1754. Johnson has helped
us to account for some part of the interval by saying that Collins
attempted to disperse the clouds gathering on his intellect 'by
travel, and passed into France; but found himself constrained to
yield to his malady, and returned'. Warton continues:

In 1754 he came to Oxford for change of air and amusement,
where he stayed a month; I saw him frequently, but he was so

weak and low, that he could not bear conversation. Once he walked from his lodgings, opposite Christ Church, to Trinity College, but supported by his servant. The same year, in September, I and my brother visited him at Chichester, where he lived in the cathedral cloisters, with his sister. The first day he was in high spirits at intervals, but exerted himself so much that he could not see us the second.

He then speaks of having been shown the 'Highland Superstitions', the 'Bell of Arragon' and the fragments, in a passage already noticed.

Of Collins's alleged madness it is impossible to say anything with certainty after two hundred years. The opinions of contemporary doctors have not been recorded, and, if they had, would be of no value. It is doubtful whether even today the study of psychiatry has made as much progress as the study of medicine had made two thousand years ago; in Collins's time it had not made a beginning. People of that generation may have been too sceptical, or too 'polite' in their own sense of the word, to believe that all madness was due to demoniacal possession, but they acted as if they believed it as firmly as their primitive ancestors had ever done. The approved remedy was chains and darkness, and there can be little doubt that many people whose real malady was a tendency to nervous depression were driven into genuine madness by their knowledge of what the treatment would be if the worst should happen.

Johnson, immediately after speaking of the inheritance of two thousand pounds by the will of Colonel Martin, says that Collins was no sooner rescued from poverty 'than his life was assailed by more dreadful calamities, disease and insanity'. Later we are told that 'he was for some time confined to a house of lunaticks, and afterwards retired to the care of his sister in Chichester, where death in 1756 came to his relief'.

The last statement is well known to be an error; Collins lived for three years after 1756. It is possible that he was for a time confined to a house of lunatics, and the most likely period is the first half of 1754. Johnson himself, referring to him on 8th May of that year, had written to Joseph Warton: 'This busy and forcible mind is now under the government of those who lately would not have been able to comprehend the least and most narrow of its designs.'(8) It was probably in the following summer or autumn, after he had been rescued by his sister and removed to Chichester, that he was visited by the Wartons, and it was probably to that visit, and his impression of Collins on that occasion, that Joseph Warton referred in a letter to Johnson which has not come down to us. On 21st December, 1754, Johnson wrote to Thomas Warton: 'I had lately the favour of a letter from your brother, with some account of poor Collins, for whom I am much concerned. I have a notion, that by very great temperance, or more properly abstinence, he may yet recover.'(9)

The hint conveyed by the last sentence, that Collins was drinking more than was good for him, is repeated in plainer language in *Lives of the English Poets*. There, without reference to the earlier statement that 'he was for some time confined to a house of lunaticks', we are told that 'his disorder was not alienation of mind, but general laxity and feebleness', that he could talk for a short time with spirit and judgement, but was soon exhausted, and that, conscious of his weakness, he 'eagerly snatched that temporary relief with which the table and the bottle flatter and seduce'. We are to suppose, then, that Collins had some mysterious trouble either causing or caused by a physical illness; some 'depression of mind', as Johnson says elsewhere, which 'enchains the faculties without destroying them, and leaves reason the knowledge of right without the power of pursuing it'. It is implied, further, that he had recourse to the bottle in the vain attempt to free himself of this unendurable burden.

It is possible that the case was one of some physical disorder reacting on the nerves, which a general practitioner today could easily have diagnosed, and if that is so there is nothing more to say. But I should like to suggest as a merely personal opinion that the bodily illness was the result of a shock to the nerves, or a series of shocks. I know that I shall be on delicate ground if I mention the Methodist Revival, and the possibility that Collins had been infected by that influence with *le délire biblique*. I am anxious to steer clear of all such controversial questions as whether Wesley's achievement, besides being a work of human genius, as it undoubtedly was, was also of divine inspiration, and I will be content to mention one simple fact which may be more relevant to the case of Collins. I have been told by old inhabitants of Cornwall, who preserve the tradition, that when Wesley described the torments of Hell in his memorable sermon at Gwennap Pit many of the listeners screamed like lunatics, and others were carried out in a state of collapse. That is borne out by a contemporary picture, in which the whole assembly is obviously tense with fright, and a woman on the edge of the crowd is seen to be fainting.

Had Collins's mind been overwhelmed by some such flood of emotion? The possibility is suggested by an incident which Johnson clearly remembered, and which evidently impressed him. It probably occurred in the spring or summer of 1754, as Johnson relates it immediately after saying that Collins tried to cure himself by foreign travel, was afterwards confined in a house of lunatics, and finally retired in the care of his sister to Chichester.

> After his return from France the writer of this character paid him a visit at Islington, where he was waiting for his sister, whom he had directed to meet him: there was then nothing of disorder discernible in his mind by any but himself, but he had withdrawn from study, and travelled with no other book than an English Testament, such as children carry to the school; when his friend took it into his hand, out of curiosity to see what companion a Man of Letters had chosen, 'I have but one book,' said Collins, 'but that is the best.'

This story was read with interest, but without surprise, by Thomas Warton, whose comment on it in his letter to Hymers reveals that Collins's mind continued to move on the same lines after his return to Chichester, and, we may suppose, for the rest of his life. 'In illustration,' he says.

> of what Dr. Johnson has related, that during his last malady he was a great reader of the Bible, I am favoured with the following anecdote from the reverend Mr. Shenton, vicar of St. Andrew's, at Chichester, by whom Collins was buried: 'Walking in my vicarial garden one Sunday evening, during Collins's

175

last illness, I heard a female (the servant, I suppose), reading the Bible in his chamber. Mr. Collins had been accustomed to rave much, and make great moanings; but while she was reading, or rather attempting to read, he was not only silent but attentive likewise, correcting her mistakes, which indeed were very frequent, through the whole of the twenty-seventh chapter of Genesis.'

Warton concludes with an afterthought not relevant to what he has just said, but interesting as a sudden reminder of the Collins whom he had known in former years:

I have just been informed, from undoubted authority, that Collins had finished a Preliminary Dissertation to be prefixed to his History of the Restoration of Learning, and that it was written with great judgment, precision, and knowledge of the subject.

In 1740, when he entered Oxford, Collins had been open to criticism as having, in the words of Gilbert White, 'too high an opinion of his school acquisitions'. After leaving Oxford he had embarked on one literary venture after another demanding all the resources of his scholarship, and, when not absorbed in his work, had been cheerful and sociable; he had mixed among actors and dramatists in the Green Room of Drury Lane, and was 'an acceptable companion everywhere'; he had made 'diverting observations' which, according to Ragsdale, had been found 'extremely entertaining', and, if we may judge by his answer when Hampton knocked over his tea-table, we shall agree that his wit was of a high order; he had played the host with grace and liberality, and had overspent his income; he had been conspicuous among the literary circle surrounding Thomson at Richmond, and, during a short acquaintance, had grown 'extremely intimate', according to Carlyle, with the brilliant and formidable John Home. That was Collins up to the beginning of the year 1751. Then something happened which caused a sudden change, and during a long period of weakness, illness and melancholy, giving rise to rumours of madness, he acknowledged that he had but one book, the Bible. Taking Warton's account in conjunction with Johnson's, we should suppose that he continued to devote himself to that one book for the rest of his life, in the intervals of mourning and raving.

We remember that in 1745, when Collins had intended or been advised to take Holy Orders, Mulso had said that he was about to become 'ye Thing he most derides'. Mulso, no doubt, spoke from personal knowledge, as he and Collins had been at school together, and would be likely to talk frankly. Even so, we should not condemn Collins for hypocrisy because he was prepared to act as any other young man in his position and of his generation might have acted. He would have been almost unique in the eighteenth century if he had considered the Church otherwise than as the means to a safe and easy profession, or had been deterred from entering it by difficulties about the Thirty-nine Articles or by any doubt of his having a genuine vocation.

We must suppose that at this time revealed religion had for him no reality. He was loyal to the Church as he was loyal to the State, and was willing to fight for both against the Jacobites; but whether he could assent to every doctrine professed by the Church was a question which troubled him no more than whether he could approve of every political principle underlying the State. He had in a high degree the religious sense common to all human beings – a sense which Wordsworth, a greater poet, was to feel more intensely – but it would not have occurred to him, any more than to Wordsworth, that that sense should find its natural expression in devotion to a visible and organized Church. His personal religion we may suppose to have been something like the religion of Horace, though without the external observances which Horace occasionally permitted himself.

Are we to suppose, then, that at some time early in 1751 Collins underwent a sudden conversion, and are we to account in that way for his raving and moaning and his renunciation of all books except the Bible? He was certainly converted, but if we ask to what faith he was converted we raise a more difficult question. It does not appear from Wesley's Diary that he himself preached at this time in any place where Collins is likely to have been, and the probability is that Collins had listened to one of those Calvinistic Methodists who left Wesley to join forces with Whitfield.

Chesterton, in arguing that poetry is an influence tending to sanity, says that Cowper was the only great English poet who went mad. He may be right,(10) for it is not certain that Collins ever actually crossed the border-line, whatever his friends may have thought. Chesterton continues:

And [Cowper] was definitely driven mad by logic, by the ugly and alien logic of predestination. Poetry was not the disease, but the medicine; poetry partly kept him in health. He could sometimes forget the red and thirsty hell to which his hideous necessitarianism dragged him amid the wide waters and the white flat lilies of the Ouse. He was damned by John Calvin; he was almost saved by John Gilpin.(11)

That, I believe, would be equally true of Collins, with the substitution of the Lavant for the Ouse and of some appropriate name – perhaps Martin Martin would serve – for John Gilpin. Though Collins's affliction came more suddenly, he may, like Cowper, have been partly kept in health by poetry. The second of the fragments discovered by Mr. Cunningham seems, as has been said already, to have been written after his retirement to Chichester, when he had good reason to speak of himself as 'luckless Collins', but before the malady had entirely overwhelmed him. The time came when even the sanative influence of poetry could no longer save him from his deepening melancholy, and when that happened, if Johnson is right, he 'eagerly snatched the temporary relief with which the table and the bottle flatter and seduce'. Very likely he did. If some profound instinct or extrarational conviction told him that it was better to die of such over indulgence than to die of Calvinism, who shall say that he was wrong?

Early in 1759 Goldsmith wrote, in *The Present State of Polite Learning:* 'The neglected author of the *Persian Eclogues,* which however inaccurate, excel any in our language, is still alive. Happy if insensible of our neglect, nor raging at our ingratitude.'(12) Within a few weeks the principal statement had ceased to be true, and the addition had acquired the force of an epitaph. According to the tablet in St. Andrew's, Chichester, Collins died on 12th June, 1759, and according to the Parish Register he was buried on the 15th.

About 1795 there was erected in the Cathedral a memorial tablet which usually attracts the attention of visitors. It is the work of Flaxman, and typical of his art, but the directing mind must have been fresh from the influence of Johnson's 'Life'. Collins is shown with a copy of the New Testament propped up before him, devoutly reading from the beginning of the Gospel of St. Matthew. Below the portrait is the following inscription:

THIS MONVMENT WAS ERECTED
BY A VOLVNTARY SUBSCRIPTION
IN HONOR OF WILLIAM COLLINS
WHO WAS BORN IN THIS CITY MDCCXXI
AND DIED IN A HOVSE ADJOINING TO THE CLOISTERS
OF THIS CHVRCH MDCCLIX.

YE! WHO THE MERITS OF THE DEAD REVERE,
WHO HOLD MISFORTVNE SACRED, GENIVS DEAR
REGARD THIS TOMB!
WHERE COLLINS, HAPLESS NAME!
SOLICITS KINDNESS WITH A DOVBLE CLAIM:
THO' NATVRE GAVE HIM, AND THO' SCIENCE TAVGHT,
THE FIRE OF FANCY, AND THE REACH OF THOVGHT,
SEVERELY DOOM'D TO PENVRY'S EXTREME,
HE PASS'D IN MADD'NING PAIN LIFE'S FEVERISH DREAM;
WHILE RAYS OF GENIUS ONLY SERV'D TO SHEW
THE THICK'NING HORROR, AND EXALT HIS WOE.
YE WALLS THAT ECHOED TO HIS FRANTIC MOAN,
GVARD THE DVE RECORD OF THIS GRATEFVL STONE!
STRANGERS TO HIM, ENAMOVR'D OF HIS LAYS,
THIS FOND MEMORIAL OF HIS TALENTS RAISE:
FOR THIS THE ASHES OF A BARD REQVIRE,
WHO TOVCHED THE TENDEREST NOTES OF PITY'S LYRE:
WHO JOIN'D PVRE FAITH TO STRONG POETIC POWERS,
WHO IN REVIVING REASON'S LVCID HOVRS,
SOVGHT ON ONE BOOK HIS TROVBLED MIND TO REST,
AND RIGHTLY DEEM'D THE BOOK OF GOD THE BEST.

179

N

Both Collins's sisters married late in life. Elizabeth became the wife of Nanthaniel Tanner, a Lieutenant in The Buffs, on 15th October, 1750.(14) The bride was forty-six and the bridegroom, probably a few years older. Tanner must have been a fine soldier, though it is difficult to imagine him as Collins's brother-in-law. He had served in the ranks for twenty years before being commissioned in 1741, and had been wounded at Fontenoy.(15) Mrs. Tanner's death in or before 1754, and the effect of her will, have already been mentioned.(16)

Anne Collins, the younger sister, was married on 28th January, 1755, to Lieutenant Hugh Sempill. On the strength of a conjecture by Moy Thomas the husband has been believed to have been the third son of the eleventh Lord Sempill, but this is an error. A glance at the two wills,(17) the one proved on 8th February, 1763, and the other on 14th September, 1764, reveals that Hugh Sempill of Chichester and Captain the Honourable Hugh Sempill of the Marines were two different persons. If there was any relationship it must have been a very distant one, as the late Lord Sempill, who personally made a search of the family papers, failed to find any trace of the Hugh Sempill who settled at Chichester. The latter, according to the Parish Register of St. Andrew's, was buried on 17th December, 1762. Afterwards the widow was married to Thomas Durnford, Rector of Bramdean and Vicar of Harting, and it is from her stepson that we have the story of Anne's destruction of certain papers belonging to her brother. To the monument to five of her relatives which she erected in 1765 an addition was made later recording her own death on 18th October, 1789, at the age of eighty-five.

If there is any truth in the interpretation suggested in these pages of certain actions attributed to her, we must suppose that Anne Collins never forgave her uncle Charles for his treatment of her in his will,(18) that she had an excessive love of money, and of the importance which goes with the possession of money, and that when her anger was roused by a grievance, real or imaginary, she lost all restraint; but there is no sufficient reason to believe that she had that aversion to her brother or to his poetry which had been alleged, and if it is true that she tended him with devotion through the last years of his life, and fought with all

180

her strength to ward off the evil which finally engulfed him, that must weigh very heavily against her faults. When she erected a marble monument to members of her family(*19*) she must have wished that the name of her brother William, among the rest, should be rescued from oblivion. That wish was to be gratified in ample measure, though not by the means which she intended.

NOTES TO CHAPTER XI

1. *Literary Anecdotes,* V. p. 53.
2. See his letter to the *Times* Literary Supplement for 1928, p. 965.
3. Ed. 1798, Vol. II, p. 584.
4. *Review of English Studies,* Vol. III, pp. 19-21.
5. That is my feeling today, though many years ago in *Notes and Queries* (14th October, 1939) I was misguided enough to argue against Collins's authorship of the poem in question. Perhaps I was prejudiced by Bronson's belief that it was one of Collins's *early* poems, which still seems to me indefensible.

   Mr. Edmund Blunden allows me to quote some remarks of his in a private letter, with which I heartily agree: 'I hope you will not succeed in one thing, viz. in frightening editors from reprinting the Verses on a Piece of Bride Cake. It is so beautiful a petition, — no doubt formed to some extent on the model of Hammond's Love Elegies, — and so instinct with a nervous sensibility, that I should not readily think Collins didn't write it — rather late in his poetical career, I take it.'
6. See pp. 166-7, above.
7. *Collins,* pp. 64-5.
8. Quoted by Birkbeck Hill, Johnson's *Lives of the English Poets,* III, 338.
9. Boswell's *Life of Johnson* (1791), I, p. 197.
10. Mr. F. L. Lucas (*Decline and Fall of the Romantic Ideal,* p. 98) observes that 'a number of eighteenth-century poets ... found it necessary, like the dog in Goldsmith's poem, to run mad'. Collins and Cowper, of course, are mentioned as two of the examples. The others — Chatterton, Smart, Clare, Blake, Shelley, Byron, Crabbe, Coleridge and De Quincey — are not very convincing. Chatterton and Smart may be admitted, but each was a law unto himself, and cannot be taken as illustrating a general rule; Mr. Lucas himself reminds us that Chatterton had madness in his family. Clare can hardly be counted as an eighteenth-century poet, as he was born in 1793 and lived to see the first twenty-seven years of the reign of Queen Victoria; and neither Shelley nor Byron nor De Quincey was more than fifteen years of age when the eighteenth century ended. Moreover, none of the three latter can be described as mad, in Mr. Lucas's phrase, 'by ordinary standards', nor

can Blake, Crabbe or Coleridge; for neither revolutionary opinions nor an addiction to drugs nor an abnormally vivid imagination is usually considered as in itself a sign of madness.

11. *Orthodoxy* (ed. 1912), p. 28.

12. Quoted by Birkbeck Hill, Johnson's *Lives of the English Poets*, III, 339.

13. Mr. F. W. Steer, County Archivist of West Sussex, to whom I am indebted for answering a private enquiry, says that there is no record of the exact date when the monument was erected, but 1795 must be approximately correct. I must also express my thanks to Canon W. K. Lowther Clarke, author of *Chichester Cathedral, its History and Art,* for drawing my attention to *Sussex Archaeological Collections*, XXXV (1887), p. 196, where there is printed a letter from Flaxman to William Hayley, dated Rome, 4th July 1791, submitting a sketch for a monument. Canon Lowther Clarke adds that he feels sure that Hayley initiated the scheme, and that Hayley is said to have had a part in composing the inscription.

14. B.M. Add. MS. 39422, f. 255.

15. C. R. B. Knight, *Historical Records of The Buffs*, Vol. III, Pt. 2, p. 669. Tanner's death is recorded in the *Gentleman's Magazine* for 1767, p. 525.

16. See pp. 47-8, above.

17. P.C.C. *Caesar*, 89, and *Simpson*, 368.

18. See pp. 52-3, above.

19. There is no obvious reason for Anne's omission from the list of the name of her sister Elizabeth. If, as one may suspect, she had a somewhat exaggerated sense of her social importance and that of her family, she may have thought that Elizabeth had made an unsuitable marriage, and may have been reluctant to commemorate her as Elizabeth Tanner. It may be remarked that there is no sign in Elizabeth's will of any estrangement from Anne.

APPENDIX ONE

Poems attributed to Collins

(The first two of these notes are reprinted with slight alterations from *Notes & Queries* for 14th October, 1939. The third is printed here for the first time.)

1. *'To Miss Aurelia C——r.'*

This poem appeared originally in the *Gentleman's Magazine* for January, 1739 (p. 41), over the signature 'Amasius', and was afterwards republished as the work of Collins in Fawkes and Woty's *Poetical Calendar*. Dr. Johnson quoted it at length, at the end of his 'Life' of Collins, as 'Mr. Collins's first production.'

We are not obliged to hold Collins responsible for this laboured trifle, which, though slight in itself, would be a heavy burden on his reputation. Johnson himself had remarked in a letter to John Nichols that 'Amasius was at that time the poetical name of Dr. Swan, and there are other poems in the *Gentleman's Magazine* over the same pseudonym. Birbeck Hill, in his edition of Johnson's *Letters*, gives the evidence for Swan's authorship exhaustively, and for that we may be grateful; though we can hardly share his regret that a composition formerly included among Collins's poems 'must no longer appear in that graceful company'.(*1*) To restore it to its true author is an act of justice to Collins no less than to the worthy Dr. Swan.

2. *'Young Damon of the Vale is Dead.'*

It was formerly believed that Collins was the author of a rhymed triviality entitled 'Song. The Sentiments Borrowed from Shakespeare', and more conveniently denoted by its first line, 'Young Damon of the Vale is dead'. In 1922 Mr. A. D. McKillop, in *Modern Language Notes* (Vol. ii, p. 181), pointed out that Beloe, a person likely to be well informed, printed the poem in the *Sexagenarian* as the work of Henry Headley. The following year, in

183

the same periodical (Vol. xxxviii, pp. 184-5), Mr. McKillop drew attention to its appearance in the *Gentleman's Magazine* for February, 1788, where it is introduced by the following letter:

Feb. 2.

Mr. Urban,

In turning over your Magazine for May, 1765, I observe a copy of most elegant verses by Collins, which are not to be found in any edition of his poems.(2) The following lines are to the best of my knowledge in the same predicament, and I believe have never yet appeared in print.

Yours, &c.

C–T–O.

This letter is generally read as evidence that 'the following lines' are also by Collins, or, in the words of Mr. E. G. Ainsworth, as 'definitely attributing the authorship to Collins'.(3) It is by no means certain that that is the meaning intended, as the writer does not use any such phrase as 'by the same author'.

We are able, fortunately, to identify 'C–T–O'. He was none other than Henry Headley,(4) who, as we have seen, was given credit for the 'Song' by Beloe. It appears, then, that it was Headley himself who sent the poem to the *Gentleman's Magazine*. In the light of this knowledge the allusion to Collins admits of an explanation. We must remember that the young Headley, a scholar and poet of great promise, had that fastidious literary sense which would be likely to reject the machine-made phrases imposed by convention upon contributors to the *Gentleman's Magazine*. The customary formula was something like this: 'Mr. Urban, – The enclosed copy of verses never having been printed, if you think them worthy of a place in your esteemed magazine, it will oblige Yours, etc.' A man of taste and originality would not drive his pen along that hard-worn groove. Headley does not disdain to follow the recognized convention, but he refuses to be a slave to it. Referring to the verses in the volume for 1765, he says, in effect: 'If the fact that this poem had not formerly been published was thought a sufficient reason for publishing it, let me offer you one which has, so far as I know, precisely that qualification for admission to your columns.'

There is one apparent difficulty in the way of this interpretation, but it is by no means so formidable as it appears at first sight. The qualifying words 'to the best of my knowledge' and 'I believe' show that Headley was in doubt whether the poem had ever been printed or not, and that, it may be said, is an indication that he could not himself have been the author. That would be a fair arugment in the conditions of today, but not in those of the later eighteenth century. The demand for light verse must have been greater at that time than it has ever been before or since, and there was very little regard for the rights of literary property. A person who came upon an elegant or ingenious trifle in manuscript would usually consider himself at liberty to publish it without asking the author's permission, and if the author had distributed copies freely, among friends of various degrees of intimacy, he might well be unable to give an assurance that the poem had never appeared in print.(5)

3. 'A Song. *Imitated from the* Midsummer-Night's Dream *of Shakespear*. Act II. Scene V.'

This poem was first claimed for Collins by Mr. I. A. Williams in an article first appearing in the *London Mercury* for May, 1923, and reprinted, with some necessary corrections suggested by Professor Garrod, by Mr. Lane Poole in the Oxford edition of Collins. It was first published anonymously in Dodsley's *Museum* for 16th August, 1746, and it remained anonymous for sixty-four years; then, in 1810, Chalmers discovered that a note in Joseph Warton's handwriting attributed it to his brother Thomas. 'That,' says Mr. Williams, 'would seem to be conclusive were it not that the internal evidence (a thing which I usually distrust) is so very strong in Collins's favour that one wonders whether Chalmers may not have made a mistake.'

Here is the poem in full:

> Lo here, beneath this hallow'd Shade,
> Within a Cowslip's Bossom deep,
> The lovely Queen of Elves is laid,
> May nought disturb her balmy Sleep!

Let not the Snake or baleful Toad
  Approach the silent Mansion near,
Or Newt profane the sweet Abode,
  Or Owl repeat her Orgies here!

No Snail or Worm shall hither come
  With noxious Filth her Bow'r to stain;
Hence be the Beetle's sullen Hum,
  And Spider's disembowel'd Train.

The love-lorn Nightingale alone
  Shall thro' *Titania's* Arbor stray,
To sooth her Sleep with melting Moan,
  And lull her with her sweetest Lay.

Mr. Williams relies mainly on the parallel between the phrase 'the Beetle's sullen Hum' (line 11) and these lines from Collins's *Ode to Evening*:

Or where the Beetle winds
  His small but sullen Horn,
As oft he rises 'midst the twilight Path,
  Against the Pilgrim borne in heedless Hum.

This parallel, he says, 'is so strong as almost to be convincing, especially when it is remembered that Collins's *Odes* did not appear until December 1746'. Professor Garrod, who in his concluding remarks is inclined to agree with Mr. Williams,(6) had already observed in speaking of the *Ode to Evening* that the first two of the lines quoted are from *Lycidas*.(7) Presumably he refers to line 28: 'What time the gray-fly winds her sultry horn'. But Thomas Warton, like his brother and like Collins, has been known to make use of a phrase from Milton, and what Collins could imitate in the *Ode to Evening* Warton might surely have imitated rather more freely.

That is offered as the clearest evidence, but, we are told, 'the parallel is not a solitary one'. We are asked to take the second and third lines of the *Song* and to compare them with these two passages:

Elves
Who slept in buds the Day.
Ode to Evening, 11. 22, 23,

.
and

His loveliest Elfin Queen.
Ode on the Poetical Character, 1. 4.

Let us by all means compare them, but let us remember at the same time that the 'elves' of the *Ode to Evening* are the 'dapper elves' of Comus, and that the 'loveliest Elfin Queen' of the *Ode on the Poetical Character* is the Fairie Queene of Spenser. The 'lovely Queen of Elves' of the *Song* is Titania, as the poem itself proclaims, but as Titania is a fairy Queen attended by elves it is not remarkable that a phrase applied to her should have some resemblance to phrases used by Collins in speaking of another fairy Queen and another company of elves. There is nothing here in any degree incompatible with Warton's authorship.

Mr. Williams continues:

And in the last verse of the *Song* there seems to be an echo of line 118 of the *Epistle to Sir Thomas Hanmer,* 'And melting music find the softest Lays', and a similarity of wording and thought to the passage about the nightingale in lines 16-18 of the *Ode to Simplicity:*

By her, whose Love-lorn Woe
In Ev'ning Musings slow
Sooth'd sweetly sad Electra's Poet's Ear.

I would draw special attention in these lines to the words 'Love-lorn', 'sooth'd' and 'sweetly'.

Here again Mr. Williams does not take into account the possibility that phrases in the *Song* resembling phrases used by Collins may have a common origin in Milton. The 'melting Moan' of the nightingale in the *Song,* the 'melting music' of Collins's

187

Epistle and the 'Love-lorn Woe' of Collins's nightingale in the *Ode to Simplicity* could all have been derived from *L'Allegro* and *Comus*:

> The melting voice through mazes running.
>
> *L'Allegro,* 1. 142

and

> Where the love-lorn nightingale
> Nightly to thee her sad song mourneth well.
>
> *Comus,* 11. 234-5

That is all that need to be said of 'melting Moan' and of the first of the three words to which Mr. Williams invites special attention, 'Love-lorn'. Of the two others, 'sooth'd' is surely a word which might occur by coincidence in any two poems in which the nightingale is mentioned. The same could be said of 'sweetly', though it could also, like 'Love-lorn', bring us back to *Comus*:

> How sweetly did they float upon the wings
> Of silence, through the empty-vaulted night.

Mr. Williams adds that 'there are other less important parallels', but I will follow his example by saying nothing about them.

The fact that in 1746 Thomas Warton was only eighteen years of age does not, as it seems to me, make his brother's statement difficult to accept. Thomas Warton was precocious, probably even more so than his brother; in any case Joseph Warton's ascription of the poem to Thomas is not incompatible with his having given a small amount of help in points of detail, and being modestly reluctant to proclaim the fact.

Of Collins's poems, the one which most easily lends itself to comparison is the *Song from Shakespear's 'Cymbelyne'*, and I cannot think that that poem and the anonymous *Song* reveal the same mind. As the case rests on internal evidence, the reader must be left to judge for himself.

NOTES TO APPENDIX I

1. Johnson's *Letters,* Vol. II, p. 185.
2. The writer refers to the verses *Written on a Paper, which Contained a Piece of Bride Cake.* See pp. 166-7, above.
3. *Poor Collins,* p. 7, note ii.
4. Henry Kett, in the 'Biographical Sketch' prefixed to his edition (1810) of Headley's *Seclect Beauties of Ancient English Poetry,* says: 'He was an occasional contributor of ingenious pieces to the *Gentleman's Magazine* under the signature of C.T.O.' See also the account of Headley in the *Dictionary of National Biography.*
5. In *Notes & Queries* for 14th October, 1939, I spun out the argument to somewhat greater length, but have not thought it necessary to repeat the remainder here.
6. *Collins,* pp. 113-5.
7. *Collins,* p. 77.

APPENDIX TWO

Collins Wills.

ROGER COLLINS.

(From the collection of Chichester Wills in the District Probate Registry, Winchester.)

IN THE NAME OF GOD AMEN May the first in the year of our Lord 1707 I ROGER COLLINS of Hunston in the County of Sussex Clerk being in perfect health and sound memory praised be God for the same and knowing the uncertainty of this life upon earth and being desireous to settle things in order doe make this my last Will and Testament in manner & forme following (that is to say) First and principally I commend my soul to Almighty God my creator assuredly by believing (*sic*) that I shall receive full pardon and full remission of all my sins and be saved by the precious death and merits of my blessed Saviour and Redeemer Christ Jesus and my body to the earth from whence it was taken to be buried in such decent and christian manner as by my Executrix hereafter named shall be thought meet and convenient and as touching such worldly estate as the Lord in Mercy hath lent me my will & meaning is the same shall be employed and bestowed as hereafter my will is expressed And first I doe revoke renounce frustrate & make void all Wills formerly be (*sic*) me made and declare & appoint this my last Will & Testament Item I give unto my son Charles all my books except those following which are mentioned. I give unto him five pounds to buy him mourning and also my silver watch I give to my son William five pounds to buy him mourning and to his daughter Elizabeth five pounds to be paid her when she comes to the age of one & twenty years Also I give to my grandson George Payne five pounds to be paid unto him at the age of one & twenty years The books I did except are those I give to my son William Pluctarcks lives Mr. Ainsworth on the pentituke Second the English Gentleman and Gentle-

190

woman Third Mr. Clarkes second volume fourth Mr. El-
boroughs two little books explaining the Divine Service I give
unto my daughter Judith Mr. Bloams history upon the Bible
Mr. Clarkes lives upon the Ancient [and] Modern Divines and also
Dr. Spark's Festivalls and fourth a Book called the House of
Mourning Lastly I give unto my daughter Judith all the rest of
my goods and chattels whom I make sole Executrix of this my
last Will and Testament paying all my debts legacies and funerall
charges In Witness whereof I have set my hand & seal the first
day of May aforesaid . . .

RO. COLLINS

Witnesses ROBERT FREEMAN
THO. SCOTT his mark
JANE FREEMAN her mark

Proved the third day of February 1708

CHARLES COLLINS (P.C.C. Edmunds 77).

IN THE NAME OF GOD AMEN I CHARLES COLLINS of the Charter House commonly called Suttons Hospital near West Smithfield Barrs in the County of Middlesex Gentleman this second day of September in the Year of our Lord one thousand seven hundred and forty one do make and declare this my last Will and Testament in manner and Form following that is to say IMPRIMIS I commend my soul into the hands of God Almighty believing remission of sins and everlasting Life by the Merits of Jesus Christ my Lord and only Saviour and I do profess to have always lived in the true Orthodox Faith of the Church of England as by Law established and I hope I shall dye a sound Member of the same Item I commit my Body to the Earth to be decently buryed by my hereafter named Executors in a good hansome Elm Coffin and Shrowed and all my Funeral Expenses not to exceed ten pounds   All my Debts I shall leave (if any) I request may be paid within a Month after my Decease and for settling my Wordly Goods such as Moneys Goods Chattels Estate and the like Item for my Freehold Estate scituate lying and being in the Parish of Saint Bartholomews without the West gate of the City of Chichester Sussex I give and bequeath to my Nephew William Collins son of Alderman William Collins of the City and County aforesaid all my said Freehold Estate with all Appurtenances belonging to it with all Rents Arrearages and Profits from it arising from one Year after my Decease to be accounted for to him   Item I give to my Neice Elizabeth Collins Daughter of Alderman William Collins aforesaid the Sum of one Shilling of good and lawfull Money of Great Britain as also my Mother Collins's Wedding Ring   Item I give to Anne Collins my Neice one shilling of good and lawfull Money of Great Britain   Item I give to my Nephew George Pain Dr in Physick of Bruton Street in the Parish of [blank in original] in the County of Middlesex the Sum of forty Pounds out of a Bond of sixty Pounds which I have on Mr. William Pannet of (*sic*) and Mr. Joseph Westborough of Kensington in the County of Middlesex   Item I give the other

remaining twenty Pounds to Charles Richard Sylvester Son of
Richard and Betty Sylvester now of Golden Lane in the Parish
of Cripplegate London and also my silver Watch I give unto the
said Charles Richard Sylvester with all my Wearing Apparel both
Linnen and Woollen all my Books of Arithmetick my late Wife
and my Picture in Frames Bed Bedding Furniture of my Room
Pewter Brass Copper Earthen and Glass Ware what Coats I shall
leave behind me I give towards the bringing up of the said Child
but whereas I said in the foregoing the Furniture of my Room I
shall here except Money Silver Plate Rings and some Pictures
Item I give to my Nephew George Paine King Charles the First
and his Queen in one Frame gilt and King Charles the Second
and Queen Ann both in Lacker or Gilt Frams (*sic*) Item I give
to my Nephew William Collins my Fathers Picture in a Frame
and my own Picture without a Frame and Alexander taking
Darius in his Tent without a Frame and the Draught of Winchester Colledge in a black Frame   Also I give to my aforesaid
Nephew William Collins my Silver Tankard with my Arms on it
and my Collection of Musick on the Score this Collection of
Church Musick as well as Songs and other Musick which if you
have no relish of it now, it may be hereafter valuable therefore
pray make much of it and keep it for the Love the Family have
born to that Faculty   The fifty Guineas that I have by me thirty
of them I give to my Nephew Dr. George Payne afore named and
ten Guineas out of the same fifty Guineas I give to Charles
Richard Sylvester to put him Apprentice to a Trade or to otherwise dispose of him to get an honest Livelyhood which I heartily
crave of my Nephew Dr. George Payne to do the best in his Power
for him which I hope he will punctually and faithfully and God
I hope will reward him for so faithfull a discharge of the Trust
resposed in him   And for the other twenty Pounds aforenamed
which I have given to Charles Richard Sylvester may remain in
my Nephew Paynes Hand until he be one and twenty Years of
Age or have served out his time which shall first happen (As for
the Lord Viscount Waymouth and his Sisters Money if there be
any likelyhood of it I give to my two Neices Elizabeth and Ann
Collins) Now as to the remaining ten Guineas I leave to my hereafter named Executors to defray my Funeral Expenses And I do

now nominate constitute and appoint my dearly beloved Nephews William Collins and Dr. George Payne Executors of this my last Will and Testament annulling and revoking all former Wills by me afore made and do ratifye and confirm this my last Will and declare it was begun according to the date recited at the beginning and not finished untill now IN WITNESS whereof I the said Charles Collins have to this my last Will and Testament set my hand and Seal this nineteenth of June one thousand seven hundred and forty two. CHARLES COLLINS – Signed Sealed and Published in the Presence of

JOHN GROSVENOR – WILL BOWERS – THO BOWYER

THIS WILL was proved at London the fifth day of March in the Year of our Lord one thousand seven hundred and forty five before the Worshipfull Robert Chapman Doctor of Laws and Surrogate of the right Worshipfull John Bettesworth also Doctor of Laws Master Keeper or Commissary of the Prerogative Court of Canterbury lawfully constituted by the Oath of George Payne the Nephew of the Deceased and one of the Executors in the said Will named to whom Administration was granted of all and singular the Goods Chattels and Credits of the said Deceased being first sworn duly to Administer Power reserved of making the like Grant to William Collins the other Executor named in the said Will when he shall apply for the same

WILLIAM COLLINS (the elder).

(From the collection of Chichester Wills in the District Probate Registry, Winchester.)

IN THE NAME OF GOD AMEN   I WILLIAM COLLINS Citizen and Alderman of the City of Chichester in the County of Sussex, being sick in body but of sound mind and memory Doe make and declare this my last Will and Testament in manner following, that is to say, FIRST I commend my soul into the hands of Almighty God believing remission of sins & everlasting life by the merits of Jesus Christ my only Saviour and Redeemer my Body I comitt to the Earth to be buried in the most private manner that may be and dispose of my Worldly Estate as follow vizt. IMPRIMIS I will that all my just Debts of every kind what soever be duly and truly paid AND WHEREAS I being seized of divers Copyhold or Customary Messuages Lands and Tenements situate lying and being within the mannor of Cackham in the County aforesaid and having this day surrendred the same before the Steward of the Courts of the same mannor to the uses of my Will, I doe in virtue of the same surrender, to the intent that all my just Debts may be paid and the better to enable my Wife and Executrix to pay the same, Will give and devise all my said Copyhold or Customary Messuages Lands and Tenements together with the use of the said surrender and all my Estate Right Title and Interest in Law and Equity of in and to the same Tenements respectively unto Elizabeth my loving Wife and her heirs desiring the same may be sold with all convenient speed and the moneys thereby arising be paid away and applyed for and towards the Discharging of my Debts   Item for the better and more sure payment of all my Debts and the better still to enable my Wife to perform and doe the same I doe give devise and bequeath unto my said Wife and to her heirs Executors Administrators and Assignes ALL and every my freehold and leasehold Messuages Lands and Tenements whatsoever and wheresoever and all my Estate right title Interest Redemption Equity and benefit of Redemption therein and unto every part thereof To the intent she may sell and dispose of the same with all convenient speed or so much thereof as shall be necessary to pay off and discharge my Debts And all the rest and residue of my goods Chattells and Estate whatsoever and wheresoever both real and personall my Debts and funerall Expenses being first paid and discharged I give devise and bequeath unto the said Elizabeth my Wife her heirs Executors Administrators and Assignes And I make constitute and appoint her my said Wife sole Executrix of this my last Will and Testament and doe hereby revoke all former Wills by me made In witness whereof I have to this my last Will and Testament sett my hand and seal the Nineteenth day of September One thousand Seven hundred and Thirty Three.

WM. COLLINS

Signed sealed and published by the said Testator in our presence who in his presence and at his request have subscribed our names as Witnesses hereunto.

WM. SOWTON Jnr.   WILL TUTTE
JAMES CLAYTON

This Will was proved before Mr. John Hancock Clerk Surrogate and so forth, on the Fifth day of November in the year of our Lord One Thousand Seven Hundred Thirty and Three By the Oath of Elizabeth Collins Widow and Relict of the said deceased and Executrix and so forth, To whom and so forth, well and truly, and so forth, sworn saving and so forth:——

196

ELIZABETH COLLINS.

(From the collection of Chichester Wills in the District Probate Registry, Winchester.)

IN THE NAME OF GOD AMEN I ELIZABETH COLLINGS of the City of Chichester in the County of Sussex Widow being of sound and disposing mind memory and understanding do make and declare this my last Will and Testament in manner following that is to say I comend my soul into the hands of Almighty God believing remission of sins and Everlasting Life by the merits of Jesus Christ my only Saviour and Redeemer my Body I comit to the Earth to be buried in a decent manner and to my Worldly Estate I Dispose thereof as follows (to wit) FIRST I will that all and every my just Debts of what kind soever be duly and truly paid In order whereunto I have this present day surrendred into the hands of the Lord of the Mannor of Cackham in the County of Sussex aforesaid by the acceptance of the Steward of the Courts of the same Mannor all and every my Copyhold or Customary Messuages Lands and Tenements situate lying and being within the Mannor aforesaid to the uses of my Will and in virtue and persuance thereof and to the intent that all my just Debts may be fully satisfied and paid and the better to enable my Daughters and Executrixes hereafter named to pay and satisfye the same accordingly I do will give and devise all and every my said Copyhold or Customary Messuages Lands and Tenements together with the use of the said surrender and all my Estate Right Title and Interest in Law and Equity of in and to the same Tenements respectively unto my loving Daughters Elizabeth Collings and Ann Collings and their heirs according to the Customs of the Mannor aforesaid desiring the same may be sold with all convenient speed and the money thereby arising paid and applyed for and towards and dischargeing of my Debts ALSO for the better and more speedy payment of my Debts and the better still to enable my said Daughters to perform and do the same and for other Causes and Considerations me hereunto moving I do give devise and bequeath unto my said two Daughters

197

Elizabeth and Ann Collings and to their heirs Executors Administrators and Assigns all and every my freehold and leasehold
Messuages Lands and Tenements whatsoever and wheresoever
and all my Estate Right Title Interest Redemption Equity and
Benefit of Redemption therein and unto every part thereof In
Trust and to the intent also and it is my Will and Desire that they
may sell and dispose of the same with all convenient speed and
by and out of the moneys thereby also ariseing pay and satisfye all
my just Debts and the rest and residue of the moneys so to be
raised and made by such sales as aforesaid And also all the rest
residue and remainder of my Goods Chattells Credits real and
personal Estate whatsoever and wheresoever after all my just
Debts aforesaid and my Funeral expenses are paid and discharged
I Give Devise and bequeath unto my said Daughters the said
Elizabeth Collings and Ann Collings and my loving son William
Collings equally to be divided between them share and share alike
And lastly I make constitute and appoint my said Daughters Eliza-
beth Collings and Ann Collings Executrixes of this my Last
Will and Testament hereby revoking all former Wills by me made.
In Witness whereof I have hereunto set my hand and seal the
Fifth day of August in the year of our Lord One Thousand Seven
Hundred and Thirty Six.   ELIZABETH COLLINS

Signed sealed published and declared by the said Elizabeth Collings the Testatrix as and for her last Will and Testament in the
presence of us who all of us in her presence and at her request
subscribed our names as witnesses hereunto
JOHN DEAR
FRA: DEAR
WILLIAM FOGDEN.

This Will was proved before the Reverend Mr. John Hancock
Surrogate &c on the Twelfth day of August in the year of our
Lord 1745 by the Oath of Elizabeth Collins natural and lawfull
Daughter of the said deceased and one of the Executrixes in the
said Will named Power being reserved to Ann Collins the other
Daughter of the said Deceased and the other of the Executrixes
also named in the said Will when she comes and so forth, well
and truly and so forth, sworn saving and so forth

EDMUND MARTIN (P.C.C. Lisle 153).

IN THE NAME OF GOD AMEN I Edmund Martin a Lieutenant Colonel in his Majesties service lying sick in the City of Chichester in the County of Sussex but in perfect Sense and Understanding do make and declare this my last Will and Testament in manner following that is to say I give and bequeath unto my Neice Elizabeth the Wife of Thomas Napper of Itchenor in the County aforesaid One hundred Pounds and my Copyhold Estates in the Mannors of Selsey and Somerly in the said County I leave to descend to my Nephew Abraham Martin Youngest Son of my late only Brother Henry Martin as I apprehend the Customs of the said several Manors to be I give and bequeath unto my Servant John Kipps Ten Pounds in money and all my Apparel both Linnen and Woollen that I usually have in wear And all the rest of my Real and Personal Estate wheresoever and whatsoever I give devise and bequeath unto my Nephew William Collins and Neices Elizabeth Collins and Ann Collins Son and Daughters of my late Sister Elizabeth Collins and to their Heirs Executors and Administrators equally to be divided between them And I make and constitute my aforesaid Neice Elizabeth Collins sole Executrix of this my Will unto which I have set my hand and Seal this nineteenth Day of April One Thousand Seven Hundred and Forty Nine. Edm. Martin. Signed Sealed and published by the said Edmund Martin as and for his last Will and Testament in the presence of us who have in his presence and at his request subscribed our Names as Witnesses.

Thos. Spenr. Wilson.　　Y. Johnson.　　Will: Tutte.

THIS WILL was proved at London on the Thirtieth Day of May in the Year of our Lord One Thousand Seven hundred and Forty nine before the Worshipful Andrew Coltee Duvarel Doctor of Laws Surrogate of the Right Worshipful John Bettesworth also Doctor of Laws Master Keeper or Commissary of the Prerogative

Court of Canterbury lawfully constituted by the Oath of Elizabeth Collins Spinster the Neice of the deceased and sole Executrix named in the said Will to whom Administration was granted of all and singular the Goods Chattels and Credits of the said deceased being first sworn duly to administer.

200

ELIZABETH TANNER (P.C.C. Pinfold 183).

IN THE NAME OF GOD AMEN I Elizabeth Tanner now Wife of Nathaniel Tanner Lieut of his Majesty's Marching Regiment of Foot called the Old Buffs (late called Elizabeth Collins Spinster) being in good health and of sound perfect and disposing mind memory and understanding do (by virtue of the Power and Authority to me reserved and given before my Intermarriage with the said Nathaniel Tanner my present Husband in and by a certain Tripartite Indenture of Settlement bearing date the Sixteenth day of October last past) make and declare this my last Will and Testament in manner and form following (that is to say) after commending my Soul unto Almighty God believing remission of Sins and Everlasting Life and committing my Body to the Earth to be decently Buried in Christian Buriel I give and dispose of all such Estates and Effects as by the Settlement aforesaid I am authorized and impowered as follows (to wit) First I give devise and bequeath all that my undivided third part in three equal parts to be divided of all and every the Freehold Messuages Lands Tenements Hereditaments and premises whatsoever whereof my late Mother Elizabeth Collins Widow died seized and whereto I am intitled or in any wise interested and particularly mentioned and described in and by the Indenture of Settlement aforesaid and also all that my undivided third part in three equal parts to be divided of all and every the leasehold Messuages Lands Tenements and Premises with the Appurtenances whatsoever whereof my said late Mother died possessed or interested in and whereto I am also intitled and also more particularly mentioned and described in and by the said Indenture of Settlement And also all that my undivided third part in three equal parts to be divided of and in all those Copyhold or Customary Lands Tenements and Premises with the Appurtenances lying and being within and held of the Mannor of Cackham in the County of Sussex whereof my said late Mother likewise died seized and whereto myself and my Sister Ann Collins Spinster were admitted upon the death of my said late Mother likewise more particularly described and mentioned in the same Indenture of Settlement and which I have this day Surrendred to the uses of this my Will And also all that my undivided third part in three equal parts to be divided of and in all those Copyhold or Customary Lands Tenements and Premises with the Appurtenances lying within and held of the Mannor aforesaid which were purchased by George Payne Esqr. of and from my Brother William Collins Gent In Trust also mentioned and described in and by the Settlement aforesaid and all my Share Part Dividend Estate Right Title Interest claim and demand whatsoever of in and to all and every the said Freehold Leasehold and Copyhold Messuages Lands Tenements Hereditaments and Premises and every part and parcel thereof with the Appurtenances whatsoever And all and every other my Freehold Leasehold and Copyhold Messuages Lands Tenements Hereditaments and Premises whatsoever and wheresoever situate lying and being in the County of Sussex or elsewhere and whereof I have Power and Authority to dispose by this my Will unto my dear and loving Husband the said Nathaniel Tanner To have and to hold all and every my undivided third part share dividend Estate right title Interest property and benefit of in and to all and every the said Freehold Leasehold and Copyhold Messuages Lands Tenements Hereditaments and Premises with the Appurtenances whereof I have Power and Authority to give and dispose unto and to the use of my said loving Husband Nathaniel Tanner and his Assigns for and during the term of his natural Life and from and immediately after his decease I give devise and bequeath the same unto my loving Brother and Sister William Collins Gentleman and Anne Collins Spinster their Heirs Executors Administrators and Assigns equally to be divided between them Share and Share alike as Tenants in common and not as joint Provided always and it is my Will and meaning and I do hereby direct that in case I shall leave any Issue one or more child or children living at the time of my decease That then the devise and Limitation over to my said Brother and Sister William Collins and Ann Collins shall cease determine and be absolutely void to all Intents and Purposes whatsoever anything before herein contained to the contrary thereof in any wise notwithstanding   And all the rest residue and remainder of my

Moneys Goods Chattels Personal Estate and Effects whereof I have the right to dispose (save and except such small pecuniary or specifick Legacies as shall be mentioned in a Paper written or signed with my own hands and annext to or left with this my Will which it is my desire and I do hereby direct my Executor to give and deliver accordingly) I give and bequeath unto my said loving Husband Nathaniel Tanner for ever whom I do hereby make constitute and appoint residuary Legatee and sole Executor of this my last Will and Testament hereby revoking all former and other Wills by me at any time heretofore made. In Witness whereof I have to this my last Will and Testament set my Hand and Seal the Eighth day of December in the Year of Our Lord One thousand Seven hundred and fifty ELIZA: TANNER Signed Sealed Published and declared by the said Elizabeth Tanner the Testatrix to be her last Will and Testament in the presence of Us who all of Us in her presence and at her request have Subscribed our Names as Witnesses hereunto. William Wade. John Dear. Mary Dear.

THIS WILL was proved at London before the Worshipfull Arthur Collier Doctor of Laws Surrogate of the Right Honourable Sir George Lee Knight Doctor of Laws & Master Keeper or Commissary of the Prerogative Court of Canterbury lawfully constituted the seventeenth day of June in the Year of Our Lord One thousand Seven hundred and fifty four by the Oath of Nathaniel Tanner the Husband of the Deceased and sole Executor named in the said Will to whom Administration was granted of all and singular the Goods Chattels and Credits of the said Deceased being first Sworn duly to administer.

Index

Ainsworth, E. G., 45, 184
Albemarle, Lord, his criticism of Colonel Martin, 55
Alcaeus, lines attributed to, 116–7
Aristogeton, 116–7
Apollo, 128–9
Aristotle: Collins's translation of his *Poetics*, 65, 66, 99; his influence on Collins's odes *To Pity, To Fear, To Simplicity*, 101–4
Armstrong, A. H., quoted, 127
Armstrong, Dr., 38, 78
Athenaeus, his *scolia*, 117, 139

Barbauld, Mrs., 125, 146
Barrow, Mrs. Mary: Alexander Carlyle's recollection of her, 152–3; her death, 153
Barrow, Mary Elizabeth, daughter of Thomas and Mary Barrow, 152
Barrow, Thomas: "very intimate" with Collins, 151; escapes from the Castle of Doune, 151, 152, 154; marries Mary Downer, 152, 167; resident at Chichester, 152; Deputy Paymaster of the Forces in North America, 152, 154; praised by Scott, 152; introduces Collins to Home, 154; his death, 153; the "cordial youth" of Collins's "Superstitions of the Highlands," 154
Bell, —, publisher, of Edinburgh, his edition of the ode "On the Superstitions of the Highlands," 158–9
Bell, Mrs. Carlyle, 87, 160
Bigg, Henry, 14
Blake, William, 106, 181
Blakiston, J. M. G., 12, 14, 21, 117, 136, 165–6

Blunden, Edmund, quoted, 3–4, 181
Bronson, Professor: his criticism of the ode *To a Lady*, 71; on *The Manners*, 99; on the ode *On the Poetical Character*, 124; on the projected "Clarendon Review," 141–2; on Bell's edition of the ode "On the Superstitions of the Highlands," 158; on the lines "Written on a Paper Which Contained a Piece of Bride Cake," 166, 181
Brydges, Sir Egerton, quoted, 67
Bundy, Elizabeth: Collins's landlady, 39; prosecutes him for debt, 64–5
Burns, Robert, quotes the ode "On the Superstitions of the Highlands," 157
Burrard, Sir Harry, 8, 10
Burrard, Paul, claims right to tythes as lessee of the Rectory of the church of St. Bartholomew, 7
Burrard, Paul (the younger), grants lease of land to Mrs. Elizabeth Collins, 7
Burrard, Sir Sidney, 8
Butcher S. H., quoted, 105

Calvin, John, 178
Carcinus, author of lines attributed to Alcaeus, 117
Cardiffe, Elizabeth, wife of Charles Collins, 48
Carlyle, Alexander: account of, 77–8; in London in 1746; meets Thomson and some of his friends in London, 78; witnesses the Battle of Prestonpans, 79; his *Fannie Weeping*, 79; his ode *To the Memory of Colonel Gardiner*, 80–2, 98; his ode *To Evening*, 82–6; evidence that he collaborated with

205

INDEX

contrasted with Gray, 108; writes to Mulso from Antwerp, 133; his Odes published, but few copies sold, 134; writes to J. G. Cooper about the projected "Clarendon Review," 138-9; certain lines in the *Castle of Indolence* may refer to him, 142; leaves Richmond, 145, 150; his letter to Dr. Hayes, 162-3; beginning of his illness, 166; temporary recovery, 172; travels in France, 172; stays at Oxford, 172; visited at Chichester by Joseph and Thomas Warton, 173; said to have been confined to a house of lunatics, 173-4; retires to the care of his sister in Chichester, 173; pre-occupation with the Bible, 175-7; nature of his illness, 174-8; religious sense and supposed conversion, 177; his death, 178-9; monument to him, 179

Poems:
Hercules, 15-17
"Sonnet," 17-18
Persian Eclogues (or *Oriental Eclogues*), 18-20, 25, 153
"Epistle to Hanmer," 25-9, 30, 41
A Song from Shakespear's Cymbelyne, 41-2, 161
Ode *To a Lady on the Death of Colonel Ross,* 70, 135
"How sleep the Brave," 70, 98
Ode *To Evening,* 84-6, 93, 95, 97-8, 101, 162
The Manners, 99-100, 101
Ode *To Pity,* 101-2
Ode *To Fear,* 101, 102-4
Ode *To Simplicity,* 104-6, 169-71
Ode *To Peace,* 110-4
Ode *To Liberty,* 110, 115-124
Ode *On the Poetical Character,* 23, 124-30
The Passions, 130-3, 162
Ode *On the Death of Mr. Thomson,* 144-6, 150
Ode *On the Popular Superstitions of the Highlands,* 153, 157, 162
Written on a Paper, Which Contained a Piece of Bride Cake, 166-7, 181

Fragments:
Battle of the Schoolbooks, 15
Lines Addressed to James Harris, 29-31
"Ye Genii who in secret state," 91, 93-6, 146
"On each new scene the Sons of ——Vertu," 123
Fragment of an Ode for Music, 163-4

"The Bell of Arragon," 164-5
To Simplicity, 168-71

Publications attributed to Collins:
Of the Essential Excellencies in Poetry, 137
To Miss Aurelia C——r, 166, 183
"Young Damon of the Vale is Dead," 166, 183-5
A Song. Imitated from the Midsummer Night's Dream of Shakespear, 185-8

Cooper, J. G., Collins's letter to, 138-9
Cooper, Mary, publisher, 41, 67
Cooper, Thomas, publisher, 41
Cooper, W. D., quoted, 9
Cowper, William: said to have been a precursor of the Romantic Movement, 106; his madness, 178
Coxed, Dr., 14
Croucher, John, 46
Cumberland, Duke of, 71-2, 110, 115
Cunningham J. S.: publishes *William Collins: Drafts and Fragments,* 13; on the "Epistle to Hanmer," 29; quoted, 74, 124, 164, 167

Dodderidge, Dr., his *Remarkable Passages in the Life of Colonel Gardiner,* 79
Dodsley, Robert: publisher, 41; publishes Collins's ode *To a Lady,* 70-1; publishes Warton's Odes but declines Collins's, 131
Downer, Mary: the "destin'd bride" of Barrow mentioned in Collins's "Superstitions of the Highlands," 153, 167: *see also* Barrow, Mrs. Mary
Druids, 92, 120-4, 146-8
Dryden, John, his *Alexander's Feast* compared with *The Passions,* 132-3
Duffield, Wilmot, (wife of Roger Collins), *see* Collins, Roger
Durnford, Thomas (the elder), marries Anne (Collins) Sempill, 180: *see also* Collins, Anne
Durnford, Thomas (the younger), his story of the destruction of certain papers, 180

Elliot, Sir Gilbert, *Fannie Weeping* wrongly attributed to him, 79
Eyre, Richard, 14

Fairfax, Edward: his translation of Tasso's *Jerusalem Delivered,* 123; Collins's admiration for, 162
Fleming, Lindsey, his *Little Churches of Chichester* quoted, 9

207

INDEX

Forbes, Duncan: hears of the death of
Charles Ross, 77; Thomson's tribute
to him, 77

Forbes, John (son of Duncan Forbes),
may have met Collins at Richmond,
77

Gardiner, Colonel: his fame perpetu-
ated in *Waverley*, 79; his conversion,
79; his purchase of Banktown, 79;
criticised by Colonel Martin, 79;
his death, 79; Alexander Carlyle's
Ode to his memory, 80–2

Garrick, David, 37, 38

Garrod, H. W.: quoted, 11; on *The
Battle of the Schoolbooks*, 15; his
criticism of Collins, 25, 32; on the
"Epistle to Hanmer," 25–6; on the
ode *To a Lady*, 72–3, 76; on the ode
To Evening, 84–6; on *The Manners*,
100; on the ode *To Peace*, 111; on the
ode *To Mercy*, 115; on the ode *To
Liberty*, 116, 119, 120; on the ode
On the Poetical Character, 125; on the
ode *On the Death of Mr. Thomson*,
144–6; on the ode *To Simplicity*,
168–70

Gibbon, Edward, 24

Goddard, Elizabeth: identified as the
"lady" of the ode *To a Lady*, 73; her
rumoured rejection of Collins and
engagement to Ross, 73; unlikely to
have lived at Harting, 74–5; whether
identical with "Delia," 74, 167–8

Goldsmith, Oliver, laments neglect of
Collins, 178

Goodger, John, owner of Southcott
Farm, 46, 69

Grant, Douglas, 17, 21, 90, 93, 142–3

Gray, Thomas: contrasted with Collins,
108; contrasts Collins's Odes with
Warton's, 135

Gray, W. Forbes, 155

Green, Richard, Rector of Birdham,
offers Collins a Curacy, 36

Hagstrum, J. H.: his *Sister Arts*, 29; on
the "Epistle to Hanmer," 30; on the
influence of painters on Collins, 93–4,
112–3; on the ode *To Peace*, 115; on
The Passions, 131–2; on Collins's
letter to J. G. Cooper, 140

Hampton, James: at Winchester, 12;
kicks over Collins's tea-table, 22

Handel G. F., his *Judas Maccabaeus*, 72

Hanmer, Sir Thomas, his edition of
Shakespeare, 25–8

Hardham, John: tobacconist, 36; a
philanthropist, 37; his brand of
snuff, 37; a lover of the theatre, 37;
dissuades Collins "from the clerical
office" and advises him to write a
tragedy, 38

Hargrave, Captain: his lamentable way
of life, 34, 39; probably identical
with Thomas Hargrave, *q. v.*

Hargrave, Dr. James, 40

Hargrave, Thomas, career and character, 40–1

Harmodius, 116–7, 121

Harris, James, Collins's verses to, 29–31

Harvey, John, 12, 14, 31

Hawley, General, his criticism of
Colonel Martin, 54–5

Hayes, William, Collins's letter to,
162–3

Hazlitt, William, 41

Headley, Henry, authorship of "Young
Damon of the Vale is Dead" attributed to him, 183–5

Heseltine, Mrs. Phyllis, 59, 63

Hill, Birkbeck, quoted, 5

Hipparchus, 116–7

Hippias, 117

Home, John: his *Douglas*, 90; his *Agis*,
151; meets Smollett, 151; meets
Collins at Chichester, 151, 154–5,
156

Horace: describes the Islands of the
Blest, 121; quoted, 129; mentioned,
177

Horner, Francis, 159

Hymers, William, 23, 24, 141, 153, 159

Inge, W. R., 136

Jennings, Miss Audrey, 60, 63

Johnson, Dr. Samuel: rescues Collins
from a bailiff, 65; helps him to
obtain an advance for a translation
of Aristotle's *Poetics*, 65; mentions
Collins's "Superstitions of the Highlands" as a lost work, 153; on
Collins's illness, 172, 173, 174; his
story of Collins's reading the Bible,
175; quoted, 6, 18, 22, 23, 29, 33, 38,
45, 55, 92, 103, 106, 109

Julius Caesar, on the Druids, 121, 147

Keats, John, 125

Kendrick, Sir Thomas, on the Druids
in *Bonduca*, 122

Ker (or Kerr), Cornet, 81

Kirby, T. F., 14, 21

208